国际市场营销

International Marketing:
Practices of Chinese Companies
Going Global

主 编／徐 亮 郭 炫
副主编／蔡 薇 刘 琳

重庆大学出版社

图书在版编目(CIP)数据

国际市场营销 / 徐亮，郭炫主编. -- 重庆：重庆
大学出版社，2023.12
（四川外国语大学新文科建设系列丛书）
ISBN 978-7-5689-3969-0

Ⅰ.①国… Ⅱ.①徐… ②郭… Ⅲ.①国际营销—英
语—高等学校—教材 Ⅳ.①F740.2

中国国家版本馆 CIP 数据核字(2023)第 104270 号

国际市场营销
GUOJI SHICHANG YINGXIAO
主　编　徐　亮　郭　炫

责任编辑：罗　亚　　版式设计：罗　亚
责任校对：谢　芳　　责任印制：赵　晟

＊

重庆大学出版社出版发行
出版人：陈晓阳
社址：重庆市沙坪坝区大学城西路 21 号
邮编：401331
电话：(023)88617190　88617185(中小学)
传真：(023)88617186　88617166
网址：http://www.cqup.com.cn
邮箱：fxk@ cqup.com.cn（营销中心）
全国新华书店经销
重庆市正前方彩色印刷有限公司印刷

＊

开本：720mm×1020mm　1/16　印张：19.5　字数：512 千
2023 年 12 月第 1 版　　2023 年 12 月第 1 次印刷
ISBN 978-7-5689-3969-0　定价：59.00 元

交叉融合，创新发展

——四川外国语大学新文科建设系列教材总序

四川外国语大学校长 董洪川

四川外国语大学，简称"川外"（英文名为 Sichuan International Studies University，缩写为 SISU），位于歌乐山麓、嘉陵江畔，是我国设立的首批外语专业院校之一。古朴、幽深的歌乐山和清澈、灵动的嘉陵江涵养了川外独特的品格。学校在邓小平、刘伯承、贺龙等老一辈无产阶级革命家的关怀和指导下创建，从最初的中国人民解放军西南军政大学俄文训练团，到中国人民解放军第二高级步兵学校俄文大队，到西南人民革命大学俄文系、西南俄文专科学校，再到四川外语学院，至 2013 年更名为四川外国语大学。学校从 1979 年开始招收硕士研究生，2013 年被国务院学位委员会批准为博士学位授予单位，2019 年经人社部批准设置外国语言文学博士后科研流动站。学校在办学历程中秉承"团结、勤奋、严谨、求实"的优良校风，弘扬"海纳百川，学贯中外"的校训精神，形成了"国际导向、外语共核、多元发展"的办学特色，探索出一条"内涵发展，质量为先，中外合作，分类培养"的办学路径，精耕细作，砥砺前行，培养了一大批外语专业人才和复合型人才。他们活跃在各条战线，为我国的外交事务、国际商贸、教学科研等各项建设做出了应有的贡献。

经过七十三年的发展，学校现已发展成为一所以外国语言文学学科为主，文学、经济学、管理学、法学、教育学、艺术学、哲学等协调发展的多科型外国语大学，具备了博士研究生教育、硕士研究生教育、本科教育、留学生教育等多形式、多层次的完备办学体系，主办了《外国语文》《英语研究》等有较高声誉的学术期刊。学校已成为西南地区外语和涉外人才培养以及外国语言文化、对外经济贸易、国际问题研究的重要基地。

进入新时代，"一带一路"倡议、"构建人类命运共同体"和"中华文化'走出去'"等国家战略赋予了外国语大学新使命、新要求和新任务。随着"六卓越一拔尖"计划

2.0(指卓越工程师、卓越医生、卓越农林人才、卓越教师、卓越法治人才、卓越新闻传播人才教育培养计划 2.0 和基础学科拔尖学生培养计划 2.0)和"双万"计划(指实施一流专业建设,建设一万个国家级一流本科专业点和一万个省级一流本科专业点)的实施,"新工科、新农科、新医科、新文科"建设(简称"四新"建设)成为国家高等教育的发展战略。2021 年,教育部发布《新文科研究与改革实践项目指南》,设置了 6 个选题领域、22 个选题方向,全面推进新文科建设研究和实践,着力构建具有世界水平、中国特色的文科人才培养体系。为全面贯彻教育部等部委系列文件精神和全国新文科建设工作会议精神,加快文科教育创新发展,构建以育人育才为中心的文科发展新格局,重庆市率先在全国设立了"高水平新文科建设高校"项目。而四川外国语大学有幸成为重庆市首批"高水平新文科建设高校"项目三个入选高校之一。这就历史性地赋予了我校探索新文科建设的责任与使命。

2020 年 11 月 3 日,全国有关高校和专家齐聚中华文化重要发祥地山东,共商新时代文科教育发展大计,共话新时代文科人才培养,共同发布《新文科建设宣言》。这里,我想引用该宣言公示的五条共识来说明新文科建设的重要意义。一是提升综合国力需要新文科。哲学社会科学发展水平反映着一个民族的思维能力、精神品格和文明素质,关系到社会的繁荣与和谐。二是坚定文化自信需要新文科。新时代,把握中华民族伟大复兴的战略全局,提升国家文化软实力,促进文化大繁荣,增强国家综合国力,新文科建设责无旁贷。为中华民族伟大复兴注入强大的精神动力,新文科建设大有可为。三是培养时代新人需要新文科。面对世界百年未有之大变局,要在大国博弈竞争中赢得优势与主动,实现中华民族复兴大业,关键在人。为党育人、为国育才是高校的职责所系。四是建设高等教育强国需要新文科。高等教育是兴国强国的"战略重器",服务国家经济社会高质量发展,根本上要求高等教育率先实现创新发展。文科占学科门类的三分之二,文科教育的振兴关乎高等教育的振兴,做强文科教育,推动高教强国建设,加快实现教育现代化,新文科建设刻不容缓。五是文科教育融合发展需要新文科。新科技和产业革命浪潮奔腾而至,社会问题日益综合化、复杂化,应对新变化、解决复杂问题亟需跨学科专业的知识整合,推动融合发展是新文科建设的必然选择。进一步打破学科专业壁垒,推动文科专业之间深度融通、文科与理工农医交叉融合,融入现代信息技术赋能文科教育,实现自我革故鼎新,新文科建设势在必行。

新文科建设是文科的创新发展,目的是培养能适应新时代需要、能承担新时代历史使命的文科新人。川外作为重庆市首批"高水平新文科建设高校"项目三个入选高校之一,需要立足"两个一百年"奋斗目标的历史交汇点,准确把握新时代发展大势、高等教育发展大势和人才培养大势,超前识变,积极应变,主动求变,以新文科理念为指引，谋划新战略，探索新路径，深入思考学校发展的战略定位、模式创新和条件保障，构建外国语大学创新发展新格局，努力培养一大批信仰坚定，外语综合能力强，具有中国情怀、国际化视野和国际治理能力的高素质复合型国际化人才。

基于上述认识，我们启动了"四川外国语大学新文科建设系列丛书"编写计划。这套丛书将收录文史哲、经管法、教育学和艺术学等多个学科专业领域的教材，以新文科理念为指导，严格筛选程序，严把质量关。在选择出版书目的标准把握上，我们既注重能体现新文科的学科交叉融合精神的学术研究成果，又注重能反映新文科背景下外语专业院校特色人才培养的教材研发成果。我们希望通过丛书出版，积极推进学校新文科建设，积极提升学校学科内涵建设，同时也为学界同仁提供一个相互学习、沟通交流的平台。

新文科教育教学改革是中国高等教育现代化的重要内容，是一项系统复杂的工作。客观地讲，这个系列目前还只是一个阶段性的成果。尽管作者们已尽心尽力，但成果转化的空间还很大。提出的一些路径和结论是否完全可靠，还需要时间和实践验证。但无论如何，这是一个良好的开始，我相信以后我们会做得越来越好。

新文科建设系列丛书的出版计划得到了学校师生的积极响应，也得到了出版社领导的大力支持。在此，我谨向他们表示衷心的感谢和崇高的敬意！当然，由于时间仓促，也囿于我们自身的学识和水平，书中肯定还有诸多不足之处，恳请方家批评指正。

2023 年 5 月 30 日
写于歌乐山下

　　改革开放四十余年来,我国社会主义现代化建设取得了伟大的成就,经济规模总量跃居世界第二,对外直接投资流量连续十年位列全球前三,中国特色社会主义进入了新时代。与此同时,世界百年未有之大变局正加速演进,以智能化和信息化为特征的新一轮技术革命正引发人类生产方式和生活模式的巨大变革。新的时代背景赋予高等学校"新文科"建设的新使命。"新文科"教育立足新时代、回应新需求,注重文科的融合化、时代性、中国化和国际化,为教育强国提供支撑引领。为了满足培养"新文科"人才的迫切需求,四川外国语大学与重庆大学出版社紧密合作,进行了大量的探索和实践,编写了这套"新文科建设系列教材"。

　　随着经济全球化发展以及新一轮技术革命的蓬勃兴起,全球营销环境正在发生深刻变化。特别是"一带一路"倡议顺利开展以来,我国企业的竞争力不断增强,越来越多优秀的中国企业"走出去"开展国际营销实践。在此背景下,作为"新文科建设系列教材"的重要组成部分,《国际市场营销》在结构设计、内容编写、案例选择等方面,整合现有国内外的相关知识内容并不断加以创新,关注全球营销环境的深刻变化,并突出我国企业"走出去"的国际营销案例,体现了新的历史条件下我国企业国际市场营销的实践发展以及与时俱进的时代特征。

　　《国际市场营销》共分为10章。其中:

　　第1章为国际市场营销概述,包括国际市场营销的概念、国际市场营销与市场营销以及国际贸易的联系与区别,以及企业开展国际市场营销的动因与过程。

　　第2章为环境分析以及国际经济环境,包括国际市场营销环境概述、国际市场营销环境分析框架、SWOT分析模型、贸易保护主义与贸易壁垒、经济发展阶段、国际经济组织以及经济特征。

　　第3章为国际市场营销的政治与法律环境,包括国际政治风险的概念和类型、政治风险的主要表现、减少政治风险的策略、法律体系基础、国际商务争端的解决方案以及知识产权保护。

　　第4章为国际市场营销的文化环境,包括如何理解文化、文化的要素、跨文化交际以及国际市场营销中的文化适应。

　　第5章为国际市场营销调研,包括国际市场营销调研的概念、过程、一手数据与二手数据以及国际营销信息系统。

第6章为国际市场营销战略,包括国际市场细分、国际目标市场选择、国际市场定位以及国际市场的进入方式。

第7至第10章为国际市场营销的产品策略、价格策略、渠道策略以及促销策略等,具体分析市场营销学"4P"方法在国际市场营销领域的应用。

本教材具有以下特点:

1. 注重专业学习与语言习得的融合。与目前国内大多数高校使用的中文教材不同,本教材用英语撰写,辅之以少量关键词汇的中文注解。教材既介绍国际营销学的专业知识,又传授本学科的英语知识,强调语言在实际商务场景中的运用,便于教师在课堂上训练本学科专业的分析方法以及与国际营销有关的英语应用技能,实现专业学习与语言习得的融合,培养"外语+专业"的复合型国际化人才。

2. 注重国际营销理论与本土企业"走出去"案例的融合。与引进版外文教材不同,本教材整理和编译了"一带一路"背景下我国企业"走出去"的素材和案例,将国际营销理论与我国企业在新的历史条件下的国际营销实践相结合,围绕我国企业的国际营销实践进行启发式、互动式探讨,增强学生的认同感、学习兴趣和课堂参与度,从而提高全英文课程的教学质量,培养学生的国际视野和家国情怀。

3. 紧扣时代前沿,实现跨学科教学与研究的交叉融合。本教材紧扣时代前沿,弥补了现有大多数教材内容陈旧、不合时宜的缺憾。随着跨境电子商务、大数据营销等实践的发展,国际营销理论需要不断更新、与时俱进。编者更新了国内外教材、教案的相关资料,在本教材反映了国内外国际市场营销课程教学研究的最新成果与发展趋势。

本教材的编写吸纳了众多国内外同行在其报告、论文、专著和教材中的精华。在此,谨向这些专家和作者表示感谢。

在本书的编写和出版过程中,四川外国语大学徐亮、郭炫、蔡薇等老师付出了辛勤的努力,重庆大学刘琳老师对书稿中的语言进行了精心校对,四川外国语大学研究生唐秋雨、邓怡然以及本科生金妍含进行了文稿整理、案例收集与翻译工作。在此,向所有编写人员表示深深的谢意。

随着中国特色社会主义新时代的到来以及全球化的纵深发展,国际市场营销作为一门蓬勃发展的新兴交叉学科,对我国企业"走出去"的理论研究和实践应用前景十分广阔。由于时间仓促,本书在理论探讨、讲述方式等方面的研究尚不够深入。书中存在的不当与疏漏之处,欢迎读者不吝指正。

徐 亮

2023 年 3 月于重庆沙坪坝

C目 录
ontents

Chapter 10　Promotion Strategy in the International Market　/ 265

References　　/ 299

Chapter 1

An Overview of International Marketing

Learning Objectives

After learning this chapter, you should be able to:

- understand the concept of international marketing;

- understand the task of international marketing;

- understand the relationship between international marketing and marketing and the relationship between international marketing and international trade;

- understand the motivations and stages of international marketing involvement;

- identify the main forms of international operation of Chinese enterprises.

//////// *Key Terms* ///////////////////////////

international marketing　国际市场营销

international trade　国际贸易

multinational corporation (MNC)　跨国公司

controllable factor　可控因素

uncontrollable factor　不可控因素

home-country/domestic environment　母国(国内)环境

host-country/foreign environment　东道国(外国)环境

cross-border　跨境的

marketplace　市场环境

customer-driven　以顾客为导向的

integrated marketing program　整合营销方案

needs　需要(专业术语,采用复数形式作名词)

wants　想要的东西(专业术语,采用复数形式作名词)

demand　需求

marketing mix　营销组合

motivation　动因

foreign direct investment (FDI)　外国直接投资

inward foreign direct investment (IFDI)　外商直接投资

outward foreign direct investment (OFDI)　对外直接投资

market diversification　市场多元化

market internalization　市场内部化

comparative advantage　竞争优势

product life cycle (PLC)　产品生命周期

resource　资源

economy of scale　规模经济

domestic marketing　国内营销

exporting marketing　出口营销

multinational marketing　多国营销

global marketing　全球营销

foreign commodity trade　对外商品贸易

licensing　许可证贸易

merger and acquisition (M&A)　兼并与收购(并购)

joint venture　合资企业

wholly-owned new enterprise　独资新建企业

sole proprietorship　独资(经营)

▶ Opening Case

China's Transsion Phones Find Success in Africa

Few Chinese have heard of Transsion, a Chinese phone maker based in Shenzhen, but the brand has millions of users in Africa, making it one of the most successful on the continent.

Transsion has more than 100 million users in Africa. Its factories have a total production capacity of 300,000 phones per day, said Arif Chowdhury, vice president of Transsion Holdings, which was founded in 2006.

"A decade ago, the sales were less than one million, mainly in India and Bangladesh. Transsion became successful only when it put almost all of its attention on the African market," said Chowdhury, who is from Bangladesh.

In 2016, Transsion produced 79.91 million phones, about 80 times the volume ten years ago.

According to technology consultant firm Counterpoint Technology Market Research, Transsion's market share in 2016 was about 40 percent in Africa, beating bigger competitors such as Samsung and Huawei. "Transsion in Africa is like what Nokia was in China years ago. Many people favor it over other phones," said Chowdhury.

"For a company to succeed, we need to find out what exactly people want. African users like selfies, multiple phone card slots, enabling local language, stable music function and longer battery life," he said.

The company organized 200 technicians to improve the camera function and calibrate the exposure to suit darker skin tones.

"We have dual-card, triple and even four-card phones, because there are many phone operators in Africa, and it is expensive to dial between networks," said Chowdhury.

Wang Yanhui, secretary-general of Mobile Phone China Association, said, "Transsion's success is rooted in its dedication to a highly segmented market."

"Many of the Chinese phone makers have explored foreign markets, but many have also failed because they did not work on the brand," Wang said.

Wang said Transsion had a big success selling cheap phones. "If they want to continue to win, they must work on technology and produce more smart phones," he said.

(A customer takes selfies with a Tecno mobile phone in downtown Nairobi,

capital of Kenya)

(Source: Adapted from Xinhuanet)

1.1 An Introduction to International Marketing

Although the world is facing unprecedented challenges such as a global pandemic, a complex economic situation, rising unilateralism and protectionism, etc., the trend of globalization is inevitable. Faced with the rapidly changing environment, enterprises can only adapt and change in order to find a space for survival and development in the intensified market competition. With the rapid development of the Internet, international trade, cross-border e-commerce and also breakthroughs in technologies, such as artificial technology, blockchain, cloud technology, big data, emerging technology (also known as ABCDE technology), the geographical and cultural distance of every corner of the planet has been greatly reduced, which objectively creates great opportunities for international marketing. These trends have jointly brought about an increase in economic and cultural exchanges, making companies' R&D, production, distribution, and marketing activities more frequently happen at international marketplaces. More and more Chinese enterprises have entered the international economic arena, greatly expanding the scope of the market. From well-known multinational corporations to unknown small and medium-sized enterprises, their decision-makers are now thinking about how to win competitions and seek development in the fierce international market.

1.1.1　How to Understand International Marketing

1. Concept of International Marketing

International marketing is the extension and expansion of domestic marketing. It refers to the business and sales activities of enterprises in more than one country. As Philip R. Cateora pointed out, "International marketing is the performance of business activities designed to plan, price, promote, and direct the flow of goods and services to consumers or users in more than one nation for a profit." Through the above-mentioned definitions of international marketing, we can see that international marketing activities take place in more than one country. The words "more than one country" account for the major difference between domestic marketing and international marketing, and this apparently minor difference explains the complexity and diversity in international marketing activities.

With the deepening process of Chinese economy to take part in the international division in the global industrial chain, increasingly more Chinese companies have changed their mindset from thinking about "where new factories should be set up or markets be established within China" to "where our products should be launched in the international marketplace". In other words, more and more Chinese enterprises are now operating across national borders, not only selling domestic products to the international market, but also investing in overseas markets to realize local production and local sales. By the end of 2019, 27,000 Chinese corporations had set up 44,000 companies in 188 countries and regions. In 2020, although the world economy had shrunk by 3.3% due to the severe impact of the COVID-19, China's outward direct investment flow reached $153.71 billion, an increase of 12.3% year-on-year, and for the first time became the world's top source of outward foreign direct investment. The investment along the Belt and Road area has increased rapidly, and has made positive contributions to the economic development of the host country. For example, Chinese construction and engineering companies are among the first to test the waters abroad. They are building railways, subways, highways, airports, ports and other infrastructure facilities in many countries. Besides, a large number of Chinese manufacturers have entered the global markets. Haier Group, one of China's largest home appliance manufacturers, for instance, has set up factories and research centers overseas.

The global market laid the stage for international marketing activities. Countries vary in political and economic systems, levels of economic development, social culture and language environment, as well as legal systems. To study the essence of international market management is not only to apply marketing skills, but also to analyze and understand the diverse marketing environments of the international market, and on this basis to adopt a variety of targeted business strategies. International marketing, to a certain extent, can be considered as an adaptation to the international market environments.

[Box 1-1]

2022 BrandZ Top 50 Chinese Global Brand Builders Ranking and Report Released, Byte Dance Ranks First

In July 2022, Google and Kantar released the ranking of the 2022 BrandZ Top 50 Chinese Global Brand Builders, which is a professional list to measure the views of overseas consumers on Chinese brands. The report shows that the overseas brand power of Chinese brands continued to grow in 2021, and Chinese brands still have the potential to expand market share and enhance brand value in the global market.

中国全球化品牌 50 强

排名	品牌	品牌力	品类
1	ll ByteDance	2,484	内容型APP
2	Alibaba Group 阿里巴巴集团	2,258	电子商务
3	Lenovo	1,898	消费电子
4	mi	1,859	消费电子
5	HUAWEI	1,674	消费电子
6	OPPO	1,349	消费电子
7	Hisense	1,241	家电
8	ONEPLUS	1,124	消费电子
9	Haier	1,098	家电
10	SHEIN	1,070	线上时尚

2. The Complexity of the Task of International Marketing

As we already know, multinational corporations operate their businesses in more than one country, and the complexity and diversity of the marketing environments of the "more than one country" means that the international marketer's task is more complicated than that of the domestic market. Since for international marketers, they have to deal with at least two levels of uncontrollable uncertainty instead of one, which include uncontrollable elements from both the home-country/domestic environment and the host-country/foreign environment.

Figure 1-1 illustrates the possible factors and elements to consider when international marketers deal with international marketing tasks. The inner circle depicts the elements that are controllable for international marketers to make international marketing decisions. The middle circle includes those uncontrollable environmental elements in the home country, which may affect the international marketing decisions. The outer circles represent the uncontrollable factors of each host-country environment within which the international marketers operate. For a single multinational corporation, international marketing decisions in one foreign market may not be applicable to another, since the uniqueness of each foreign market requires different solutions.

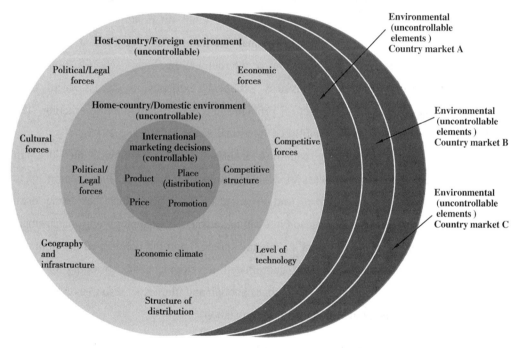

Figure 1-1   The Complexity of the Task of International Marketing

3. The Formation and Development of the Theory of International Marketing

With the development of the theories and practices of marketing and international trade and the increasing international marketing practices, the study of international marketing began to arouse scholars' attention. In the late 1950s and early 1960s, academia began to apply theories of marketing and international trade to solve problems arising in international economic activities. The theory of international marketing began to form in the 1960s.

Two of the symbolizing works for the formation of the theory of international marketing are as follows: In 1959, Professor R. L. Kramer from the University of Pennsylvania first proposed the term "international marketing". In 1966, *International Marketing* by Professor Philip R. Cateora from the University of Colorado established a systematic framework for international marketing, which is a representative work of this discipline.

With the continuous deepening of studies and practices, the theory of international marketing further developed in the 1970s, and the theoretical framework of international marketing was gradually formed in the late 1970s.

In the 1980s, the cross-border investment and business activities were very active. Multinational corporations' experiences in international marketing activities further promoted the theoretical study of international marketing, and enabled it to receive worldwide attention. In June 1982, well-known international marketing scholars from North America and Europe gathered at Business School Netherlands to discuss deeply and extensively some theoretical and practical problems faced by international marketing. The study of international marketing established its global status by the late 1980s.

Since the 1980s, developing countries, including China, introduced the ideas of international marketing in the process of developing national economy and opening up to the outside world. Since the reform and opening up in 1978, China has made great achievements by actively introducing foreign capital, advanced technology and management experience. The enhancement of China's economic strength and the accelerated development of economic globalization require the coordinated development of "bringing in" and "going out", to make full use of both international and domestic resources and better participate in the competition of economic globalization.

1.1.2 International Marketing and Marketing

As mentioned above, international marketing has developed based on marketing. Hence, international marketing is an extension and the application of the principles of marketing, and there are similarities between international marketing and marketing. However, as international marketing is a cross-border economic and trade activity, it has many differences compared with domestic marketing.

1. The Relationship between International Marketing and Marketing

The relationship between international marketing and marketing is mainly reflected in the following three aspects.

① The same principle

Both international marketing and marketing are based on the basic principles of economics and the contents of modern management, statistics, mathematics, accounting, sociology, psychology and many other disciplines. Such methodologies can be applied not only to domestic marketing activities, but also to international marketing.

Besides, as international marketing is the overseas extension of marketing, the basic principles, strategies and methods used to guide domestic marketing, such as marketing research, market segmentation, target markets selection, and marketing mix strategies etc., are also applicable to international marketing.

② The focus on the needs of consumers

Both international marketing and domestic marketing have experienced a development process from "production concept" to "marketing concept", from producer-centered to consumer/user-centered. Today's companies are more aware of not only meeting the needs of consumers and users for the value of goods or services, but also satisfying the psychological needs of consumers and users. Therefore, whether in the domestic market or in the international market, enterprises must start their marketing activities by understanding the marketplace, focusing on satisfying customer needs, and following the sequential steps of a marketing process:

Step 1: Understand the marketplace and customer needs and wants.

Step 2: Design a customer-driven marketing strategy.

Step 3: Construct an integrated marketing program that delivers superior value.

Step 4: Build profitable relationships and create customer delight.

Step 5: Capture value from customers to create profits.

③ International marketing is the extension of domestic marketing

Generally speaking, enterprises first engage in domestic marketing, and then gradually get involved in international marketing activities. In other words, the development of enterprises from a domestic company to a multinational corporation is a gradual process. At first, the enterprise only faces the domestic market, and its business scope, development strategy and marketing mix strategy are all oriented to the domestic market demand. Some products are exported to the international market due to accidental factors. Subsequently, enterprises are forced to look for sales in foreign markets and seek opportunities to enter the international market due to the increasingly fierce competition or the decreasing demand in the domestic market, although the domestic market is still their primary and main market. With the gradual deepening of the international target market, enterprises become more sensitive to the information of the international market, and more agile in responding to the changes in the demand of the international marketplace. Enterprises begin to arrange production and sales for the demand of the international market, and produce more products for the international market. With the adoption of advanced technology, the enlargement of production scale, and the accumulation of international marketing experiences, enterprises have the capability to face the international market, carry out global marketing strategy and implement international marketing decisions. From the above process, we can see that enterprises generally start from its domestic operation, gradually expand to the international market, and continue to enlarge the scope of the international market.

2. The Differences between International Marketing and Marketing

① Different marketing environments and contexts

This is the main and most significant difference between international marketing and domestic marketing. Different countries have very diverse social and cultural backgrounds, in which customs, languages, religious beliefs, values, thinking processes and behavior patterns differ from one to another. The political and legal systems of different countries also vary significantly. Due to the influence of the marketing environment and context, consumers in different countries have different consumption patterns and demand focuses, so they have different understandings of even the same product or the same piece of information, which directly affects product design and acceptance, information transmission methods, distribution and promotion measures, etc.

Domestic marketing is carried out within the borders of a home country. The environmental differences within regions of one country are much smaller than those of international marketing. In particular, the political and legal environment is basically consistent within a country. However, since international marketing activities are carried out across different countries, the varying nature of the environment and the context of different marketplaces have a significant impact on the marketing activities of enterprises.

▶ **Case 1-1**

Why Are Dishwashers Not Popular in China?

Dishwashers are very popular in European and U.S. households, with a market coverage of over 70%. Dishwashers, like gas stoves, are almost the must-have kitchen electrical products in every household in the Western market.

In China, the first fully automatic cabinet dishwasher was introduced by Little Swan

Company in 1998. At present, some other dishwasher brands have also appeared in the Chinese market, such as Siemens, Midea, Glanz, etc. Household dishwashers usually cost several thousand yuan.

The machine can run with hot water at 60 ℃ for several times, which can completely remove the residues and grease on the surface of the dishes, and common viruses and bacteria can also be killed. However, if we wash dishes by hand, the repeated use of rags will breed a lot of bacteria.

The running time of a dishwasher is generally about 1 hour, the consumption of water is about 10-12 liters, and 47 pieces can be washed. However, washing 47 pieces by hand usually needs 103 liters of water, which is 10 times the consumption of the machine.

So household dishwashers have many advantages, such as being healthier, more water-saving and so on. However, in China, the dishwasher market has not been fully developed. At present, even with the high level of consumption in urban areas in China, the coverage rate of the dishwasher is only about 3%.

Think about the following question:

Why are dishwashers so popular in Europe and the United States, but not in China?

Implications: From the above examples of the low popularity of dishwashers in the Chinese market, we can see that in international marketers must consider the characteristics, preferences and customs of consumers in the target market countries. Because of the particularity of the local consumer's consumption behavior, it is difficult to succeed in overseas markets if products are not improved to meet customer needs in those markets.

The difference in the marketplaces' environment requires international marketers to pay more attention to the investigation and analysis of the international market environment. The needs, values and utility of consumers of target countries should be considered, specifically, in aspects like functional design, appearance design, quality, variety, specification, and packaging of products. It will be risky to stick to enterprises' own domestic criteria.

Therefore, when an enterprise enters into the market of more than one country, the strategies, tactics, procedures, and methods of the international marketing activities will have to change due to the varying environment, which will obviously increase the difficulty and cost of adjustment. Only by considering and analyzing various international environments carefully, can enterprises find practical ways to carry out international marketing activities with pertinence.

② Different processes of marketing management

Marketing management plays a key role in the global strategy of multinational corporations. Marketing managers in multinational corporations need to design and formulate marketing strategies and execute the company's marketing strategy plan. In the marketing management process of multinational companies, what roles should their headquarters and subsidiaries play? To what extent should the management authority be distributed between the headquarters and subsidiaries? From the perspective of the centralized management approach, direct participation of the headquarters staff in the formulation, execution and supervision of local marketing programmes can improve the efficiency of the subsidiary, and help them to understand the possible marketing plans worldwide and avoid potential crises. In contrast, the decentralization view holds that the subsidiary needs to have autonomy or decision-making authority, because the manager of the local company has the best understanding of the local market demand. In short, the management process of international marketing is very complicated, and the decision-making authority of the headquarters and subsidiaries needs to be comprehensively determined according to the characteristics of the industry and products, the features of the local market demand, the competition in the local market and other factors.

③ Different marketing mix strategies

Domestic marketing merely faces uncontrollable factors of the home country's environment, and the marketing mix strategy is relatively simple and easy. International marketing activities are affected by uncontrollable elements from both the foreign and domestic environments, especially the environmental uncertainties in the host country, making the marketing mix strategy much more difficult and complicated.

More specifically, for example, in terms of product strategy, international marketing faces the choice of either standardization or differentiation strategy. In most cases, differentiation strategy is the primarily concerned strategy because of the huge differences in market demand between different countries and regions. Only by adapting to the needs of the local market can the products meet the wants of local customers. On the other hand, when the market needs are quite similar, companies can choose a product standardization strategy. If enterprises neglect the complexity and diversification of international market demands, international marketing decisions will be problematic.

In terms of pricing strategy, international market pricing is much more complicated than domestic market pricing. Domestic market pricing generally considers the cost, the supply and demand of the market, and the competitive situation. It is easier for domestic marketers to notice the changes in domestic market prices. However, for international market pricing, companies will consider not only the above-mentioned factors of the cost, demand, supply and competition of different countries, but also others such as the transportation fees, tariffs, foreign exchange rates and insurance premiums, etc. In addition, enterprises should also consider the laws and regulations of governments on price control. Therefore, international market pricing is more complex and complicated, and it is more difficult for marketers to manage the price changes.

In terms of distribution strategy, domestic marketers are familiar with domestic distribution channels, so it is easier for them to make decisions to select, control and manage domestic distribution channels. For international marketing marketers, they should choose not only domestic exporters, but also foreign distributors. Due to the differences of distribution systems in different countries, the width and length of distribution channels vary. For example, there is a comparatively long distribution channel in the Japanese market, where it takes five or six links for goods to go from producers to customers, which makes it more difficult for enterprises to enter the Japanese market.

In terms of promotion strategies, due to different cultures, laws, policies, languages, and media, it is more complicated and more difficult for companies to choose advertising strategies and other communication strategies.

④ Different extents of utilizing resources

Enterprises engaged in domestic marketing tend to use the resources provided within the domestic market. However, through international marketing, multinational corporations can utilize the resources of the first country, capital of the second country, technology of the third country, labor of the fourth country and so on. International marketing enables companies to allocate resources among different countries, and combine their strengths to manufacture competitive and comprehensive products. The integration of international factors such as resources, capital, technology and labor can improve efficiency, reduce costs, and obtain greater comparative advantages than domestic marketing.

⑤ Different degrees of risk

The differences in the environment and the complexity of the marketing management process inevitably bring a lot of uncertain factors, making it riskier than domestic marketing. The uncertainty of international marketing is evident in almost every step. For example, there are great differences in the needs of consumers in various countries, which leads to the increase in the flexibility of product design, and factors such as the changes in international market exchange rates affect international pricing. In a word, international marketing is riskier than domestic marketing.

1.1.3 International Marketing and International Trade

Both international marketing and international trade are economic activities across national borders for obtaining profit, but there are obvious differences between each other. These differences are mainly reflected in aspects such as theoretical basis, the motivation, the subject, the orientation, being cross-border or not, information sources, market activities and so on. Based on the comparison by the economist Vem Terpstra, Table 1-1 lists the differences in more details.

Table 1-1   Comparison of International Marketing and International Trade

Content	International Trade	International Marketing
Theoretical basis	"Absolute Advantage Theory" by Adam Smith, "Comparative Cost Theory" by David Ricardo, etc.	Theories of Marketing and International Trade
Motivation	Comparative interest	Profits
The subject	A country	A company
The orientation	Product-oriented	Demand-oriented
Whether across national borders	Yes	Not necessarily
Source of Information	Balance of payment statement	Company account
Marketing Activity		

Continued

Content	International Trade	International Marketing
Purchasing	Yes	Yes
Warehousing and transportation	Yes	Yes
Pricing	Yes	Yes
Market Research	Generally not	Yes
Product Development	Generally not	Yes
Promotion	Generally not	Yes
Channel Management	No	Yes

As can be seen from Table 1-1, the differences between international marketing and international trade are as follows:

① Theoretical basis

The theoretical basis of modern international trade was born more than two hundred years ago, among which the "absolute advantage theory" by the classical political economist Adam Smith and the "comparative cost theory" by David Ricardo are representative ones. However, the foundation and development of marketing theory was only at the beginning of the 20th century, and it had been only a few decades since international marketing was separated from marketing as a specialized subject.

② The motivation

The foundational theory of international trade is based is comparative interest. As long as there is comparative interest, goods can be transported from one country to another. However, international marketing is from the point of view of the enterprise, and the question focused is how to maximize the profit of the enterprise.

③ The subject of the exchange of goods (services)

International trade is the exchange of products or services between two countries. Generally speaking, a country is the organizer of international trade, and the country is the subject of the exchange behavior. On the other hand, international marketing is organized and carried out by enterprises, which is also the main body of the exchange behavior. In other words, for international marketing, the seller of products or services is an enterprise, and the buyer may be a country, an enterprise or individuals.

④ Orientation of the activity

International trade is a country's trading behavior based on its own resource advantages and factor endowments. It is a macro-level economic behavior with the country as the main body, and it is product-oriented. However, international marketing is the management process of a series of marketing strategies and tactics carried out by the company to satisfy the needs of consumers. It is a micro-level management behavior with the company as the main body, and it is consumer demand-oriented.

⑤ Whether across national borders

In terms of international trade, the exchange of products or services must transcend national boundaries and transfer from one country to another. On the other hand, international marketing, as a marketing activity that crosses national borders, means that its activities transcend national borders, but the products or services may or may not need to transcend national borders. For example, a multinational corporation has subsidiaries in several countries, and the products are produced and sold locally. Although the products produced by the local subsidiary do not move across national borders, the marketing activities carried out are transnational. This can be reflected in the statistics. The turnover of overseas enterprises is recorded in the company's marketing records, but not in the international trade volume. Therefore, the total sales volume of international marketing for enterprises often exceeds the export volume in international trade.

⑥ Source of information

The source of information to evaluate the performance of international trade is a country's balance of payments, from which we can see a country's import and export trade situation, whereas the information source for evaluating international marketing performance is the international marketing record and the account of the company.

⑦ Marketing activities

Although international trade involves marketing activities such as product purchase and sales, physical distribution, and product pricing, it lacks overall marketing planning, organization, and control; while international marketing activities involve not only product purchase and sales, physical distribution, product pricing, marketing research, product development, but also the formulation, execution and control of marketing plans. That is to say, international marketing focuses on the management of the overall marketing activities of the enterprise.

1.2 The Motivation and Process of International Marketing Involvement

1.2.1 The Motivation of International Marketing Involvement

In recent years, with the development of global industrial supply chains and the explosive economic growth of China, investing abroad and going global, not only to developing countries but also to developed ones, has become an unstoppable trend for Chinese companies. Over the past 20 years since China entered the World Trade Organization (WTO), China's foreign direct investment (FDI) has risen from 26th to the first place in the world. Different industry environments, companies' own conditions and specific goals determine that Chinese companies have different motivations for international marketing.

1. Market Motivation

The primary motivation for companies to carry out international marketing activities is to obtain a larger market. Specifically, it is manifested in the following four aspects:

① Successfully enter foreign markets

In order to protect their own markets and support the production and operation of domestic enterprises, governments often adopt a series of trade protection measures. Therefore, through technology transfer and foreign direct investment, enterprises can transfer production to an international market or a third country that is not subject to trade barriers, so as to avoid tariff and non-tariff barriers and enable products to enter the country's market smoothly.

② Expand the market

Since the market capacity within the domestic country is always limited, in order to expand the market and gain greater space for survival and development, companies need to enlarge markets through international marketing activities.

③ Diversify the market

The domestic environment is extremely competitive; it is better to go out to emerging markets or developed markets to diversify with Chinese markets. When a company sets up branches or subsidiaries in various markets, the flexibility of business activities will increase, and the adaptability to the entire market will also increase. Diversification of the market can reduce the operating risk of the company.

④ Internalize the market

Through international marketing activities, especially the trading activities between subsidiaries of international companies scattered in the world markets, the original externalized exchanges can be internalized as much as possible, incorporated into the management system of the company, so as to realize the domination and control of the market. Therefore, internalizing the international market and giving full play to its advantages is the deep motivation of international marketing.

2. Competitive Motivation

Another important reason for enterprises to explore the international market is to win the increasingly fierce market competition.

① Avoid competition

Nowadays, the dynamics of the domestic corporation environment have changed dramatically. For example, costs are increasing, the market demand for products is becoming increasingly saturated and overcapacity exists in many industries. In order to avoid the extremely fierce competition in the domestic market, enterprises begin to go abroad and seek more market space.

② Chase competitors

In the oligopolistic market structure, there are only a few large competitors, and these competitors keep a wary eye on each other's behavior. If one takes the lead in investing overseas, other competitors will follow suit and chase the leading enterprise to invest overseas, which is a kind of oligopolistic reaction. There are certainly attractive reasons for overseas investment, but it is more important to maintain the balance of competitive relations. For example, in the fast-food industry, KFC was the first to enter the Chinese market in 1987 when it opened its first KFC restaurant in Beijing. Three years later, in 1990, its rival McDonald's also entered the Chinese market by opening its 500-seat flagship store in Shenzhen.

③ Exercise competence

Operating in the international market can help to enhance the ability of international marketers to communicate effectively with employees, customers and suppliers coming from different languages, cultures, values and working methods, and to gain the international management experiences to coordinate the cultural differences and conflicts. Through the global brand strategy, it can fill the trust gap, enhance the brand influence, and improve the brand awareness and brand value. Through entry forms such as mergers and acquisitions (M&A), Chinese companies look for advanced technology that makes them more sophisticated and more competitive in the global market.

④ Extend the product life cycle (PLC)

Due to the different stages of economic development and technological progress in various countries, sometimes a product is at different stages of its life cycle in different countries. The product that no longer has an advantage in one country's market may still have a significant competitive advantage in another country. Some products with declining market competitiveness in the domestic market may be in short supply and in a growth stage in the market of another country. Therefore, companies can transfer products that have no advantage in the domestic market to foreign markets, extend the life cycle of products, and give full play to their competitive advantages.

3. Resource Motivation

Each country has its own resource advantages, and multinational corporations can make full use of these resource advantages through international marketing to maximize global benefits.

① Exploit natural resources

Countries have different natural resource conditions. Enterprises can make up for the shortage of domestic resources by developing foreign natural resources through international direct investment. Therefore, for resource-poor countries, the use of foreign resources has become an important investment purpose. In addition, the development of foreign resources may be less costly and more effective than the development of domestic resources. For example, the participation of China's oil companies in the exploration and development of global oil and gas market can alleviate the shortage of domestic oil and gas resources and ensure national energy security.

② Utilize labor resources

Since China's reform and opening up, many multinational corporations from developed countries have come to invest in China and directly engage in production and business activities. Apart from being attracted by China's huge market, they also intended to take advantage of China's relatively cheap labor resources.

③ Obtain technology resources

International marketing campaigns also enable companies to acquire advanced technologies that are not available through other means. This has very positive implications for enterprises in developing countries as it helps to narrow down the technological gap with developed countries.

④ Win information resources

On the one hand, facing the international market directly, enterprises can collect the relevant information of the international market in a timely manner, which creates conditions for enterprises to seize opportunities and make scientific decisions. On the other hand, when enterprises go abroad and go global, they can also deliver information to overseas markets more directly and strengthen communication with foreign consumers and users.

4. Profit Motivation

Enterprises' fundamental purpose of carrying out international marketing activities is to maximize their global benefit. International enterprises can make greater profits by exploiting the market and taking advantage of foreign resources.

① Gaining profit through economies of scale

When the company's product sales increase, the cost of a single product can be reduced, so as to achieve economies of scale. Through international marketing activities, by selling products to foreign markets, companies can achieve economies of scale. At present, there is overcapacity in many industries in the domestic market. In this context, many Chinese companies go abroad to actively explore and expand the international market to gain profits through economies of scale.

② Gaining profit through resource advantage

International companies can reduce costs by taking the resource advantages of the host country, including the above-mentioned natural, labor, and information resources, etc., thereby achieving greater benefits.

③ Gaining profit through favorable policies

A huge driving force for enterprises to go abroad is the government's favorable policies. In order to encourage domestic enterprises to go overseas, the government formulated preferential policies, for example, taxation policies such as tax reduction policy, tax refund policy, financial and monetary policies such as low-interest loans, guaranteed loans and export price subsidies, etc. The government can also provide many services for enterprises, such as providing foreign trade consulting and international market information. All these supports are conducive to strengthening the competitiveness of enterprises in the international market.

At the same time, in order to attract foreign investment, host governments may also introduce a series of preferential policies such as taxation policies, financial and monetary policies, and relevant services. Therefore, when Chinese companies going aboard, they can gain profits through favorable policies from the governments of both the home country and the host country.

1.2.2 The Process of International Marketing Involvement

The process of companies' international marketing involvement is closely linked with the integration of the world economy and the development of the domestic market economy. The following five stages can indicate how a domestic company can grow into a global one through its international marketing involvement.

1. Domestic Marketing

A company at this stage mainly faces with the domestic market and does not actively cultivate customers outside national boundaries. The focus, orientation and operating activities are still concentrated on domestic consumers, suppliers and competitors. However, products may still enter foreign markets indirectly through trading companies, foreign customers contacting companies, wholesalers, distributors, websites, etc. For example, a company may receive international orders from the Internet users through its website. With the development of network technology and new media, the emergence of new channels such as live streaming and purchasing on behalf has further expanded the possibility of domestically marketed products reaching overseas markets.

2. Exporting Marketing

This is the first stage for companies to enter the international market. As the capacity and scale of production increase and the domestic demand changes, there might be temporary surpluses to be exported to foreign markets. However, this stage is a transitional one, for when the domestic demand increases over the surpluses, the exporting activity may be reduced or suspended. Since the surpluses and exporting activity can be characterized by a temporary nature, a company at this stage has little or no intention of setting up and maintaining overseas market representation. The awareness of international market research and product development is not enough and the exporting of products is only an extension of domestic products. Its target market is still the domestic market, and products are produced to meet the needs of domestic markets. Hence, at this stage, there is little change in the company organization or product line. Profits from foreign markets are seen as a bonus in addition to regular domestic profits.

3. International Marketing

This is the second stage for companies entering the international market. With the accumulation of export marketing experience and the further improvement of production capacity, the company at this stage has a long-term production capacity for selling goods and services in foreign markets. As the overseas demand grows, the company may establish factories and production capacity in overseas markets. Besides, the company may employ overseas intermediary agencies, or establish its own sales team or sales subsidiaries in important markets. The company becomes dependent on foreign sales and profits.

Although companies are more involved in international strategic planning at the stage of international marketing, they are also characterized by the tendency of ethnocentrism or home-country centrism. Ethnocentrism is the notion that people in one's own company, culture, or country know best how to do things. It is believed that the home country is superior, and the needs of home country are more relevant. It is also characterized by taking the interests and cultural values of the home country and the parent company as the fundamental guidance. Product development, profit allocation, and personnel policies are all "home country-centered". Most of the marketing planning authority is concentrated in the domestic head office. The marketing strategies adopted in the overseas market are quite similar to those in the domestic market.

4. Multinational Marketing

As companies become more and more experienced in international marketing, international marketers increasingly pay attention to studying the international target market and adapting the product to the special requirements of each country. This is the third stage for companies entering the international market. Companies at this stage are fully involved in international marketing and become multinational marketing firms. In this stage, companies tend to have an orientation of polycentrism. Polycentrism assumes that overseas markets are different and unique. Therefore, each overseas market should be targeted in a different way, and differentiation strategy should be used in order to succeed in international marketing. The product strategy at this stage is to adapt to the markets of various countries.

5. Global Marketing

This is the most advanced stage of a company's transnational operation. At this stage, companies take the world as their target market, and regard the world, including the domestic market, as one market. Instead of focusing on national boundaries, the segmentation of the international market is usually determined by factors such as geographical proximity, income level, cultural similarity, etc., which usually span across national boundaries. Instead of focusing on the uniqueness of each market, global marketing concentrates on both the commonality and the differences in the global market. At this stage, a global company implements unified marketing strategies based on the commonality of culture. At the same time, it also pays attention to taking diversified local marketing strategies to meet the needs of different markets. The firm may offer global product concepts but with local adaptation with the idea of "think globally, act locally". Besides, when a company develops from international marketing to the global marketing stage, it can be noticed that more than half of its sales revenue comes from overseas markets. A global company begins to take a global perspective on the entire business operations, such as R&D, purchasing, manufacturing, marketing, organizational structure, sources of finance, personnel, and so on.

Lenovo's transformation into a global company is instructive. As a global leader in the PC market, it develops, manufactures and markets cutting-edge PC products and value-added professional services. Lenovo serves more than 180 markets. The company's global manufacturing allows tailored offerings to regional markets and includes more than 30 manufacturing facilities, including in-house, joint venture, original design manufacturer, and contract manufacturer sites in Argentina, Brazil, China, Germany, Hungary, India, Japan, Mexico, and the U.S. In May 2005, Lenovo completed the acquisition of IBM's Personal Computing Division, making the company the world's third largest computer manufacturer (after Hewlett-Packard and Dell). Lenovo not only succeeded in its acquisition of ThinkPad Line, but also had successful international acquisitions in countries like Germany, Brazil, etc. Besides, Lenovo takes a global approach in their business. For example, the company brings in excellent international management talents from the U.S., Europe, Asia, etc., and sets up a management team with a global perspective. Lenovo has successful experience in global marketing. It does not just view itself as a Chinese company that has gone global, but also positions itself as a global firm in the international marketplace.

► **Case 1-2**

Tsingtao Beer Set Up Its First Overseas
Production Plant in Thailand

On October 17, 2011, Tsingtao Beer signed a factory building agreement in Bangkok, Thailand, which declared Tsingtao Beer's entry into the Southeast Asian market.

In 2011, the company had 59 breweries in 19 provinces of China, and its iconic product Tsingtao Beer was distributed in more than 70 countries and regions around the world. With the gradual maturity of the domestic beer industry and the rising demand for Tsingtao beer in the international market, the company believes that the time to accelerate the internationalization process is ripe. Jin Zhiguo, chairman of the company, said that the company would first establish supply chains in countries with similar cultures, change the previous export mode into "local production and local sales". It not only reduces production and transportation costs, improves freshness and is conducive to product promotion, but also enjoys advantages such as government support and tariff preferences.

Thailand is located in the center of Southeast Asia, with a sound market economy and an open investment and business environment. As an emerging market, Thailand has a huge market capacity and development space. With the political stability of Thailand and the increasing popularity and sales of Tsingtao Beer in Thailand in recent years, the company chose Thailand as its first overseas destination of "first market, then factory".

Tsingtao Beer's Thailand factory will make full use of Thailand's preferential trade advantages in Southeast Asia to gain cost competitiveness. Building factories in Thailand, is to enter the Southeast Asian market as the first stop to expand the international market in Europe, and even Oceania.

1.2.3　The Forms of International Operation of Chinese Enterprises

The internationalization of Chinese enterprises is a process of gradual integration into the international economy. It is mainly developed through the forms of international trade, licensing, absorbing and utilizing foreign capital, and foreign direct investment.

1. Foreign Commodity Trade

The cross-border commodity exchange activities between economic entities of different countries and regions are the most primary and important market entry mode in the process of international operation.

There are three types of commodity export: direct export, indirect export and barter trade. Indirect export has the advantages such as less investment, less risk and greater flexibility. It is a shortcut for enterprises that have just started their international market business or most small- and medium-sized enterprises. However, the disadvantage is that it is hard for export enterprises to quickly and accurately access the information of the international market, to directly obtain business experience in the international market, to control market share and price, and to improve the enterprise's reputation.

Direct export involves greater investment, greater risk and higher potential rewards. However, exporting production enterprises need to have the right to operate import and export independently, have their own international marketing channels, and assign special personnel to take charge of export marketing management, such as setting up export departments, establishing overseas offices or foreign subsidiaries, etc.

The form of barter trade is highly complementary. It is a transaction method that combines import and export. The delivery speed is fast, and no cash payment is required. It is suitable for exchanges with the neighboring countries. In the case of insufficient funds of the buyer, the equipment exporter can export equipment and technology by means of compensation trade, and use the other party's cheap labor, raw materials, or re-sale products to make profits.

2. Licensing

Licensing is the most important and basic form of technology trade, and its trade targets include patent, trademark and know-how. With the continuous improvement of the technological innovation capabilities of Chinese enterprises, licensing has become a new profit growth point for Chinese enterprises.

Licensing offers technology exporters a low-cost, low-risk form to access the international markets. Especially when the target country's currency depreciates, import restrictions or investment restrictions are imposed, licensing may be the most effective way to enter the international market.

For companies that import technology, licensing provides an effective way for enterprises to expand their business. Some companies make use of the key technologies and knowledge obtained by licensing to achieve breakthroughs in production efficiency and product quality. Some enterprises also complete diversifications into new business areas through licensing.

There are also some disadvantages such as technology leakage, cultivating potential market competitors, uncertainty of the licensor's reputation and limited benefits of licensing, etc.

3. Absorbing and Utilizing Foreign Capital

According to statistics, China's actual use of foreign capital in 2021 exceeded trillion yuan for the first time, reaching 1.1 trillion yuan, an increase of 14.9%. 48,000 new foreign-funded enterprises were established, an increase of 23.5%, achieving "double improvement" in the scale and quality of foreign investment.

In the past two years, due to the impact of the pandemic and the readjustment of global industrial and supply chains, global transnational investment has fluctuated greatly. The reconstruction of the international industrial chain is characterized by near-shore, localization and regionalization. The competition among countries to attract investment is becoming increasingly fierce. Meanwhile, domestic companies are also facing pressure from rising prices of labor, land and raw materials. Despite these challenges, China has favorable conditions such as complete industrial support, sound infrastructure, abundant human resources, stable foreign investment policies and an improved business environment. Hence, China has a super-large attractive market for foreign investment, and the overall expectation of foreign investment in China is good.

[Box 1-2]

The Status Quo of China's Utilization of
Foreign Capital Market in 2022

Since China's reform and opening up, famous multinational companies around the world have started to shift their attention to China and launched large-scale investments in China. The utilization of foreign capital in China keeps on rising. The status quo of China's utilization of foreign capital market in 2022 are as follows:

① China has become the second largest destination of foreign direct investment in the world.

② Asia is the main source of foreign direct investment in China.

③ The service industry has replaced the manufacturing industry as the main field of foreign investment.

4. Foreign Direct Investment

Foreign direct investment mainly takes the forms of international mergers and acquisitions, joint ventures and wholly-owned new enterprises.

① Merger & Acquisition

Mergers and acquisitions have now become the main form of international direct investment. There are advantages of international mergers and acquisitions:

- It can help multinational corporations to organize production and sales abroad by avoiding tariff and non-tariff barriers.
- It can help to improve the scale economy of enterprises and reduce their production costs.
- It can help enterprises to enter new industries at a lower cost.
- It can help to achieve the "localization" of operations.
- It can help to obtain technical information, management knowledge and know-how, and other scarce resources that are not easily available in the external market.

② Joint Venture

The form of the joint venture is widely adopted, not only by large multinational companies, but also by many small- and medium-sized companies and companies that have just gone abroad.

In the following situations, companies can consider adopting the form of joint ventures when entering the international market.

- When there are restrictions on the form of ownership of foreign enterprises by laws and regulations in the host country.
- When the multinational corporation needs long-term access to local raw materials and resources.
- When the multinational corporation needs to rely on the assistance of local enterprises to enter and expand the local market.
- When the multinational corporation intends to enter more overseas markets but its capital and operating capability are insufficient.

③ Wholly-owned Enterprise

Wholly foreign-owned operation means that the multinational company independently controls the production and marketing in the foreign market. The sole proprietorship can ensure 100% ownership and all profits, and can integrate the marketing strategy of foreign subsidiaries with the overall strategies of the multinational corporation. At the same time, however, the wholly foreign-owned operation requires the largest amount of capital investment and takes the highest degree of risk.

Since the reform and opening up and accession to the WTO, China has made great achievements in both inward foreign direct investment (IFDI) and outward foreign direct investment (OFDI), and has become a major recipient of global foreign direct investment, as well as a major provider of foreign direct investment. In 2020, China attracted $144.37 billion in foreign direct investment, with over one million multinational companies invested in China, making China the second largest country of inward foreign direct investment (IFDI). In 2020, China's foreign direct investment reached $153.71 billion, and has become the world's top source of outward foreign direct investment (OFDI). The investment in countries along the Belt and Road has increased steadily. Outward foreign direct investment not only drives the export of Chinese products, but also promotes the increase in local finance, tax revenue and employment opportunities.

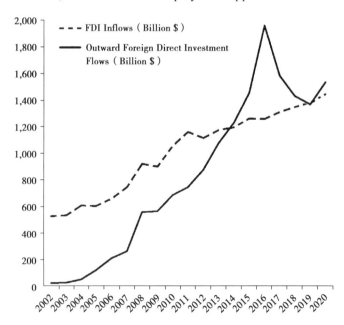

Figure 1-2   China's FDI Inflows and Outward Foreign Direct Investment Flows

(Source: China Statistical Yearbook 2021)

Chapter Summary

- International Marketing is the extension and expansion of domestic marketing. It refers to the business and sales activities of enterprises in more than one country.

- For international marketers, they have to deal with at least two levels of uncontrollable uncertainty instead of one, which includes uncontrollable elements from both the home-country/domestic environment and the host-country/foreign environment.
- The theory of International Marketing began to form in the 1960s.
- The basic principles of international marketing and marketing are the same; both of them focus on the needs of consumers; from the process of business development, international marketing is an extension of domestic marketing. Meanwhile, international marketing and domestic marketing also differ in marketing environments and contexts, processes of marketing management, marketing mix strategies, extents of utilizing resources, and degrees of risk.
- Both of the international marketing and the international trade are economic activities across national borders for obtaining profits, and the differences are mainly reflected in aspects such as the theoretical basis, the motivation, the subject, the orientation, being cross-border or not, information sources, market activities and so on.
- The motivations of the international operation of enterprises are mainly for the market, the competition, the resources and the profits.
- The process of an enterprise's involvement in international marketing generally goes through the stages of domestic marketing, export marketing, international marketing, multinational marketing and global marketing.
- The forms of international operation of Chinese enterprises mainly include international trade, licensing, absorbing and utilizing foreign capital, and foreign direct investment.

Main Concepts

international marketing, international trade, ethnocentrism, polycentrism

Think and Practice

1. Explain the complexity of the task of international marketing.
2. Discuss the similarities and differences between international marketing and domestic marketing.
3. Briefly describe the similarities and differences between international marketing and international trade.
4. Discuss the motivations of the Chinese companies' going global with some examples.

5. Identify the stages of Chinese companies' going global and describe the characteristics of each stage.

6. List the main forms of internationalization adopted by Chinese enterprises.

7. Look up relevant literature or information and think about the indicators to measure the degree of globalization of multinational enterprises. Can you use these indicators to calculate the degree of globalization of China's multinational corporations?

8. Look up an example of a Chinese enterprise going abroad, and analyze its motivation, development stages, and lessons learned from its success or failure.

9. Compare the advantages and disadvantages of different routes of "easy first and then difficult" and "difficult first and then easy" of Chinese enterprises' "going abroad" strategy.

 ## Case Study

The Process of International Marketing
Development of Chinese Enterprises

The international marketing development of Chinese companies has gone through three phases:

- The phase of export marketing;
- The phase of OEM-oriented marketing;
- The phase of cross-border mergers and acquisitions.

The way Chinese companies enter the foreign markets has evolved from a single export trade to a combination of export, overseas direct investment, and joint ventures. Marketing strategies in overseas markets have also shifted from passive processing to self-built brands and sales channels.

1. The Phase of Export Marketing (1979–1990)

In 1979, China began implementing the reform and opening-up policy. Some domestic enterprises began to enter the international market to earn foreign exchange through exports. Domestic products mainly entered the international market through export. Some enterprises set up their own sales organizations, overseas representative offices, or joint ventures. The number of enterprises participating in the international market was relatively small, and those participants were more likely state-owned large- and medium-sized industrial enterprises and foreign trade companies. Chinese companies' overseas investments were small-scale and the industrial scope was quite narrow. The investment regions were mainly concentrated in developing countries.

2. The Phase of OEM-oriented Marketing (1991–2001)

In order to make products more suitable for local market demands and to bypass barriers to entering overseas markets, many Chinese companies began to invest directly in foreign countries. After the 1990s, the proportion of manufactured product exports increased significantly, and the products' technological level was greatly improved. Some companies increased their investment in scientific research, carried out technological innovations, created brands, and even gained a large market share in some developed countries. The number of companies participating in international operations grew rapidly, with diversified industry fields and geographical expansion. The investment regions expanded from developing countries to some developed countries. The investment agents transformed from foreign trade companies to manufacturing enterprises.

Besides, the rise of private enterprises significantly contributed to the internationalization of Chinese enterprises. Among the large-scale private enterprises in China, Wanxiang, Huawei, New Hope, Zhengtai, and other companies have accessed the international market inordinately. These companies currently invest in more than 40 countries worldwide. To create complementary advantages, private enterprises formed strategic alliances with foreign companies through mergers and acquisitions, joint ventures, and other forms. Private enterprises were mostly small in scale and adopted the OEM model to enter the overseas market. In recent years, some successful private enterprises created anti- "OEM" mode, which has achieved great success. Additionally, private manufacturing enterprises have obtained the right to operate import and export independently, and become a new growth point for China's foreign trade exports.

3. The Phrase of Cross-border Mergers and Acquisitions (2002–present)

As a new form of "going out", cross-border M&A has developed rapidly in China. 2002 was the first year of China's accession to the WTO, and Chinese companies were more profoundly and comprehensively involved in the trend of globalization. The pace of Chinese companies entering the international market has dramatically accelerated, and overseas mergers and acquisitions have surged. Some powerful domestic enterprises have acquired foreign sales channels and famous brands through acquisitions and international strategic alliances, forming complementary advantages and entering the local market faster. The trend of domestic companies entering the global market with their own brands has become more evident. Lenovo, Xiaxin, and other companies all changed their corporate logos to better penetrate the brand into the international market.

Discuss the following questions.

1. Look up the term "OEM" on the Internet and outline the characteristics of OEM of Chinese enterprises.

2. Does a company's cross-border merger and acquisition mean that it has entered into a global marketing stage? Explain your reasons.

Chapter 2

Environmental Analysis and Economic Environment of International Marketing

////////// *Learning Objectives* ////////////////////// · · · · · · · · · · · · · · ·

- Understand the elements of analyzing the macro and micro environment of international marketing;

- Analyze the international marketing environment by using the SWOT model;

- Understand the impact of the international marketing environment on international marketing activities;

- Identify the main forms of trade barriers;

- Understand the theory of economic growth stages;

- Identify the main forms of economic integration;
- Understand economic characteristics.

/////// *Key Terms* /////////////////////////

macro environment　宏观环境

Political, Economic, Social and Technological Analysis　PEST 分析

micro environment　微观环境

supplier　供应商

company　公司

marketing intermediary　营销中介机构

customer　顾客

competitor　竞争者

public　公众

Strength, Weakness, Opportunity, Threat Analysis　SWOT 分析

protectionism　贸易保护主义

trade barrier　贸易壁垒

tariff　关税

ad valorem duty　从价税

specific duty　从量税

compound duty　复合税

nontariff barrier　非关税壁垒

import quota　进口配额

foreign exchange control　外汇管制

anti-dumping　反倾销

technological barrier　技术壁垒

green barrier　绿色壁垒

discriminatory government procurement policy　歧视性的政府采购政策

boycott and embargo　抵制与禁运

monetary barrier　货币壁垒

export subsidy　出口补贴

theory of economic growth stages　经济成长阶段理论

traditional society　传统社会

preconditions for take-off　起飞前夕

economic take-off stage　起飞阶段

drive to maturity　趋于成熟

high mass consumption　高度消费阶段

the United Nations　联合国

industrialization　工业化

per capita income　人均收入

less-developed countries (LDCs)　欠发达国家

more-developed countries (MDCs)　较发达国家

least-developed countries (LLDCs)　最不发达国家

newly industrialized countries (NICs)　新兴工业化国家

World Trade Organization (WTO)　世界贸易组织

International Monetary Fund (IMF)　国际货币基金组织

World Bank Group (WBG)　世界银行集团

The United Nations Conference on Trade and Development (UNCATD)　联合国贸易和发展会议

European Union (EU) 欧盟

North American Free Trade Area (NAFTA) 北美自由贸易区

Association of Southeast Asian Nations (ASEAN) 东南亚国家联盟

Asia-Pacific Economic Cooperation (APEC) 亚太经合组织

Regional Comprehensive Economic Partnership (RCEP) 区域全面经济伙伴关系

forms of economic integration in regional markets 区域市场上经济一体化的形式

free trade area 自由贸易区

customs union 关税同盟

common market 共同市场

economic union 经济联盟

personal disposable income 个人可支配收入

Engel's Law 恩格尔法则

▶ Opening Case

15 Nations Sign RCEP Trade Pact—World's Biggest FTA

The long-awaited Regional Comprehensive Economic Partnership (RCEP), covering nearly a third of the global population and about 30 percent of global GDP, was signed by its 15 members on Sunday at the fourth RCEP summit in Hanoi.

It is the world's biggest free trade agreement (FTA) measured in terms of GDP, larger than the Comprehensive and Progressive Agreement for Trans-Pacific Partnership (CPTPP), the European Union, the recent U.S.-Mexico-Canada Free Trade Agreement or Mercosur, according to Rajiv Biswas, chief economist for the Asia-Pacific region of IHS Markit.

The agreement will promote fewer tariffs on trade in goods, and better rules for trade in services, including market access provisions for service sector suppliers from other RCEP countries. Besides, non-tariff barriers to trade among its members, such as customs and quarantine procedures and technical standards, will be reduced.

It will also allow for one set of rules of origin to qualify for tariff reduction with RCEP members. A common set of regulations mean fewer procedures and easier movement of goods.

Chinese Premier Li Keqiang stressed that "the signing of the RCEP is not only a landmark achievement of East Asian regional cooperation, but also a victory of multilateralism and free trade."

The signing of RCEP plays an extremely important role in the economic recovery of its members in the post-epidemic period besides promoting long-term prosperity and development, the statement said.

Moreover, the preferential results of the agreement directly benefit consumers and enterprises and will play an important role in enriching consumer market choices and reducing enterprises' trade costs.

(Source: Adapted from CGTN)

2.1 An Introduction to the International Marketing Environment

Firms engaged in international marketing often face unfamiliar foreign market environments. The key to successful international marketing lies in adapting to a constantly changing, mostly uncontrollable, and unexperienced environment. Before formulating the correct international marketing strategy, international marketers should first understand how the economic, political, societal, cultural, technological and other environmental factors have a great impact on the internationalization strategy of firms.

2.1.1 How to Understand the International Marketing Environment

Before an international company enters into a foreign market, it should first try to understand the marketplace by analyzing the environment of the foreign market. The environment of a foreign market consists of all the forces and elements that affect companies' international marketing activities and the achievement of objectives. These environmental factors can be categorized into macro-level forces and micro-level elements.

The macro-level environment refers to the general international marketing environment which is difficult to control and influence, and can bring opportunities and threats to enterprises' international marketing activities. Enterprises and the other participants in the micro marketing environment are all surrounded by the macro-level environment.

The macro-level environment can be explained and understood by factors such as political, legal, economic, cultural, demographic, technological and natural forces. Generally, four major external environmental factors can affect the industry and firms; they are political, economic, social and technological factors. In brief, it is called PEST analysis, as shown in Figure 2-1.

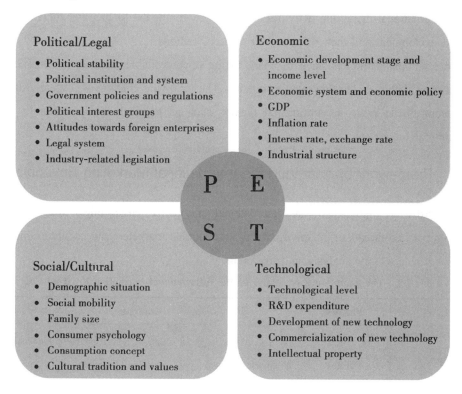

Figure 2-1 PEST Analysis Model

The micro-environment consists of relevant participants in the industrial chain. The factors in the micro-environment can affect a company's ability to serve its overseas customers, which include suppliers, the company itself, marketing intermediaries, customers, competitors, the public, etc.

The macro-environmental and micro-environmental factors are shown in Figure 2-2.

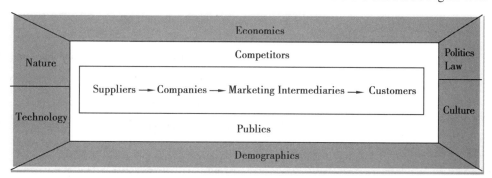

Figure 2-2 The International Environment of International Marketing

The international marketing environment influences marketing activities by providing opportunities or posing threats to firms. Market opportunities are attractive and beneficial to firms' international marketing activities, whereas environmental threats are unfavorable to firms' development and their international market positions.

International marketers have to adapt to the uncontrollable international marketing environment within which they plan to operate. The following chapters will mainly discuss the uncontrollable macro-environmental factors, such as political, legal, economic, and sociocultural forces, etc.

2.1.2　Framework of Analyzing the International Marketing Environment

In order to understand the international marketing environment and find the opportunities and threats of the environment, international marketers can use the framework shown in Table 2-1 for analysis and prediction.

Table 2-1　The Framework of Analyzing the International Marketing Environment

Level	Factors	Content
Macro-level environment	Politics	political system, political situation, related policies, administrative efficiency, political groups, social order, ruling party, relationship between host country and home country, etc.
	Law	legal system, legislative status, law enforcement status, judicial system, intellectual property rights (IPR) protection, etc.
	Demographics	population scale, gender structure, age structure, geographical distribution, family size, urban and rural structure, mobility rate, ethnic structure, education level, occupation, birth rate, death rate, growth rate, family life cycle, etc.
	Economics	GDP, national income, market interest rate, inflation rate, economic development stage, industrial structure, regional development status, consumer income, disposable income per capita, consumption structure, etc.
	Culture	values, rituals, symbols, beliefs, thought processes, etc.

Continued

Level	Factors	Content
Macro-level environment	Technology	new materials, new processes, new equipment, new techniques, logistics techniques, new payment methods, new media techniques, etc.
	Nature	climate, geography, ecological environment, resources, energy, pollution, environmental protection, topography, geographical location, traffic conditions, etc.
Micro-level environment	Target customer	groups of target customers, customer needs, customer psychology, customer behavior, purchasing power, social class, cultural concept, age, family life cycle stage, occupation, economic status, etc.
	Competitor	brand competitor, market leader, market challenger, market follower, substitute producer, etc.
	Supplier	supply capacity, supply quality, credit system, supply price, supply cycle, supply policy, etc.
	Intermediary	distributors, agents, logistics firms, consulting firms, insurance firms, wholesalers, retailers, etc.
	Public	financial institutions, media, the government, communities, etc.
	Internal conditions of the firm	production capacity, marketing ability, management ability, staff quality, financial situation, technological level, firm organizational structure, leadership style, firm scale and strength, etc.
	Industry	industrial life cycle stage, industrial competition structure, industrial market structure, industry development trend, barriers to entering into and exiting from the industry, etc.
	Region	local policy, supply of production factors, supporting equipment, industrial cluster, residents' income level, etc.

2.1.3 SWOT Analysis Model

Analyzing the international marketing environment aims to seek marketing opportunities and to avoid environmental threats. Marketing opportunity means the market possibilities for firms to obtain competitive advantages and differential benefits. The environmental threat is the adverse trend in the environment, which may lead to the decline or elimination of a brand, a product or even the whole firm if there are no appropriate response measures. In practice, opportunities and threats often coexist. The same environmental change may be a threat to some companies while providing opportunities for others.

The task of international marketing managers is to seize opportunities, meet challenges and avoid threats in the market with powerful measures. Especially nowadays, enterprises are operating in a more volatile, uncertain, complex, ambiguous (VUCA) environment. Environmental changes in the VUCA era are having a profound impact on almost all businesses. In this case, environmental analysis is an increasingly important business function. How should international marketing managers respond to the market opportunities and environmental threats they face? The following describes a commonly used environmental analysis method—SWOT analysis.

1. An Overview of the SWOT Model

The letters of SWOT represent Strength, Weakness, Opportunity, and Threat. SWOT is the analysis of the strengths, weaknesses, opportunities and threats of a business.

SWOT can be divided into two parts: the first part is SW, which is mainly used to analyze internal conditions; the second part is OT, which is mainly used to analyze external conditions. Therefore, SWOT analysis is actually a method of synthesizing and summarizing all aspects of the internal and external conditions of the enterprise, and then analyzing the strengths and weaknesses, opportunities and threats of the organization.

It should be noted that the analysis of strengths and weaknesses mainly focuses on the advantages and disadvantages of the internal conditions of the enterprise itself compared with its competitors, while the analysis of opportunities and threats focuses on the changes in the external environment and the possible impact on the enterprise. At the same time, the same changes in the external environment may bring completely different opportunities and threats to enterprises with different resources and capabilities. Therefore, there is a close connection between the external and internal conditions.

2. The Basic Steps of SWOT Analysis

① Analyze environmental factors

Use various research methods to analyze various environmental factors of the company, namely external environmental factors and internal ability factors.

- Analyze the external environment of the enterprise. External environmental factors include opportunity factors and threat factors, which are favorable and unfavorable factors directly affecting the development of the company. They generally include economic, political, social, population, technology, market, competition and other factors.

- Analyze the internal conditions of the enterprise. Internal environmental factors include strength and weakness factors, which are positive and negative conditions compared with competitors. They generally include products and services, management, organization, finance, sales, human resources and other internal aspects.

② Construct SWOT matrix

Match the external opportunities and threats with the internal strength and weakness of the enterprise, and comprehensively analyze the internal and external environment of the enterprise. In this process, those factors that have a direct, important, massive, urgent and long-term influence on the development of the company shall be prioritized, while those indirect, secondary, minor, minor, non-urgent and short-term influencing factors shall be listed in the back.

③ Select competitive strategy

Build a SWOT matrix (Figure 2-3) to form feasible alternative strategies. The above comprehensive analysis of the internal and external of the enterprise can show the overall and concise situation of the enterprise, the position the enterprise is currently in, and the further corresponding measures that should be taken. This can play an important reference role in the formulation, implementation and inspection of enterprise development strategies.

	Strength	**Weakness**
Opportunity	SO strategies	WO strategies
Threat	ST strategies	WT strategies

Figure 2-3　SWOT Analysis Matrix

2.2　Economic Environment of International Marketing

The economic environment of international marketing is a collection of economic factors that directly or indirectly affect and restrict international marketing, and it is an important part of the international marketing environment. It can be understood from three different perspectives.

Firstly, from a global perspective, it refers to the basic situation of the world economy such as the international financial environment, the international trade environment, the economic cycle, the world economic structure, etc. The second is from the perspective of regional organizations, which consists of a series of countries and regions with similar cultural backgrounds, comparable economic development levels, and close relations with each other. The third is from the perspective of a country and its economic impact on the national level of international marketing.

Generally speaking, the economic environment has the greatest impact on international marketing, which directly affects where, how, and how much of a company's products are sold. Therefore, an analysis of the economic environment is very important.

2.2.1　Protectionism and Trade Barriers

1. Protectionism

While economic globalization and regional economic integration have deepened the liberalization and facilitation of global investment and trade, they have also been accompanied by the emergence of unilateralism, trade protectionism and anti-globalization thoughts and actions. Trade protectionism measures not only make consumers pay higher prices, but also have a significant negative impact on the global economy and trade.

Trade protectionism refers to the theory or policy of international trade that restricts imports through tariffs and various non-tariff barriers in order to protect domestic industries from competitions with foreign companies. The fundamental purpose of trade protectionism is to safeguard national economic interests by restricting other countries' goods and services to participate in the domestic market competition. Tariffs, import quotas, foreign exchange controls, anti-dumping, technical barriers, green barriers, and discriminatory government procurement policies are some means of international trade protection.

Countries take trade protection measures to protect the home market and infant industries, maintain employment, control trade deficits, conserve natural resources and develop national economies. However, in the long run, especially in the era of globalization, trade protectionism will not only be detrimental for the countries implementing the protection measures, but also harm the development of the world economy. The arguments are as follows.

- For countries implementing the protection measures, trade protectionism raises the price of imported goods, distorts the price signals of goods or services, and prevents the effective allocation of resources, which is detrimental to the domestic economic development.

- While trade protectionism provides a "protective umbrella" for domestic national industries, the lack of market competition also results in the shortage of innovative motivation in domestic market. Afterwards, it is difficult to improve the quality of products and services, which will also have a negative impact on the healthy development of domestic industries.

- Trade protectionism hinders the improvement of international specialization and production efficiency, impedes the free movement of goods and services, capital and technology and other factors around the globe, and goes against the trend of economic globalization.

Therefore, opposing trade protectionism is one of the cooperation themes actively supported and advocated by international and regional organizations, such as the World Trade Organization (WTO), Asia-Pacific Economic Cooperation (APEC) and the Organization for Economic Cooperation (OECD), and global governance mechanisms, such as the G20.

Since its reform and opening up, China has made remarkable economic achievements. In recent years, a new pattern of international economic cooperation and competition is taking shape and evolving at an accelerated pace. China will continue to promote theoretical and practical innovation in opening up, establish a new concept of open development, implement the initiative of jointly building the Belt and Road, speed up the construction of a new and open economic system, advocate the development of an open world economy, and actively participate in global economic governance.

2. Trade Barriers

In general, trade protection measures can be grouped into two categories: import restrictive measures and export incentive measures.

① Tariffs

A tariff is a tax imposed by a government on goods crossing its borders. Tariff rates are based on the value, quantity, or a combination of both of the imported goods. There are generally three types of tariffs:

- **Ad valorem duty**, which is based on the price of imported goods, and expressed as a percentage of the price of goods. The formula for calculating the ad valorem tax is: ad valorem tax = total value of goods × ad valorem tax rate.
- **Specific duty**, which is based on the quantity, volume, weight and other units of measurement of goods. The formula for calculating the specific duty is: specific duty = quantity of goods × specific duty per unit.
- **Compound duty**, which combines both methods of the ad valorem tax and the specific tax on a particular imported item. The formula for calculating the compound tax is: compound tax = quantity of goods × specific duty per unit + quantity of goods × value per unit × Ad valorem tax rate.

② Import quotas

An import quota refers to the absolute restriction on the import quantity or value of a certain type of commodity for a certain period of time in order to protect the domestic industry.

③ Foreign exchange controls

The government may adopt different forms of foreign exchange management measures such as currency blockade and government approval to establish monetary barriers for trade protection. Currency blockade is to block imports by prohibiting importers from exchanging their national currency for the seller's currency. Government approval is that when a country is in severe shortage of foreign exchanges, an exchange permission is required by the government for the exchange of a certain amount of local currency for foreign currency.

④ Anti-dumping

Anti-dumping refers to the measures taken against the dumping of foreign goods in the domestic market, whereas dumping is the act of exporting a product to another country at a price lower than its normal value with the purpose of seizing the market and causing damage to the industry of the same or similar products in the importing country. In order to prevent such kind of "predatory pricing", extra duties beyond general import duties are imposed on dumped foreign commodities to prevent them from being sold cheaply, and such additional duties are called "anti-dumping duties".

⑤ Technological barriers

Focusing on some technological characteristics of the imported products, a government may impose technical barriers through establishing compulsory or non-compulsory standards or inspection procedures, with the purpose of protecting national security, human health, the ecological environment, product quality and so on.

⑥ Green barriers

A green trade barrier refers to those import restriction measures with the specific aim of protecting natural resources, ecological environment, human health, etc. For developed countries, as the scientific and technological content of products and the public's environmental awareness are generally high, they have very strict requirements on environmental standards for imports, which are applied not only to the products, but also to the entire process, such as product development, production, packaging, transportation, using, recycling, etc.

▶ **Case 2-1**

The EU's "Eco-design Requirements for Household Washing Machines" Greatly Increase the Cost of Exporting Companies

On 31 March 2009, the EU Eco-Design Regulation Committee adopted the draft of implementation measures on the "Eco-design requirements for household washing machines", which mainly focus on the eco-design requirements and energy efficiency labeling of washing machines. Eco-design specifies the program time, indicative information of water and electricity consumption in various modes, and requires that products must be labeled with energy efficiency and dehydration efficiency levels, with complex pattern templates attached.

Europe is the second-largest market for China's washing machine exports. In 2009, the export volume of China's washing machine was 1,134,600 units, and the export value was 197.5 million U.S. dollars. Qingdao is an important manufacturing and export base of household washing machines, and has large-scale electrical products export enterprises such as Haier and Hisense. Once the European Union implements the energy efficiency labeling and ecological design requirements, Chinese export enterprises for household appliances will have to pay high fees for product energy efficiency and eco-design consultation. It will directly lead to a large increase in production costs and greatly affect the export of the domestic appliance industry.

---

⑦ Discriminatory government procurement policies

In the procurement and investment plans, the government may give priority to purchasing domestic products, so as to achieve the goal of restricting the import of similar products from foreign countries. This has become a new form of trade protectionism.

⑧ Boycotts and embargoes

Boycotts and embargoes are the extreme forms of trade protectionism for economic blockade and sanctions against countries with disputes. Specifically, government boycott is a restriction concerning the purchase and importation of certain types of goods or services from certain countries. An embargo is a ban on the export or import of certain or all goods to or from a specific country. For example, for over half a century, the American blockade of Cuba and trade embargo against it have caused great damage to the Cuban economy and people's lives.

⑨ Export subsidies

In addition to the above-mentioned import restrictive measures, there are also measures taken to stimulate exports, such as export subsidies. Export subsidies refer to the measures taken by a government, such as giving cash allowances or financial incentives to exporters, so as to reduce the price of exported goods and improve the international competitiveness of exported goods.

2.2.2　Stages of Economic Development

The marketing activities of firms are restricted by the average economic development level of a country or region. In host countries of different stages of economic development, residents' income and customers' demand for products vary a lot, which will affect the international marketing activities to a certain extent.

For example, in the consumer market, customers in regions of a relatively high economic development level tend to be concerned about the product style, performance and characteristics, and therefore quality competition is more common than price competition. In regions of a low level of economic development, customers pay more attention to the function and practicability of products, and the price factor is more important than product quality. In terms of producer market, users in regions of a higher level of economic development prefer advanced, sophisticated, highly automated and high-performance production equipment, which requires large investment and labor saving. Therefore, firms should adopt different marketing strategies in regions of different levels of economic development.

1. The Theory of "Stages of Economic Growth"

According to the theory of "Stages of Economic Growth" proposed by Walt Whitman Rostow in 1960, there are five steps in the process of economic development through which all countries will pass.

① Traditional society

This stage is characterized by a subsistent, agricultural based and isolated economy, with intensive labor and low levels of trading. At this stage, the productivity level is low, modern scientific and technological methods are not adopted for production, and the literacy rate is low.

② Preconditions for take-off

This phase is the transitional period of the economic take-off stage. At this stage, modern scientific and technological knowledge began to be applied to industrial and agricultural production. Public services such as transport, communications, electricity, education and health care have begun to develop. The dominant industry at this stage is usually the primary sector or labor-intensive manufacturing industries.

③ Take-off

This stage is a period of intensive economic growth, in which industrialization begins to occur. The application of science & technology, social facilities and human resources have been able to promote the steady development of industrial and agricultural productivity and maintain the stable development of the economy. With the improvement of agricultural labor productivity, a large number of labors have been transferred from the primary sector to the manufacturing industries, and foreign investment has increased significantly. The country's comparative advantage in international trade has shifted from agricultural exports to the export of labor-intensive products, such as clothing, shoes, toys, small handicrafts, standardized home appliances, etc.

④ Drive to maturity

At this stage, modern technology is effectively applied to most industries. High value-added export industries continue to increase. Manufacturers and consumers are keen on new technologies and products. The focus of investment has shifted from labor-intensive industries to capital-intensive industries. National welfare, transportation and communication facilities are significantly improved, and the economic growth benefits the entire society. Companies begin to invest abroad.

⑤ High mass consumption

At this stage, the main economic sector has shifted from manufacturing to services. Per capita income reaches a high level, and residents have considerable discretionary income, with the rising consumption of luxury goods. Both producers and consumers begin to make use of the achievements of high technology. People spend more money on leisure, education, health care, national security, social security programs, and begin to welcome the entry of foreign products. At present, major developed countries have entered this stage of development.

2. The United Nations' Classification

The United Nations divides the process of a country's economic development into the following three categories according to the degree of industrialization:

① Least-developed countries (LLDCs)

Least-developed countries (LLDCs) refer to industrially underdeveloped, agrarian, self-sufficient societies with rural populations and extremely low per capita income levels. Countries in this category rarely participate in world trade, represented by some countries in

Central Africa and parts of Asia.

② Less-developed countries (LDCs)

Less-developed countries (LDCs) refer to industrially developing countries that have just entered world trade with relatively low per capita income, such as many countries in Asia and Latin America.

Newly industrialized countries and regions (NICs) refer to those developing countries and regions whose economic development level is between developed countries and developing countries, with a higher level of industrialization close to developed countries, such as China, India, South Korea, Singapore, Malaysia, Thailand, Chile, Argentina, and Brazil, etc. These NICs experienced rapid industrialization, maintained a high rate of economic growth, and their per capita income exceeds that of other developing countries. They carried out a free market reform instead of imposing restrictive trade, attracted both trade and foreign direct investment, and had become strong exporters of many products such as steel, automobiles, machines, components, clothing, and electronics, as well as huge import markets.

③ More-developed countries (MDCs)

More-developed countries (MDCs) refer to industrialized countries with high per capita income, such as Canada, the United Kingdom, France, Germany, Japan, and the United States.

2.2.3　International Economic Organization

International Economic Organization (IEO) refers to the organization established through the conclusion of or accession to international treaties or agreements between two or more national governments or non-governmental organizations in order to achieve common economic goals. International economic organizations have appeared in various fields, such as transportation, postal service, communication, trading and so on.

1. Classifications of International Economic Organizations

① Classification by the scope of participation

According to the scope of participation, international economic organizations can be grouped into worldwide international economic organizations and regional international economic organizations. A worldwide international economic organization refers to an economic organization whose participants include governmental or non-governmental organizations from all or most continents of the world. The worldwide international economic organizations mainly include the World Trade Organization (WTO), the International Monetary Fund (IMF), the World Bank Group (WBG), the United Nations Conference on Trade and Development (UNCATD), etc.

Regional international economic organizations refer to the organizations whose participants are limited to governmental or non-governmental organizations in a certain continent or region. The trend of regional economic integration is rising globally, and regions such as Europe, the Americas, Asia, the Middle East and Africa are all experiencing varying degrees of regional economic integration. Some representative regional international economic organizations include the European Union (EU), the North American Free Trade Area (NAFTA), the Association of Southeast Asian Nations (ASEAN), Asia-Pacific Economic Cooperation (APEC), and the Regional Comprehensive Economic Partnership (RCEP), etc.

② Classification by the commodity structure

According to the commodity structure, there are also various international economic organizations established on the basis of the characteristics of a particular commodity. These categories are also known as professional international economic organizations, mostly producers or exporters of a particular commodity. It is characterized by the purpose of coordinating the export policies (including the export quantity and price) of each member and making unified arrangements for the production, and sales of commodities, so as to safeguard the common economic interests of the members in the international trade of relevant commodities. At present, almost all raw materials and primary products have their own international economic organizations, such as the Organization of Petroleum Exporting Countries, the International Council of Wheat, the International Tea Commission, the International Sugar Organization, the International Coffee Organization, etc.

2. Forms of Economic Integration in Regional Markets

Regional economic integration is a significant trend of world economic development, and regional economic organizations play an important role in promoting regional economic development. Understanding the different forms of regional economic integration has insightful implications for international marketers to identify and exploit opportunities in regional and global markets. Figure 2-4 shows the major forms of regional economic integration according to the varying degrees of formality within which countries' regional economic cooperation activities take place.

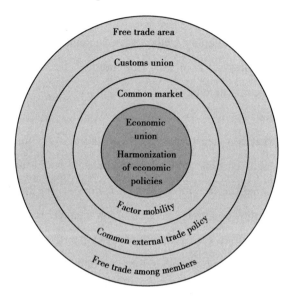

Figure 2-4   Major Forms of Regional Economic Integration

(Source: Adapted from Hollensen, 2021)

① Free trade area (FTA)

The free trade area is the least restrictive and loosest form of regional economic integration. In a FTA, all trade barriers between member countries are eliminated, and each member country maintains its own trade barriers to non-member countries.

On January 1, 1994, the North American Free Trade Agreement (NAFTA), signed by the United States, Canada and Mexico, came into effect, and the North American Free Trade Area was announced to be established. The three member countries must abide by the principles and rules stipulated in the agreement, such as national treatment, most-favored-nation treatment and procedural transparency, to achieve their objectives and eliminate trade barriers. The goods of member countries within the FTA can flow through each other with tariff reduction and exemption, while maintaining the original tariffs and barriers for the countries outside the FTA.

② Customs union

A customs union is a form of closer economic cooperation among member countries, with a higher degree of economic integration than a free trade area. As in the FTA, goods and services are freely traded among members. In addition, however, the member countries stipulate a unified trade policy for imports from non-member countries. Specifically, imports from countries outside of the customs union are subject to the same tariff regardless of which member country they enter.

The Benelux countries (Belgium; Netherlands; Luxembourg) formed a customs union in 1921, and the early "European Economic Community" and "East African Community" are also examples of customs unions.

③ Common market

The common market is a step further based on the customs union. It is characterized by the elimination of tariff barriers among member countries, the unification of tariffs for non-member countries, and the free movement of factors of production (labor, capital and technology) among member countries. In a common market, restrictions on immigration and cross-border investment are removed, and factors of production, such as labor, capital, technology, etc., are mobile and can therefore be allocated efficiently in the regional economy.

An example of a common market is the European Common Market, also commonly known as the European Economic Community (EEC), which was the predecessor of the European Union. In 1957, the six founding members, Belgium, France, Germany, Italy, Luxembourg and the Netherlands, signed the Treaty of Rome and established the EEC. The Single European Act, ratified in 1987, made important modifications and supplements to the Treaty of Rome, stipulating that by the end of 1992 a single internal market with free movement of goods, services, capital and people without borders would be established within the European Community.

④ Economic union

The form of economic union not only realizes the free movement of goods and production factors, establishes a common external tariff, but also formulates and implements certain common external economic and social policies by gradually abolishing the differences in policies among member countries. The economic integration has therefore expanded from commodity exchange to production, distribution and even the national economy, forming an organic economic entity within the economic union. In addition to the features of a common market, member countries in the economic union further coordinate their fiscal, monetary and exchange rate policies. Typically, a common currency is adopted within the economic union. Since the coordination and cooperation among member countries usually go beyond the economic dimension, to some extent, the economic union is also a political union.

The most representative example of an economic union is the European Union. In December 1991, the member countries of the European Community adopted the Treaty on the European Union in the Netherlands, commonly known as the Maastricht Treaty. On November 1, 1993, the Maastricht Treaty entered into force and the European Union was officially born. The Maastricht Treaty also resulted in the European Economic and Monetary Union (EMU), which introduced the euro, a common currency for the European Union, on January 1, 1999. On January 31, 2020, the United Kingdom officially "Br-exited", and the European Union currently has 27 member states.

2.2.4　Economic Characteristics

Economic characteristics are the most important indicators in international marketing. Indicators of economic characteristics include demographics, income, consumer savings, credit level, consumption structure, the degree of urbanization, etc.

Demographics can reflect the scale and structure of the market, and is the basic factor that constitutes demands. The market is composed of customers who have purchasing desires and purchasing power. The larger population a market has, the larger scale of the market there will be. At present, population growth rates in developed countries such as the United States and Western Europe are declining. Many developing countries including China are also facing an aging population. According to the seventh national census conducted in 2020, the total population of Chinese people on the mainland aged 60 or above has reached 264.02 million, including 190.64 million people aged 65 or above, or 13.5 percent of the total population. China's elderly market is huge.

Technological progress and economic development have extended the average life span and reduced the death rate. Therefore, the market for health care products, tourism and entertainment will be promising. The process of urbanization in many developing countries has led to population mobility, resulting in changes in population density and distribution. Furthermore, these changes have a significant impact on the scale, structure, and level of consumption, business models as well as service modes.

When analyzing and evaluating the economic environment of the international market, international marketers need to pay particular attention to the purchasing power of the target market. The purchasing power of the market is mainly affected by the income level, expenditure structure, savings and credit level and urbanization degree of the country or region, among which the income level is the most important factor. Factors that may affect the income level are as follows.

① **Gross National Product (GNP)**. It can reflect the level of national economic development and the size of the overall market of a country or a region.

② **Per capita income**. It can measure the average purchasing power of consumers and infer the level and structure of the consumption.

③ **Personal income**. It can measure the purchasing power of a local consumer market.

④ **Personal disposable income**. It can reflect the ability of consumers to spend and save.

In addition to the income level, the factor of consumption structure also affects the market purchasing power.

⑤ **Consumption structure**. It can be reflected by the Engel's coefficient. The formula for calculating the Engel's coefficient is as follows: Engel's coefficient (%) = total food expenditure (household or individual)/total consumption expenditure (household or individual) × 100%.

In the 19th century, German statistician Engel drew a rule on the change of the consumption structure based on statistical data, namely that the less a family's income, the greater the proportion of expenditure on food in the family income (or total expenditure). On the other hand, however, with the increase of family income, the proportion of expenditure on food in the family income (or the total expenditure) will decrease. This is called Engel's Law.

By applying Engel's coefficient, the Food and Agriculture Organization of the United Nations proposed the following criteria:

Poverty: Engel coefficient > 59%

Adequate food and clothing: Engel coefficient 50% − 59%

Well-off: Engel coefficient 40% − 50%

Wealthy: Engel coefficient 30% − 40%

The richest: Engel coefficient < 30%

❯❯ Chapter Summary

- Environmental factors can be categorized into macro-level factors and micro-level elements.

- The macro-level environment can be explained and understood by factors such as political, legal, economic, cultural, demographic, technological and natural factors.

- The micro-environment consists of relevant participants in the industrial chain. The factors in the micro-environment can affect a company's ability to serve its overseas customers, which include suppliers, the company itself, marketing intermediaries, customers, competitors, the public, etc.

- The international marketing environment influences marketing activities by providing opportunities or posing threats to firms.

- SWOT is an analysis of the strengths, weaknesses, opportunities and threats of a business. SWOT analysis is actually a method of synthesizing and summarizing all aspects of the internal and external conditions of the enterprise, and then analyzing the strengths and weaknesses, opportunities and threats of the organization.

- Trade protectionism refers to the theory or policy of international trade that restricts imports through tariffs and various non-tariff barriers in order to protect domestic industries from competitions with foreign companies.

- Trade protection measures can be grouped into two categories: import restrictive measures and export incentive measures, such as tariffs, import quotas, foreign exchange controls, anti-dumping, technological barriers, green barriers, discriminatory government procurement policies, boycotts and embargoes, export subsidies, etc.

- According to the theory of "Stages of Economic Growth", there are five stages of economic development, including traditional society, preconditions for take-off, take-off, drive to maturity, and high mass consumption.

- UN's classification of countries' economic development includes least-developed countries (LLDCs), less-developed countries (LDCs), and more-developed countries (MDCs).

- Forms of economic integration in regional markets include free trade area (FTA), customs union, common market, economic union, etc.

- Factors that may affect the income level include Gross National Product (GNP), per capita income, personal income, personal disposable income, and consumption structure, etc.
- The consumption structure can be reflected by the Engel's coefficient.

Main Concepts

international marketing environment, protectionism, trade barriers, Theory of Economic Growth Stages, Engel's Law

Think and Practice

1. List the elements of analyzing the macro- and micro-environment of international marketing.

2. What are the basic steps of SWOT analysis? Can you analyze the internal and external environment of a multinational corporation by applying the SWOT model?

3. Discuss the impact of the international marketing environment on international marketing activities.

4. List the main forms of trade barriers and types of tariffs.

5. List the stages of countries' economic growth and describe the characteristics of each stage.

6. List the main forms of economic integration in regional markets and describe the characteristics of each form.

7. Collect information on examples of the world economic organizations and regional economic organizations. Share with your classmates the full name, establishment time and purpose of these organizations.

8. Search for information on the Belt and Road market and analyze the macro environment of the market. What are the opportunities and threats in this market?

9. Understand the factors of economic characteristics.

10. Describe Engel's Law.

11. Collect the data of newly industrialized countries and analyze the opportunities for international marketing in the markets of NICs.

Case Study

Industry 4.0 in BRICS: What Is the Fourth Industrial Revolution? Why Does It Matter to Developing Countries?

During April 2013's Hannover Fair, the idea of "Industry 4.0" was officially presented by Germany and soon became a tag that every industrialized society wants to attach itself to. People in the private sectors welcome it as a revolution in manufacturing, and governments see it as a stimulant to the sluggish economy.

Unlike the first three Industrial Revolutions which were driven by one specific discovery or breakthrough, the fourth one is based on "combinations of technologies", as Klaus Schwab, the founder of the World Economic Forum, once pointed out.

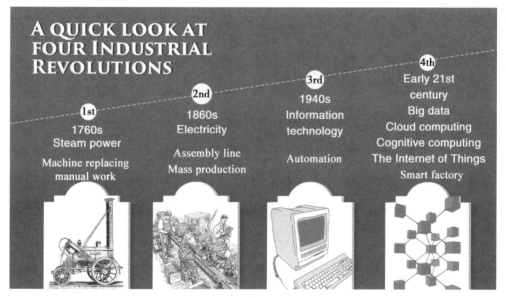

Observing the development timeline, we can find that the Industrial Revolution started with the advent of machines and climbed up one stage after another when human beings tried to harness them to achieve larger and more complex output with less input. The final result, as far as we can see, for now, is the "smart factory".

A factory is where mass production happens and being smart can be regarded as an advanced state of automation, meaning that we can teach machines to "think", which enables them to perform self-diagnosis, self-configuration and self-optimization, a lot more than doing repetitive work. As a result, the amount of time, energy and labor saved during that process can be put elsewhere to bring more productivity and generate far higher value.

For developing countries—for example, the BRICS countries—Industry 4.0 poses challenges but also provides opportunities.

(Source: Adapted from CGTN)

Discuss the following questions.

1. What are the main characteristics of Industry 4.0? What is the biggest difference between Industry 4.0 and the other three industrial revolutions?
2. What opportunities can Industry 4.0 bring to developing countries such as BRICS? What are the opportunities for international marketing companies?

Chapter 3

Political and Legal Environment of International Marketing

Chapter Outline

Political Environment of International Marketing

◇ The Concept and Types of International Political Risk

◇ Main Manifestations of Political Risk

◇ Other Manifestations of Political Risk in the Economic Field

◇ Strategies to Reduce Political Risk

Legal Environment of International Marketing

◇ Bases of Legal Systems

◇ Resolutions of International Business Disputes

◇ Protection of Intellectual Property Rights

Learning Objectives

- Understand the importance of the international political environment and its impact on foreign investment;
- Understand the concept of international political risk and identify the types;
- Understand the manifestations of political risk;
- Be familiar with the strategies to reduce political risk;
- Be familiar with the scope and characteristics of legal systems in the world;
- Be familiar with the resolutions of international business disputes;
- Have a basic understanding of the types of intellectual property and how to protect IPR.

/////// **Key Terms** ///////////////////

political risk　政治风险

nationalism　民族主义

overall political risk　总体政治风险

ownership/control risk　所有权/控制权风险

operating risk　经营风险

transfer risk　转移风险

confiscation　没收

expropriation　征用

nationalization　国有化

domestication　本土化

government ban　政府禁令

host government default　东道国政府毁约

political unrest　政治动乱

terrorism　恐怖主义

import restriction　进口限制

local-content requirement　当地含量要求

tax control　税收管制

security review　安全审查

labor problem　劳工问题

Intellectual Property Rights (IPR)　知识产权

environmental protection　环保

quasi-insurance of political risk　政治风险准保险

franchising　特许经营

International Investment Agreements (IIAs)　国际投资协定

Bilateral Investment Treaty (BIT)　双边投资条约

code law (civil law)　大陆法系

common law　英美法系

first to use　使用在先

first to register　注册在先

force majeure　不可抗力

international business disputes　国际商务争端

mediation/conciliation　调解

arbitration　仲裁

litigation　诉讼

jurisdiction　司法管辖权

patent　专利

Patent Cooperation Treaty (PCT)　专利合作条约

invention　发明

utility model　实用新型

trademark　商标

copyright　版权

▶ **Opening Case**

Huawei Expands Patent Licensing Amid Sales Revenue Slush

Chinese technology giant Huawei has expanded patent licensing with global firms, as the company seeks new sources of revenue after being added to Washington's trade blacklist in 2019.

Huawei announced the renewal of the patent license agreement with Finnish company Nokia. Nokia began booking licensing revenue from Huawei back in 2017, the latest extension reflects Huawei's prowess, which continues to grow despite the U.S. pressure. Huawei and OPPO also announced the signing of a global patent cross-licensing deal, which covers basic patents for cellular communication standards, including 5G standards. Huawei and Samsung Group have signed a similar deal on their respective standard essential patent packages. In automobiles, the tech giant has reached royalty agreements with automakers, including Audi, Mercedes-Benz and BMW, to add communications technologies to their vehicles.

In 2022, Huawei has signed or renewed more than 20 patent licensing deals in industries including smartphones, automobiles and telecommunications. Huawei's global patent licensing revenue was about $1.2 billion from 2019 to 2021, or hundreds of millions of dollars annually. For the second year in a row, the company will receive more patent revenue in 2022 than it pays out to other companies.

Huawei posted a total revenue of 636.8 billion yuan ($191.1 billion) in 2021, a decline of 28.6 percent from a year earlier, as the U.S. curbs on Chinese technology influenced its sales in places such as the U.S. and Europe.

Huawei CEO & founder Ren Zhengfei told the company's intellectual property team to step up efforts to turn its vast pool of patents into revenue through "reasonable pricing", according to a company memo made public in April 2022.

For five straight years, Huawei has ranked first in the world in terms of Patent Cooperation Treaty (PCT) applications, said Alan Fan, head of Huawei's IPR Department.

(China's telecom giant Huawei displays 5G technology at the 2018 Mobile World Congress in Barcelona, Spain, February 26, 2018)

(Source: Adapted from CGTN)

3.1　Political Environment of International Marketing

The impact of government on the environment is effected through government policies, laws and regulations, as well as other restrictive measures. The government's foreign trade policies and attitudes reflect its fundamental idea of improving national interests. Therefore, companies must assess the political and legal environment of the country as much as possible before entering a country.

A country's political environment mainly includes the government and party system, government policy, nationalism, political risks, etc. International marketers should pay attention to the composition of the current government and its main policies for the operations of foreign businesses. Is the government conservative, neutral or far-left? Does the current commercial policy encourage free operation systems or state ownership? To answer these questions, companies must also consider the views of the ruling party. To well understand the political climate of a foreign government, a company must study what the government stands for and consider, as far as possible, the long-term direction of its political development. The stability of government policy directly affects the long-term management strategy of enterprises. Therefore, the primary concern of enterprises is to focus on the fundamental change in a country's foreign policy.

Admittedly, the change of political parties and governments may cause unstable relationship between the government and enterprises, but the most critical political factor affecting international marketing in the world today should be strong economic nationalism. The influence of nationalism on foreign companies is the same in both developed and developing countries, but only in varying degrees of intensity.

3.1.1　The Concept and Types of International Political Risk

In the past, only large multinational companies were concerned about political risk. However, as more and more companies are purchasing and selling globally, political risk has gradually become a common topic. Nowadays, political risk management is playing an increasingly important role in the agenda of most senior decision-makers.

Political risk is the possibility of an adverse effect of political events occurring in one country or changes in a country's political relations with other countries. It is a risk that companies often encounter when operating across borders, and occurs not only in developing countries in general, but also in developed countries from time to time. For example, in 1980, Canada adopted a new energy policy that reduced foreign participation in energy from 75 percent to 50 percent, thus drastically altering its traditional approach of welcoming foreign investment in the oil industry to the detriment of foreign investors.

There are two main reasons for the generation of political risk. Firstly, there is a goal conflict between the multinational company and the host country. When companies operate internationally, they seek to maximize their economic interests and to satisfy the interests of their shareholders, suppliers, customers and creditors. The host government, on the other hand, does not only concern with the development of its own economy, but also has political, social, cultural and ideological objectives. Therefore, there is often a conflict of objectives between the two sides, such as the issue of ownership and control, the inflow of foreign capital and the outflow of capital from the host country, etc. Secondly, there is a conflict between the business operations and the host government's regulations. In order to meet the country's intended objectives, host governments often enact laws and regulations to restrict the operation of businesses in their jurisdictions. The implementation of these measures often poses risks to foreign enterprises. It can be seen that political risk is closely related to the political system, economic policy, culture and law of the host country and is beyond the control of corporate investors.

Political risk comes from the uncertainty of the host country's political change in the future and the uncertainty of damaging the interests of the foreign enterprise charged by the host government. It generally comprises four categories: overall political risk, ownership/control risk, operating risk, and transfer risk.

Overall political risk arises from the uncertainty of a company's perception of the prospects of the host country's political system. The overall political instability does not necessarily force companies to abandon investment projects, but it will certainly interfere with business decision-making and profitability.

Ownership/Control risk arises from the uncertainty of the host government's control over or restriction on foreign companies' property.

Operating risk is the risk of the host government's interference with the ongoing operations of a firm. It is mainly manifested in restrictions on operational functions such as production, sales and finance.

Transfer risk mainly occurs when companies want to transfer capital between countries. Transfer risk arises primarily from the host government's restrictions on the repatriation of operating income and capital from foreign enterprises. Transfer risk also includes the risk of currency devaluation.

▶ Case 3-1

China Urges Myanmar to Stop Violence

On March 14, 2021, the Chinese Embassy in Myanmar urged Myanmar to take effective measures to stop violence and punish perpetrators after several Chinese-funded factories were smashed and burned by lawbreakers on Sunday, which led to several Chinese being injured.

Chinese investment in the textile industry in Myanmar has created nearly 400,000 jobs for Myanmar, and such behavior will also damage the interests of Myanmar people, the embassy said.

The statement came after over 10 factories, including some Chinese-funded enterprises, were vandalized and set on fire at an industrial zone in Myanmar's Yangon city on March 14, 2021.

Carrying iron rods, axes and gasoline, the arsonists smashed the security personnel and set fires at the factories' entrances and in warehouses.

Vehicles and nearby shops were also vandalized.

(Source: Adapted from *China Daily*)

3.1.2   Main Manifestations of Political Risk

1. Confiscation

Confiscation is the most severe political risk, referring to the official seizure of a foreign company's assets without payment. There were two notable confiscations. When Fidel Castro became the political leader of Cuba and later when the Shah of Iran was overthrown, U.S. enterprises' property were confiscated. Confiscation was most prevalent in the 1950s and 1960s.

2. Expropriation (Nationalization)

Expropriation is a political risk when the host government seizes the foreign investment but makes some reimbursement for the assets. The purpose of expropriation is nationalization, which refers to the takeover of foreign companies by the host government.

In 2008, then Venezuelan President Hugo Chavez announced the nationalization of Cemex (Mexico), Holcin (Switzerland) and Lafarge (France). The Venezuelan government formed joint ventures with the above companies and controlled more than 60% of the shares. Thus, the Chavez government expropriated Mexico's Cemex operations, paying a negotiated price.

3. Domestication

Domestication can be understood as a gradual process of expropriation. By domestication, host countries gradually transfer the foreign investment to national control and ownership through a series of government decrees that mandate the local ownership and greater national involvement, and reduce the control of foreign companies.

4. Government Bans

The host country affects the operation of investors in many ways, such as losing control of investment and the opportunity to make profits. Therefore, their decision-making is completely dependent on the government's requirements and policies, not on market conditions.

▶ Case 3-2

Coca-Cola Is Back with the Recipe Still Being a Secret

Since 1991, the recipe for Coca-Cola had been kept strictly confidential. The Indian government had ordered Coca-Cola to disclose its formula or it must cease its operations in India. It is said that a secret ingredient called 7-X makes Coca-Cola unique. The Indian Industry Minister informed the Indian parliament that Coca-Cola's branch in India had to transfer its 60% shareholding to the Indians and hand over its production technology by April 1978 or close down its business.

Although Coca-Cola's sales in India accounted for less than 1% of its global sales, a potential market of 800 million people was huge. The Coca-Cola Company expressed its reluctance to give up the formula. The Indian government refused to allow Coca-Cola to import the necessary raw materials. In 1977, Coca-Cola was deported by the Indian government.

16 years later, Coca-Cola re-entered the Indian market as the government's attitude toward foreign investment changed. This time it was no longer necessary to publish its formula.

5. The Host Government Defaults

Overseas investment projects tend to have a long operating period. During that period, the change of relevant policies, regulations, the ruling party or even the government in the host country may occur. In such circumstances, the host government may not fulfill the relevant commitments in the project agreement. The commitments can range from building infrastructure, such as roads, pipelines and export terminals, to labor agreements and the elimination of some government regulations and fees.

6. Political Unrest

Political unrest includes wars, revolutions, subversion, coups, civil strife, violence, and terrorism. Terrorists often target multinational companies for reasons such as humiliating the government and its relationship with foreign companies, kidnapping foreign company managers to raise funds for terrorist activities, or creating fear within a country.

The Institute for Economics and Peace released the Global Terrorism Index 2022 in March 2022. The index provides a comprehensive summary of the main trends and patterns of global terrorism over the past 14 years. By examining indicators such as the number of terrorist attacks and casualties, the report ranks 163 countries (99.7% of the world's population) according to the impact of terrorism. Among them, the 10 countries most affected by terrorism in 2021 are Afghanistan, Iraq, Somalia, Burkina Faso, Syria, Nigeria, Mali, Niger, Myanmar and Pakistan.

[Box 3-1]

Country Risk Rating Report on China's Overseas Investments (2022) Released

The world is undergoing unprecedented changes in a century and suffering from the COVID-19 epidemic, so the risks of the global investment environment deserve vigilance. In 2020, China's outward FDI flows and stocks ranked the first and third place in the world, respectively. China's influence in the field of foreign direct investment continued to expand. From the perspective of the overseas investment of Chinese enterprises and sovereign wealth, this report constructs an evaluation system with a total of 42 sub-indicators including five major indicators: economic foundation, solvency, social resilience, political risk and relations with China. Covering 114 countries and regions, this report provides a comprehensive and quantitative assessment of the main risks faced by Chinese companies.

The results show that for developed economies, the Economic Foundation is better than the developing countries, the Political Risk is lower, the Social Resilience is higher, the Solvency is stronger, and the overall investment risk is lower than that of emerging economies. The highest rated country in 2022 is Switzerland, with the other countries in the top ten being New Zealand, Denmark, Qatar, South Korea, Norway, Sweden, the UAE, Germany and Australia. For emerging economies, although the gap between their Economic Foundation and Political Risk scores and that of developed countries is still relatively obvious, in the long term they will remain the most promising destination for Chinese overseas investment, as the demand for investment within the emerging economies, especially the RCEP region, rises. At present, the Belt and Road region has become a new growth point for China's outward direct investment. Specifically, among the countries along the Belt and Road, investment risks are low in East Asia, generally higher in Africa and South Asia, higher in some countries in Central and West Asia, and more varied in West Asia.

Political risks have the characteristics of wide coverage, strong radiation, large losses and irresistibility, so the management of political risks should be strengthened in overseas investments. For political risks in host countries, an assessment of political risks should be made based on an understanding of the risks, and preventive measures should be formulated according to the characteristics and the magnitude of the risks.

3.1.3 Other Manifestations of Political Risk in the Economic Field

Political risk not only results from government actions, but also has its consequences and impacts reflected in the economic field.

1. Import Restrictions

Import restrictions refer to a government's direct restriction on the quantity or amount of import of certain consumer goods or products such as raw materials, machinery and spare parts for a certain period of time. Within a specified period, goods within a quota may be imported, while those above the quota may not be imported, or may be imported only after higher tariffs or fines have been imposed. The aim is to force foreign companies to buy more of the host country's products and thus create a market for local industries, establish or accelerate the establishment of specific domestic industries and promote the technological progress and industrial upgrading in the country.

2. Local-content Requirements

A local content requirement specifies that certain parts of a commodity must be produced within the importing country, either in a specific number or in value. Through the regulation of local content requirements, the host country attempts to achieve the goals of improving local technology, promoting the development of related industries, increasing labor force employment, and accumulating local capital. But at the same time, it also faces the risk of a decline in the level of domestic consumer welfare.

In South Africa, the automobile industry is the second largest industry and the largest manufacturing segment. Its output value accounts for 7.5% of the gross domestic product (GDP), 30% of manufacturing output and 10% of exported products. Due to the developed automobile industry, South Africa is also known as "Detroit in Africa". In 2019, the South African government formulated the overall plan for South Africa's automobiles, with the goal of increasing the content of local automobiles from 39% to 60% by 2035.

3. Foreign Exchange Control

Foreign exchange control refers to the international trade policy that a government adopts laws and regulations to restrict international settlement and foreign exchange trading in order to balance international payments and maintain its own currency exchange rate.

Foreign investors' investment and operations in the host country inevitably involve foreign exchange transactions. Foreign investors will encounter foreign exchange controls and transfer risks when investing their capital and transferring their profits. Foreign investors are required to comply with the relevant foreign exchange regulations of the host country, otherwise the transaction may be hindered and may even attract anti-money laundering, anti-tax avoidance and other investigations.

4. Tax Control

The use of tax to control foreign investment is also a manifestation of political risk. When going abroad to participate in overseas investment and international marketing activities, Chinese enterprises need to understand the general local business environment, the main tax types, the taxation system and the bilateral tax treaties (agreements or arrangements) in the host country.

In practice, some energy and mineral exporting countries have imposed additional high taxes on local energy and infrastructure projects of Chinese enterprises by modifying domestic laws and regulations or issuing new administrative orders for geopolitical reasons, which seriously affect the normal operation and investment interests of Chinese enterprises in the local area.

5. Security Review

Security review risk is a political risk that the host country rejects foreign investors on the grounds of safeguarding national security and interests. It is mainly manifested in the access to special industries, such as nuclear technology, information technology, public utilities, strategic resources, etc., which may be limited due to the sensitivity of the industry. The U.S., Australia, Canada and some European countries often have governmental review systems and corresponding review bodies that stipulate that foreign investment must not threaten national security.

In the global competition for 5G technology and new infrastructure, Chinese companies such as Huawei and ZTE have been subjected to sanctions by the U.S. and other Western countries. Through the geopolitical influence built up by its allies, the U.S. has imposed a series of sanctions on Chinese enterprises, such as prohibiting or restricting economic entities in third countries from conducting economic and trade exchanges with Chinese counterparts, which has adversely affected the global infrastructure investment of

Chinese enterprises.

6. Labor Problems

The risk of labor protection is the risk that enterprises suffer losses due to the punishment of the host country, or the boycott of the trade union for the violation of the labor laws and regulations of the host country.

This is a typical legal problem encountered by Chinese companies in overseas M&A. In most developed countries, labor protection laws are sound and trade unions are strong, so they have a great influence in the process of investment and M&A, in post-investment management, and even in the process of layoffs. However, labor disputes are often overlooked by Chinese companies. If the personnel of the enterprise are arbitrarily adjusted or laid off, the enterprise may violate local labor laws, leading to labor union protests, strikes and even government punishment or litigation.

▶ **Case 3-3**

Fuyao and UAW

In January 2014, Cao Dewang, Fuyao's global chairman, announced that he planned to build an automotive glass manufacturing plant on the site of the former General Motors Moraine plant. Fuyao Glass employed 2000 American workers in Moraine, exceeding the number of employees originally agreed with Moraine and the Ohio government.

In 2016, the U.S. Occupational Safety and Health Administration (OSHA) received a letter of complaint from a group of 11 workers at the Fuyao Glass Plant. The letter of complaint was signed by the UAW (United Auto Workers, the largest union of auto workers in the U.S.). The OSHA fined Fuyao $226,000 for safety violations.

In April 2017, at the push of the union, Fuyao raised hourly wages for all its American employees from about $10 an hour to about $12.

----

7. Intellectual Property Rights

Intellectual property risk refers to the risk that an enterprise may infringe others' intellectual property due to its ignorance of the host country's intellectual property laws and regulations, or suffer losses due to its weak protection of its own intellectual property rights or lack of independent intellectual property rights.

The biggest impact of intellectual property risks comes from European and American markets. For example, the United States International Trade Commission often launches Article 337 to investigate intellectual property rights of foreign investors.

8. Environmental Protection

Environmental protection risk is mainly the risk of loss of overseas investments due to environmental protection issues. For example, hydropower plants acquired in Africa need to be approved by the World Bank, as well as by green organizations in Germany, France, etc. For Chinese companies, a breach of the relevant regulations on environmental protection in the host country could mean a huge fine and could even lead to an order to close down.

3.1.4　Strategies to Reduce Political Risk

Although the political risk of the host country cannot be changed, there are some strategies that can help international marketing enterprises reduce the impact of political risk.

1. Quasi-insurance of Political Risk

Quasi-insurance of political risk is a subtle way to resist political risks by keeping the government out of the project and thus reducing the chances of expropriation and confiscation by the host government, known as "soft political risk insurance". Specific methods include licensing or franchising, establishing joint ventures with local companies and expanding the investment base.

① Licensing or franchising

When a company owns unique technology and the political risk is high, it may be possible to license the technology or patent to obtain a license fee. A company can use licensing agreements with a foreign firm to supplement its domestic bottom line with almost no capital or marketing costs.

Franchising is similar to licensing, especially when it comes to the use of a business name and a business model for a specified period, and possibly covering a geographical area.

More details of licensing and franchising will be discussed later in Chapter 6.

② Establishing joint ventures

Joint ventures can be with local firms or other third-country multinational corporations.

Joint ventures with local companies help reduce anti-MNC sentiment, promote local employment and increase local revenues, while joint ventures with another third-country MNC add additional bargaining power for third countries.

③ Expanding the investment base

By expanding the investment base, the international marketing company can seek multiple investors, banks and multilateral institutions to participate in the project, form consortia with funds from the host country and other countries to invest, and ensure that the funding for the project comes from a wider range of sources, including host country banks.

The advantage of this strategy is that it can mobilize the strength of all the investors and stakeholders of the project whenever there is any threat of government takeover or expropriation. This strategy becomes particularly powerful especially if the bank has provided a loan to the host country. If more investors from within and outside the host country as well as multilateral institutions are involved, the host government will also be less likely to take direct control of project assets because of pressure from relevant interest groups as well as the international community.

2. Institutional Protection

There are strategies for taking advantage of institutional protection such as IIAs and BITs.

① International Investment Agreements

International Investment Agreements（IIAs） are international treaties concluded by countries or regions to protect and promote cross-border investment by foreign investors. Investment protection agreements can usually provide foreign investors with a number of core substantive investment protections, including fair and equitable treatment, national treatment and most-favored-nation treatment, government expropriation compensation, profit repatriation, etc. The host country's acts of impeding and restricting cross-border investment projects due to geopolitical considerations may fall into the scope of the above-mentioned substantive protection.

② Bilateral Investment Treaty

The political risk is significantly reduced if a **Bilateral Investment Treaty（BIT）** is concluded between the host government and the home government of the investor. It stipulates the relevant rules for mutual protection and promotion of two-way investment. By 2022, there are 108 investment agreements signed and currently in force between China and relevant countries and regions. If the host country violates its obligations in investment protection and causes losses to the enterprise, the enterprise can safeguard its legitimate rights and interests according to the dispute settlement mechanism in the applicable investment agreement.

These treaties are effective mechanisms for the host government to fulfill its obligations. In fact, if the host government attempts to infringe the rights of investors, it will not only violate the prevailing standards of international law, but also violate the treaties signed with the investor's home country. In other words, the existence of these treaties increases the balance of interests of the host government.

3. Insurance of Political Risk

The access for investors to obtain insurance of political risk includes commercial insurance companies, export credit agencies, and multilateral institutions.

① Insurance from commercial insurance companies

This is to purchase common commercial property insurance from commercial insurance institutions, such as all risk insurance for property, business interruption insurance, third-party liability insurance, etc.

② Insurance from export credit agencies

This is policy insurance for investments in areas with high political risks. For example, China Export and Credit Insurance Corporation, as a policy insurance agency in China, underwrites export credit insurance, covering the scope of political risks including expropriation and nationalization, exchange events, wars, government default, etc.

③ Insurance from multilateral institutions

The Multilateral Investment Guarantee Agency (MIGA), established by the World Bank in 1988, encourages foreign capital flows into developing countries by providing investment guarantees to prevent risks such as civil war and strife, property expropriation, currency transfers, and host country default.

▶ Case 3-4

Chinese Enterprises Suffered Great Losses in Libya

Libya is one of the important markets for China's foreign contracted engineering business. As of 2011, China has undertaken a total of about 50 large-scale projects in

Libya, involving a contract value of US $18.8 billion. The investments of the 13 central SOEs (China Railway Construction Engineering Corporation and others) cover housing construction, supporting municipalities, railway construction, oil and telecommunications. The war in Libya exposed Chinese enterprises to a series of risks, such as loss of fixed assets, loss of expected earnings, loss of withdrawal costs and loss of future exchange rate settlement.

The reasons why Chinese enterprises suffered great losses in Libya are as follows: First, they only invested in engineering insurance, but war is the exclusion of engineering insurance. Secondly, in addition to commercial insurance, there is also policy insurance that can bear the economic losses caused by war. In addition, currently China has not signed any form of Bilateral Investment Treaty with the Libyan government.

3.2 Legal Environment of International Marketing

The legal environment refers to a variety of laws, rules, and regulations to be followed when a corporation develops economic relations with others. The law is the legal basis for maintaining normal business activities. Companies can only be effectively protected by law if they carry out various marketing activities under the law.

As various countries have obvious differences in their political philosophy, judicial systems, historical traditions and social norms, their laws and regulations may vary. For example, the U.S. and E.U. countries have relatively stricter laws on product quality, product liability, intellectual property rights, environmental pollution and treatment of employees, which undoubtedly increases the complexity of the legal environment in which multinational companies operate. Multinational companies must therefore learn how to adapt to different legal regimes in the global marketplace.

In recent years, as Chinese brands are going global, it is not uncommon for Chinese brands and trademarks to be registered overseas by others. When entering an international market, a Chinese company may find that a foreign competitor has already used its brand in that market, or that there are no trademark protection measures in that market. For example,

"Dabao" "Changhong" "Wang Zhihe" and many other well-known Chinese trademarks have been registered overseas.

Therefore, when engaged in international marketing activities, enterprises should not only abide by their legal system but also understand and comply with the legal system of the host country as well as relevant international regulations, international practices, and guidelines.

3.2.1 Bases of Legal Systems

International marketing activities are subject to laws, rules, and regulations formulated by diverse legal systems. There are three heritages of legal systems in the world, which are code law, common law and Islamic law.

1. An Overview of the Three Heritages of Legal Systems

① Code law (Civil law)

Code law (or Civil law) originated in ancient Rome in the 5th century BCE, and it is the earliest and most widely used legal system in the world. Code law systems are based mainly on Roman law heritage and are found in European countries such as Germany, France, Italy, Spain, Belgium, Netherlands, Switzerland, etc., Asian countries such as Japan, etc., and most Latin American countries.

Code law is based on an all-inclusive system of written rules of law. It consists of a comprehensive system of legislation, with the rules usually codified. The legal system under the code law is generally divided into three separate codes, including commercial law, civil law and criminal law.

② Common law

The common law system originated in England in the 11th century. It applies to over 20 countries, including the U.K., the U.S. (The exception is the state of Louisiana, which adopts the civil law system.), Canada (The exception is the province of Quebec, which adopts the civil law system), Australia, New Zealand, India, Malaysia, Singapore, Kenya, South Africa, Zimbabwe and other countries once under English influence.

The most important feature of the common law system is its predominantly tradition-oriented approach. The basis for common law is traditions, past practices and legal precedents established by higher courts through interpretation of regulations, laws and past rulings. Common law attaches great importance to custom and cases, and the judgments of past cases are binding on the decisions of similar cases in the future, namely the so-called principle of precedent.

In recent years, countries with common law systems have formulated a large number of written laws as a supplement to case law.

③ Islamic law

Islamic law is based on Islamic doctrines and the interpretation of the *Koran*. The content of Islamic law (Sharia) began to take shape around the 10th century. At present, more than half of Islamic countries in the world practice Islamic law, such as Iran, Saudi Arabia, etc. There are also certain Islamic law countries in the Belt and Road area. Nevertheless, Islamic countries in the Gulf region has currently established codified corporate laws.

This legal system is mixed with many Islamic religious precepts. For example, the laws of most Islamic countries prohibit investment in the alcohol or tobacco industry, banks cannot charge interest, etc.

2. The Comparison between Code Law and Common Law

The following three differences between civil law and common law systems may be involved in international businesses.

In terms of the **basis for the two legal systems**, code law is based on a comprehensive system of written rules and provisions with possibly broad interpretations. On the other hand, common law is recognized as not being comprehensive or all-inclusive, since it is based on tradition, past practices and legal precedents.

Another difference lies in the **issue of intellectual property protection**. Specifically the principle of determining the ownership of a brand or trademark in civil law countries is quite different from that in common law countries. Most civil-law countries apply a "first to register" approach, meaning the ownership is established by registration. On the other hand, most common-law countries adopt a "first to use" approach, meaning the ownership is established by prior use. It is therefore important to understand where and under what circumstances an infringement might occur.

In addition, common law and civil law also differ in the **scope of determining force majeure** when it comes to the impossibility of performing a contract. In common-law countries, force majeure is strictly limited to unforeseeable natural events such as earthquakes, mudslides, tsunamis, tornadoes, floods, etc. In civil-law countries, however, force majeure encompasses not only unforeseeable natural events but also unforeseeable human conducts, such as labor strikes, riots, etc. Therefore, compared with the civil law system, the criteria for identifying force majeure in the common law system are more stringent, whereas in civil-law countries, the scope of contract non-performance may be expanded.

Table 3-1　A Comparison between Code Law and Common Law

Content	Code Law	Common Law
Basis	written rules and catchall provisions with broad interpretations possible	tradition, past practices and legal precedents, not all-inclusive
Ownership of intellectual property	first to register	first to use
Force majeure	unforeseeable occurrences of natural and human acts	unforeseeable occurrences of natural acts

[Box 3-2]

Can COVID-19 Be Considered as Force Majeure?

The outbreak of the COVID-19 epidemic in early 2020 had a significant negative impact on many aspects of international business activities. The parties to an international commercial contract were inevitably unable to perform their contractual obligations due to market price fluctuations, difficulties in the transportation of goods, and non-compliance with quarantine standards, and there were situations of delay in performance, inability to perform, or even termination of the contract.

On February 1, 2020, the China International Trade Arbitration Commission issued a force majeure certificate to companies. Issuing a force majeure certificate was a powerful way to exempt international commercial contracts from the breach of contract under the influence of the epidemic, but the force majeure certificate was not recognized by all other countries around the world. For example, on February 7, 2020, the Dutch companies Royal Dutch Shell PLC and TOTAL SA issued a statement rejecting the force majeure certificate provided by China National Offshore Oil Corporation. Besides, in common law countries, if there was no force majeure clause, the court would apply more stringent rules to examine whether COVID-19 could constitute an exemption.

Therefore, in practice, whether the liability can be exempted through force majeure needs to be combined with the identified laws and specific cases.

3.2.2 Resolutions of International Business Disputes

In international businesses, disputes inevitably arise over a refusal to pay by purchasers, poor quality supplies, delays in shipping goods, rising raw material costs and so on. When faced with an international business dispute, the basic resolution methods include negotiation, conciliation, arbitration and litigation. The settlement of any dispute shall take the following steps: first, communicate and negotiate informally; If communication and negotiation do not work, mediation, arbitration, or even litigation may be conducted. Only when all else fails is the last resort—litigation. In practice, if the parties to a dispute fail to reach a conciliation agreement, most international marketers prefer to settle the dispute through arbitration rather than litigation.

1. Mediation/Conciliation

Mediation (or conciliation) is a process whereby two parties to a dispute ask a third party to mediate their divergences in order to reach an agreement. Mediation is private and meetings between the parties and the mediator are confidential.

Mediation can be classified into non-governmental mediation, arbitration mediation, and court mediation according to the institution and procedure by which it is handled. Non-governmental mediation is a mediation conducted with the participation or under the auspices of individuals or non-governmental organizations, such as chambers of commerce, associations, and other non-governmental organizations. Non-governmental mediation has no legal effect, and the mediation agreement reached can only be voluntarily implemented by the parties. Arbitration mediation refers to mediation conducted with the participation or under the auspices of an arbitration institution. Once the agreement of arbitration mediation is reached, it is binding on the parties. A court mediation is a mediation conducted with the participation or under the auspices of the court. Court conciliation is a litigation activity in itself, and its conciliation has the same legal effect as a judgment.

Therefore, under formal mediation methods such as arbitration mediation and court mediation, the mediation agreement has a legal effect and is binding on the parties.

2. Arbitration

If mediation is not conducted or fails, then the next step is arbitration. Arbitration means that both parties concerned choose a fair and informed party or parties as the arbitrator. The arbitrator decides the merits of the case and makes an award that both parties agree to implement. Most arbitration is conducted under the auspices of professional arbitration institutions. In most countries, decisions reached through formal arbitration are legally valid.

The advantages of arbitration include:

- Fast adjudication and low cost.
- The arbitration process is confidential and there is no hostile act, so there is no damaging effect on reputation.
- Arbitration has the characteristics of mediation, so about 1/3 of cases in international businesses have been settled through direct dialogues between the parties before the award.
- Arbitrators do not appear as judges and are experienced, so the arbitration result is fair and easy to accept by the parties.
- During the arbitration, both parties are allowed to continue business while disputing, so that greater loss can be avoided.
- The arbitration is not based on legal provisions but on a fair treatment of the facts, and the parties are satisfied that they do not have to resort to the national courts of the other party.
- If the parties to a contract settle their dispute by arbitration, an arbitration clause should be included as part of the contract. A typical arbitration clause can be included in the contract such as: Any controversy or claim arising out or relating to this contract shall be determined by arbitration in accordance with the International Arbitration Rules of ICC.

For the above-mentioned reasons, arbitration plays an increasingly important role in solving international commercial disputes.

[**Box 3-3**]

International Commercial Arbitration Institutions

There are more than 100 countries and regions in the world with permanent international commercial arbitration institutions, which can generally be classified into international, regional, national and industrial arbitration institutions.

① International arbitration institution

- The International Court of Arbitration of the International Chamber of Commerce (ICC). Founded in 1923 and headquartered in Paris, it is a permanent arbitration institution under the International Chamber of Commerce. The ICC is the world's leading and most influential international arbitration institution providing international economic and trade arbitration services, and is a major center for international commercial arbitration.

- The International Center for the Settlement of Investment Disputes (ICSID)

② Regional arbitration institution

- Inter-American International Commercial Arbitration Commission

- Commercial Arbitration Center of the Economic Commission for Asia and the Far East

③ National arbitration institution

- The Arbitration Institute of Stockholm Chamber of Commerce (AISCC). The agency has rich arbitration experience and a good operation mechanism with handling cases quickly and timely, which has led to an increasing number of international economic and trade contracts for arbitration in Sweden.

- London Court of International Arbitration (LCIA)

- Court of Arbitration of the Zurich Chamber of Commerce

- American Arbitration Association (AAA)

- Japan Commercial Arbitration Association (ZCC)

- The Hong Kong International Arbitration Centre (HKIAC)

- China International Economic and Trade Arbitration Commission (CIETAC)

④ Industrial arbitration institution

There are the various specialist arbitration agencies set up by various trade associations, such as the arbitration bodies set up under the London Grain Association and the London Rubber Exchange, the Dutch Coffee Trade Arbitration Committee, etc.

3. Litigation

There are many reasons why companies are reluctant to litigate in court, such as:

- Relatively high cost and long duration when going through litigation.
- Fear of creating a bad reputation and damaging public relations.
- Fear of unfair treatment in a foreign court.
- Fear of the loss of confidentiality.

Therefore, companies are often more willing to resolve international business disputes through peaceful means such as mediation, arbitration, etc.

When settling commercial disputes between parties in two different countries by means of litigation, one key issue is to clarify which country's law and which country's court to resort to, namely the jurisdictional issue. In order to reduce uncertainty and avoid unnecessary conflicts, international marketers should specify the jurisdiction clause when signing contracts. In the absence of such a clause, the parties to the dispute may rely on the law of the country where the contract is established or on the law of the country where the contract is performed. Generally speaking, if there is no jurisdiction clause in the contract, the law of the place where the contract is signed shall govern.

3.2.3 Protection of Intellectual Property Rights

As more and more Chinese companies go global and participate in international competition and cooperation, cross-border protection of intellectual property rights has become a mandatory course for innovative companies to develop international markets. According to the data released by the World Intellectual Property Organization, China has ranked first in the world in the number of international patent applications under the PCT (Patent Cooperation Treaty) for three consecutive years in 2022. Chinese enterprises have been very active in international patent applications.

1. Types of Intellectual Property

Intellectual property is a general term for the legal rights based on creative achievements as well as industrial and commercial marks. The three main types of intellectual property rights are patent right, trademark right, and copyright, among which patent right and trademark right are also collectively referred as industrial property rights.

① Patent right

Patent right is an exclusive right granted to an inventor or designer within a certain period of time according to legal procedures. Patents include invention patents, utility model patents and appearance design patents.

An **invention** is a new technical solution to a product, method or improvement thereof. Compared with the other two types of patents, an invention patent allows for a longer period of protection, but the granting criteria are higher and the procedure is more time-consuming.

A **utility model** is a new technical solution for the shape or construction of a product or a combination thereof, which is suitable for practical use. Utility model patents have a shorter term of protection, but are granted with a lower standard and a less time-consuming procedure.

A **design** refers to the new design of the shape, pattern, color and combination of the whole or part of the product, which is aesthetic and suitable for industrial application.

② Trademark

A trademark is a mark used by an operator to distinguish his or her goods or services from those of others. The most important function of a trademark is that of source identification.

③ Copyright

Copyright refers to the rights (including property rights and personal rights) enjoyed by the authors of literary, artistic and scientific works.

2. How to Protect Intellectual Property Rights Overseas

① The need for patenting abroad

Before entering overseas markets, international marketing enterprises should carefully consider the layout of overseas patents in advance, for obtaining patent protection overseas has the following benefits:

- International patenting can help companies build up patent strength to counteract or restrain competitors.

- International patenting can help companies to obtain valuable patents with the potential for gaining profits through licensing, patent transfer, etc.
- International patenting can increase the added value of products and further promote the brand value.
- International patenting can help to improve a company's bargaining power over suppliers and its ability to control risk in the supply chain.
- International patenting can promote the incorporation of relevant patents into international technical standards and improve the company's industry influence.
- Patenting abroad can gain more social and cultural identities in the local market.

② The principles of "first to register" or "first to use"

As we mentioned earlier, there are differences in the principles of protecting intellectual property rights in various legal systems. In many civil law countries, the ownership of intellectual property rights is established on a "first-to-register" basis, i.e. whoever registers a trademark or other intellectual property right first is deemed to be the legal owner. In common law countries, however, the ownership of intellectual property rights is established on a "first to use" basis, i.e. whoever can prove that they used it first is usually considered the legal owner. If companies are not aware of the differences in the principles of intellectual property protection between different legal systems, they may easily be exposed to intellectual property infringement in the international marketplace.

▶ Case 3-5

Lenovo Changed Its Logo

Before 2003, Lenovo used to have "Legend" as its English brand name. In 2002, Lenovo extended its products from the mainboard field to the PC field and planned to enter the European market of laptops. However, there were difficulties in using the Legend brand in Europe.

At that time, Lenovo had six branches in Europe, including the UK, the Netherlands, Spain, Germany, France and Austria. The brand of Legend had been registered by more than one company locally, and by at least a dozen companies worldwide. In the U.S., the Lenovo trademark had been registered even earlier than in China.

In 2003, Lenovo changed its English brand name from "Legend" to "Lenovo".

Old Brand Name   New Brand Name

③ Ways of patenting abroad

There are three main ways to apply for overseas patents, namely, direct application, Paris Convention application and Patent Cooperation Treaty (PCT) application.

- **Direct application**. The applicant may fill in the patent application form, translate it into the official language of the target country or region, and submit it to the patent office of the target country or region. For the direct application route, a confidential examination is required at the China Intellectual Property Office prior to the submission to the target country or region.

- **Paris Convention application**. The applicant needs to fill in different forms for various countries through separate applications, and the application materials need to be in the designated language. The application process of this approach is more complicated than PCT application.

- **Patent Cooperation Treaty（PCT）application**. Through the PCT, an applicant can apply for patent protection in multiple countries by filing a single "international" patent application without the need to submit separate patent applications to each country. The application materials can be prepared in the native language, which provides convenience for applicants to apply for patents in foreign countries.

Chapter Summary

- Political risk is the possibility of an adverse effect of political events occurring in one country or changes in a country's political relations with other countries.
- Political risk comes from the uncertainty of the host country's political change in the future and the uncertainty of damaging the interests of the foreign enterprise charged by the host government. It generally comprises four categories, overall political risk, ownership/control risk, operating risk, and transfer risk.
- The main manifestations of political risk include confiscation, expropriation

(nationalization), domestication, government bans, host government defaults, political unrest, etc.

- Other manifestations of political risk in the economic field include import restrictions, local-content requirements, foreign exchange control, tax control, security review, labor problems, intellectual property rights, environmental protection, etc.

- There are some strategies that can help international marketing enterprises reduce the impact of political risk, such as quasi-insurance of political risk (e. g., licensing or franchising, establishing joint ventures, expanding the investment base), institutional protection (e. g., IIAs, BITs), and insurance of political risk (e. g., insurance from commercial insurance companies, export credit agencies, or multilateral institutions)

- The legal environment refers to a variety of laws, rules, and regulations to be followed when a corporation develops economic relations with others.

- There are three heritages of legal systems in the world, which are code law (civil law), common law and Islamic law.

- Code law is based on an all-inclusive system of written rules of law. It consists of a comprehensive system of legislation, with the rules usually codified.

- The most important feature of the common law system is its predominantly tradition-oriented approach.

- In terms of the principle of determining the ownership of intellectual property, most civil-law countries apply a "first to register" approach, whereas most common-law countries adopt a "first to use" principle.

- In common-law countries, force majeure is strictly limited to unforeseeable natural events. Whereas in civil-law countries, force majeure encompasses not only unforeseeable natural events but also unforeseeable human conduct.

- When faced with an international business dispute, the basic resolution methods include negotiation, conciliation, arbitration and litigation.

- In practice, if the parties to a dispute fail to reach a conciliation agreement, most international marketers prefer to settle the dispute through arbitration rather than litigation.

- When settling commercial disputes by means of litigation, it would involve jurisdictional issues to clarify which country's law and which country's court to apply.

- The three main types of intellectual property rights are patent right, trademark right, and copyright, among which patent right and trademark right are also collectively referred as industrial property rights.

- There are three main ways to apply for overseas patents, namely, direct application, Paris Convention application and PCT (Patent Cooperation Treaty) application.

Main Concepts

political risk, code law (civil law), common law, force majeure, international bussiness disputes

Think and Practice

1. Discuss the impact of the international political environment on international marketing activities.
2. Explain the concept and the types of political risk.
3. What are the main manifestations of political risk? And what are the other manifestations in the economic field? Can you illustrate with some examples?
4. In which regions of the world are terrorist activities more frequent?
5. Can you suggest strategies to reduce political risks?
6. Collect data and make a map of political risks in an intended international market (can be measured by optional indicators).
7. If you are an executive in a multinational corporation, select a country that you are interested in and analyze its political environment.
8. What are the scope, characteristics and differences of the civil law system and the common law system?
9. What are the possible resolutions to an international business dispute?
10. What are the principles of intellectual property protection in the civil law system and the common law system?
11. What are intellectual property rights? What types of intellectual property can be classified into? Why should a multinational company protect IPR in an international market?

Case Study

China Tops the World in PCT International Patent Applications

Chinese applicants filed the highest number of international patent applications in the world through Patent Cooperation Treaty (PCT) in 2020, reaching 69,000, China National Intellectual Property Administration (CNIPA) said.

"The average ownership of invention patents in 2020 reached 15.8 patents per 10,000 people. China was the top user in the world of the PCT with about 69,000 applications pending," said Shen Changyu, the head of CNIPA.

The review for examining intellectual property (IP) patents was made more efficient by shortening the average processing time by 2 months to 20 months, according to Shen, while the review time of trademark registrations was shortened by half, so international cooperation on IP has also been stepped up.

"President Xi Jinping and European Union leaders signed the China-EU agreement on geographical indications. China participated in the negotiations on intellectual property with RCEP. We also renewed the Belt and Road IP cooperation deal with the World Intellectual Property Organization," added Shen.

Efforts to strengthen IP protection saw some 42,000 patent infringement complaints handled in 2020 in China, as more Chinese companies are encountering a rising number of IP disputes overseas. The administration has also established 10 centers across the country to help deal with such disputes.

Shen further mentioned that China will provide more services for Chinese enterprises going global by strengthening its mechanism for handling IP disputes overseas.

Discuss the following questions.

1. What are the motives behind the surge in the number of PCT patent applications by Chinese companies?

2. What are the ways for Chinese enterprises to apply for international patents?

Chapter 4

Cultural Environment of International Marketing

/////// **Learning Objectives** ///////////////////

- Understand the importance of culture to international marketers;

- Understand the concept, Iceberg Model, and characteristics of culture;

- Understand how elements of culture affect consumer purchasing behavior;

- Understand Hofstede's cross-cultural dimension theory;

- Understand Hall's high-context/low-context theory;

- Understand the relationships between cultural dimensions;

- Be aware of the obstacles to cultural adaption;

- Have a sense of developing global awareness and cultural sensitivity.

////// *Key Terms* //////////////////////

iceberg model of culture　文化的冰山模型

etiquette and custom　礼仪与习俗

symbol　符号

aesthetic　审美观

thought process　思维方式

values　价值观

religious belief　宗教信仰

Hofstede　霍夫斯泰德

power distance　权力距离

uncertainty avoidance　不确定性规避

individualism/collectivism　个人主义/集体主义

masculinity/femininity　男性化/女性化

religious taboo　宗教禁忌

religious practice　宗教习俗

cross-cultural communication　跨文化沟通

Hall　霍尔

high-context/low-context culture　高语境/低语境文化

perception of time　时间观念

polychronic time (P-time)　多重时间利用方式

monochronic time (M-time)　单一时间利用方式

information-oriented　信息导向

relationship-oriented　关系导向

cultural adaptation　文化适应

ethnocentrism　母国中心主义

Self-Reference Criterion (SRC)　自我参照标准

global awareness　全球意识

cultural sensitivity　文化敏感性

▶ Opening Case

A "Perfect" Look for the Asian Market

Perfect Diary, a Guangzhou-based company, sells its products in several Southeast Asian markets, including Vietnam, Malaysia, Singapore and the Philippines, through Perfect Diary's website as well as via local e-commerce platforms such as Shopee.

Despite being in the market for only a year, Perfect Diary is already the largest vendor of color cosmetics on Shopee in Singapore and Vietnam, in terms of sales as at the end of May 2021. It also topped other foreign brands in the face powder category in the Philippines.

Southeast Asia is considered a hot spot for the global cosmetics industry. With the support of local e-commerce platforms such as Lazada and Shopee, the beauty and cosmetics industry has been growing at an unprecedented speed.

For the planned Southeast Asian market expansion, the biggest challenge for Perfect Diary is "localization", as consumers from various markets there have different religious beliefs and preferences.

To better localize in the Southeast Asian market, the Chinese company cooperated with Sanrio, a company that designs, licenses and produces products focusing on the cute aspect of Japanese popular culture, to launch a series of products. With cute packaging and reasonably priced products, the series soon became a hit there.

Perfect Diary also developed color numbers that are more suitable for local consumers, in products such as loose powder and lip gloss, according to their skin color. They also upgraded oil control technologies used in makeup-related foundation products to better suit local demands. Compared with leading Western brands, Perfect Diary's products are more suitable for the skin of Asian people.

Perfect Diary has become a first mover in the marketing method of DTC, or direct-to-consumer, where it cooperates with KOLs or key opinion leaders, including charismatic influencers like "Lipstick King" Li Jiaqi to sell products on social media platforms like Douyin, TikTok for China, WeChat and the Little Red Book. The main consumer group, the young consumers, is more receptive to marketing through KOLs that they identify with.

In Southeast Asia, Perfect Diary develops a broad range of KOLs from TikTok and Facebook, as well as celebrity partners, to drive viral online social marketing campaigns and rapidly build vast and loyal fan followings for their brands and products. In Vietnam, for instance, Amee, a popular music singer of Vietnam, has become a lipstick artist for Perfect Diary, which attracted many young consumers to buy the lipstick used by the online star.

(Source: Adapted from *China Daily*)

One of the most significant differences between cross-border marketing activities and domestic marketing is how to deal with people in different cultural environments. People in different cultural environments have differences in language, religious beliefs, values, thinking processes, customs, etc., so the needs, wants, and demands for goods and services are quite different. The design, style, packaging, advertising, promotion and other marketing activities of a product should be culturally acceptable in the local market. Marketing methods that work in a particular cultural environment may not work in another and may even lead to misunderstandings, friction and conflicts. When conducting international marketing activities, companies must pay attention to the cultural environment, analyze the influence of cultural factors, and adapt to these different cultural environments.

4.1 Understanding Culture

1. The Concept of Culture

The concept of culture is extremely abstract and complicated. Scholars have described the concept of culture in different ways. Culture has been defined as "the collective programming of the mind that distinguishes the members of one group or people from another", or "the human-made part of the human environment—the sum total of knowledge, beliefs, art, morals, laws, customs, and any other capabilities and habits acquired by humans as members of society".

2. The Iceberg Model of Culture

The iceberg model (or iceberg theory) can help us further understand the different levels of culture. According to the iceberg theory, each culture is like a huge iceberg, which can be divided into two parts: the culture above the water surface and the culture below the water surface.

The culture above the water surface (or surface culture) only accounts for a small part of the overall culture, but it is more visible, tangible and easy to change over time. Surface culture mainly involves people's daily behaviors, habits, lifestyle and customs that can be observed. This is also the part that international marketing activities can exert influence on, which brings opportunities to international marketers.

The culture below the water surface (or deep culture) accounts for the majority of the whole culture. The elements of this part of culture are invisible and difficult to change over time. The part of deep culture which is closer to the surface contains beliefs, values and patterns of thinking, such as aesthetics, concepts of family, marriage and time, as well as attitudes towards elders, cooperation and competition, etc. The deepest part under the surface is the root of culture formation and the basic assumptions in culture, such as national identity, ethnic culture and religion, etc. Deep culture can influence surface culture, but it is difficult to be influenced or changed by international marketing activities. Deep culture can sink the ship of an international business if international marketers mistakenly run into it.

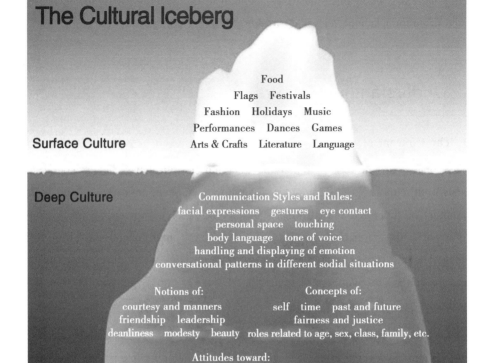

The Cultural Iceberg

Surface Culture

Food
Flags   Festivals
Fashion   Holidays   Music
Performances   Dances   Games
Arts & Crafts   Literature   Language

Deep Culture

Communication Styles and Rules:
facial expressions   gestures   eye contact
personal space   touching
body language   tone of voice
handling and displaying of emotion
conversational patterns in different sodial situations

Notions of: Concepts of:
courtesy and manners   self   time   past and future
friendship   leadership   fairness and justice
deanliness   modesty   beauty   roles related to age, sex, class, family, etc.

Attitudes toward:
elders   adolescents   dependents
rule   expectations   work   authority
cooperation vs. competition
relationships with animals   age   sin   death

Approaches to:
religion   courtship   marriage   raising children
decision-making   problem-solving

Figure 4-1   The Iceberg Model of Culture

3. Characteristics of Culture

The characteristics of culture can be described from the following aspects.

① Historical

A culture is formed and developed under certain social and historical conditions, so it has social historicity and distinctive characteristics of the times. Therefore, culture has been evolving and developing with the changes in society and history over time.

② Inherited

Social history is constantly changing and any subsequent culture reflects the inheritance of previous culture. People learn, share and transmit culture from generation to generation through social institutions such as families, schools, communities, etc. Chinese culture has inherited a cultural tradition since the Pre-Qin Dynasty, while Western European culture has inherited a cultural tradition since ancient Greece and Rome.

③ Patterned

The accumulation of culture follows the emergence and development of a nation, so culture has a national character. This national or regional character is reflected in the cultural pattern. For example, Chinese nation has been living under stable and self-sufficient economic conditions for a long time, thus forming the cultural characteristics of courtesy and modesty in Chinese culture. The United States is a country of immigrants, which has resulted in a diverse cultural identity.

4.2　Elements of Culture

The cultural elements that may have an impact on international marketing activities mainly include etiquette and customers, symbols, ways of thinking, values, religious beliefs, etc.

4.2.1　Etiquette and Customs

As the visible part of the "iceberg" of culture, customs are patterns of behavior and interaction that are learned and repeated. When conducting business activities in another cultural context, it is very important to understand local etiquette and customs, which can not only help international marketers avoid embarrassment or making mistakes that offend local people, but also improve their ability of cross-cultural negotiation and communication, and make a success in their international businesses.

Etiquette is the collective term for manners, courtesy, gestures, and rituals. It refers to the process of disciplining oneself and respecting others in a certain agreed-upon procedural manner in interpersonal interactions, such as dressing, interaction, communication, etc. For example, in Chinese culture, a handshake is usually used in meeting etiquette, while in French culture, people give a bisous and hug when they greet each other.

Customs are patterns of behaviors, norms and habits that are generally followed by people on special occasions. They are transmitted from generation to generation, and are mainly embodied through national customs or folk practices, festive customs, traditional rituals, etc.

International marketing is deeply influenced by etiquette and customs in the following aspects.

1. Food Culture

When it comes to food, beverage and medicine, international marketers must be culturally sensitive. A deep understanding of food-related cultural preferences is essential for every company engaged in international marketing of food or beverages.

[Box 4-1]

Survey Says Chinese Cuisines Represent China's Culture Best

Chinese cuisines have become the most favorable element representing China's rich culture among foreigners, according to the 2016－2017 China National Image Global Survey released on Friday.

The survey interviewed citizens in 22 countries, with 500 respondents from each country. Among the 11,000 surveyed, 52 percent picked Chinese cuisines as a representative of Chinese culture, while almost 80 percent said they had tried it, with the majority of whom speaking highly of it.

Chinese medicine and martial arts also stood out as significant representatives of Chinese culture, picked by 47 and 44 percent, respectively.

Over half of the respondents who said they had tried Chinese medicine gave it the thumbs up as well.

(Source: Adapted from *China Daily*)

2. Etiquette and Daily Routine

International marketers also need to be familiar with the etiquette, rituals, and daily routines of international partners of businesses. For example, the working hours in Germany are generally from 9 a.m. to 5 p.m., so it is inappropriate to make an appointment before 10 a.m. and after 4 p.m.

3. Festive Customs

International marketers can make full use of festivals and customs in various cultures for timely displays, promotions and sales. For example, during the Christmas season in Western countries, cross-border e-commerce companies can promote products such as Christmas cards, wrapping paper, disposable tableware, kitchenware, clothing, shoes, hats, jewelry, home furnishings, colored lights, baby products, consumer electronics, etc.

4. Business Gifting

In business gifting activities, it is important not only to choose the right business gift but also to pay attention to the gift packaging and how the gift is presented. In Japan, for example, gifts must be delicately wrapped. In Germany, it is usually appropriate for guests to bring flowers to hosts, and the number of flowers must be odd number.

4.2.2　Symbols

Language and aesthetics, as symbols of culture, play an important role in international marketing activities such as the translation of brand names, the aesthetic design of products, etc.

1. Language

Language is the means of expression by which human beings communicate and interact. There are about 7,000 languages spoken in the world. Generally speaking, each nation has its own language, which is one of the important characteristics of national culture. Chinese, English, Spanish, Russian, Arabic and French are the main working languages of the United Nations. Among them, Chinese is the language with the largest number of native speakers worldwide, and English is the most widely spoken language in the world. As of January 2021, the most spoken language in the world is English with over 1. 3 billion speakers, followed closely by Mandarin Chinese with over 1. 128 billion speakers, and in the third place by Hindi with almost 646 million speakers.

When exporting products in the process of international marketing involves language issues, international marketers not only need to grasp the literal meaning of words, but also understand the customary usage in various cultures. For example, biscuits in British English are called cookies in American English. In addition, it is necessary to pay attention to the idiomatic and symbolic meanings. Some export trademarks have not been very well researched and translated. For example, the brand of Golden Rooster has the meaning of good luck in Chinese culture, but it is not appropriate to translate it into Golden Cock in English, because "Cock" is a dirty word in contemporary English slang, and it makes British and American people feel uncomfortable as a trademark. The Sailboat brand, translated as Junk, is not popular in foreign markets either, since it also has a meaning of rubbish.

2. Aesthetics

It is reputed that Confucius once said that a picture is worth a thousand words, which implies that the symbolic system of culture can be described by aesthetics. Aesthetics is a culture-specific view of beauty in general, including views, attitudes and evaluations of art, images, colors, graphics or symbols. The influence of aesthetics on international marketing activities is mainly reflected in issues such as advertising development, product design, color selection, etc.

The appearance of a product makes the most intuitive impression on consumers in the first place. Therefore, whether an international marketing product can become a commercial success is closely related to whether its design can meet the aesthetic needs of local consumers. The appearance design of products should not only meet the functional requirements of products, but also meet the aesthetic and emotional needs of local consumers. Cultural elements and symbolic meaning in product industrial design have become the main design factors. For example, in terms of product design styles, in some Western countries the aesthetic emphasis is on novelty, uniqueness and the expression of individuality, while in the East the emphasis is on modesty and elegance.

Amongst the different product categories, products such as cosmetics and clothing are more influenced by aesthetics. Skincare products from different countries combine local culture and skincare philosophies to create their own characteristics. For example, Asian cosmetics emphasize whitening benefits, while European and American skincare products place more emphasis on anti-aging benefits.

In addition, a culture may have a preference for certain colors due to its own history and tradition. For example, Chinese people like the color red and use "Chinese Red" to show their beautiful affection for red. Green is favored by the people of Islamic countries. Japanese are fond of purple, and Thais express their love and admiration for their King with their love for yellow.

In the process of international marketing, companies should consider how their products are influenced by aesthetics, and in particular, they should accurately understand the aesthetic views of the host country in terms of product design, production and packaging decisions, etc.

4.2.3 Thought Processes

Thought processes are the thinking habits that people use to process information and perceive the world around them. Thought processes are the relatively fixed metacognitive patterns that a nation has developed over a long time. In a sense, thought processes reflect the cultural characteristics of a nation and are one of the core elements of its culture.

The difference in thought processes in Eastern and Western cultures can be reflected in the way of painting. The freehand brushwork of Chinese painting tends to appreciate the whole picture and show the background as well as the foreground. In Chinese freehand brushwork, "to be both real and unreal" is an important aesthetic principle, which reflects an abstract way of thinking. Western paintings, on the other hand, are more descriptive, in a way that the focus is on the foreground with more details of the central image and less attention on the background, reflecting a perceptual way of thinking. This difference between the perception-focus and big picture reflects the very different thinking habits and preferences of Eastern and Western cultures.

Eastern and Western paintings also demonstrate their various thinking patterns. The thought processes of Eastern culture tend to be holistic and see the connection between things from the perspective of the whole. This holistic way of thinking emphasizes the harmony between the subject and the environment as well as the influence of the environment, recognizes contradictions, and views the world in the perspective of contradiction. The Western way of thinking, on the other hand, is analytical and one-dimensional. It focuses on the characteristics of things themselves, and emphasizes the use of logical or non-contradictory perspectives to view and analyze problems. In a sense, the

Western way of thinking is "seeing the trees but not the forest", while the Eastern way is "seeing both the trees and the forest".

In general, the Eastern way of thinking emphasizes the whole picture, the context, the environment and universal connections, while the Western way of thinking emphasizes the individuals. As the famous Chinese cultural master Mr. Ji Xianlin said, the Eastern way of thinking is integrative, while the Western way of thinking is analytical.

4.2.4　Values

As an invisible part of the cultural "iceberg", values are the general views on what is good and bad, right and wrong, important and unimportant, an enduring thought, belief, and attitude, as well as a specific behavior pattern preferred by individuals and society. Once formed, values are in a relatively stable state, and directly or indirectly affect the behavior choice of society and individuals.

In the field of cross-cultural research, Hofstede's Cultural Dimensions Theory, proposed by the Dutch psychologist Geert Hofstede, is an influential analytical framework. While working at IBM, Hofstede found that despite the corporate culture, the cultural values of IBM employees varied greatly across its branches around the world. From 1967 to 1973, Hofstede conducted a large-scale survey in IBM on the cross-cultural differences in the values of employees across different countries. More than 116,000 questionnaires were distributed in more than 20 different languages in 72 countries and regions.

Hofstede found that the cultural values of the nations studied differed along four primary dimensions: the individualism/collectivism index (IDV), the power distance index (PDI), the uncertainty avoidance index (UAI), and the masculinity/femininity index (MAS).

Hofstede's cultural dimension theory provides a coordinate system for observing and understanding the differences among cultural values, and provides a tool for international marketers engaged in cross-cultural business and management to understand the values and norms of behavior of people from different cultures.

1. Power Distance

Power distance focuses on authority orientation, which refers to the extent to which members of a lower status in a society or organization accept the unequal distribution of power.

In cultures with high power distance, power distribution is more centralized, the inequality between superiors and subordinates is greater and top-down decision-making is favored. In such cultures, organizations tend to be more hierarchical with a "taller" structure. Higher power distance ratings were observed in some countries in Asia and Latin America, such as India, Nepal, Philippines, Mexico, Venezuela, Colombia, etc.

On the other hand, in cultures with low power distance, power distribution is decentralized, the organizational structure is flatter with little difference in social hierarchy, and there is a preference for bottom-up decision-making. Some countries exhibit much lower PDI scores, such as the U.S., Canada, Australia, New Zealand, Israel, Denmark, the U.K., Ireland, Sweden, Norway, Finland, Switzerland, etc.

2. Individualism/Collectivism

Individualism/Collectivism focuses on self-orientation, which measures whether a society as a whole is concerned with the interests of the individual or the collective.

In individualistic cultures, people tend to be more self-centered, and only look after themselves and immediate family. People tend to have an "I" mentality, feel little need for dependency on others, and seek the achievement of individual goals rather than collective goals. The society tends to reward and accept individual initiatives. Some Western countries, such as the U.S., Canada, the U.K., Australia, etc., show high scores on IDV.

On the other hand, in collectivistic societies, people focus on collective relationships and care for the extended family. They have a "we" mentality, are interdependent on each other, and tend to accommodate each other in order to maintain group harmony. Some Asian and Latin American countries, such as Japan, Thailand, Indonesia, Brazil, Colombia, Chile, Venezuela, etc., exhibit low ratings at this dimension.

3. Uncertainty Avoidance

Uncertainty Avoidance focuses on risk orientation, which refers to whether a society can avoid and control uncertainty through formal channels when it is threatened by uncertain events and unconventional environmental threats. This dimension reflects the extent to which a culture avoids uncertainty and ambiguity.

In cultures with a high uncertainty avoidance index, people have a higher need for security. Society members tend to appear more anxious and worried about uncertain situations, and try to avoid uncertainties through rules and regulations, safety measures, expert opinions, etc. In such countries (or regions), there are more written rules and regulations in an organization, the employee turnover rate is lower, and the organization largely provides employees with a sense of job security. Such cultural characteristics are more obvious in some European, Latin American and Asian countries, such as Greece, Portugal, Belgium, France, Spain, Peru, Chile, Argentina, Japan, etc.

On the contrary, in a culture with a low uncertainty avoidance index, social members are less anxious and nervous about uncertainty. They are more tolerant of different and new ideas, more receptive to reform, and willing to take risks. There are few written rules and regulations in an organization, and the employee turnover rate is relatively high. Countries that fall into this cultural category include the U.S., the U.K., Ireland, Singapore, Denmark, Sweden, India, etc.

4. Masculinity/Femininity

Masculinity/Femininity focuses on achievement orientation, which describes whether the society's dominant values place more emphasis on masculine qualities such as personal achievement and materialism, or feminine qualities such as caring for others and quality of life.

In countries with a high masculinity index, there is a strong sense of social competition, and the criteria for success are fame, wealth, and material achievement, etc. People appreciate assertiveness, self-confidence, control, competition, earning money, and recognize improvement and challenges. There is an emphasis on competition in organizations and a focus on job performance. Men have a relatively dominant position in social and organizational affairs. The results of Hofstede's research show that countries such as the U.S., Japan, Austria, etc., have a relatively high masculinity index.

In countries with prominent femininity, people attach more importance to the quality of life and are generally willing to resolve conflicts through reconciliation and negotiation. People value cooperation and friendship, pursue quality of work and life, and believe that success is determined by interpersonal relationships and living environments. The workplace has lower stress and less job conflicts, and women can hold higher managerial positions. Suppliers and customers are in close partnerships with each other. Countries such as Denmark, Sweden, Norway, Finland, etc., are among the most feminine societies.

4.2.5   Religious Beliefs

As the deepest layer of the cultural "iceberg", religious beliefs are a source of values and behavioral preferences, which have a profound impact on people's lifestyles, choices of goods to buy and purchasing behavior patterns. Religious contexts can present opportunities or constraints to international marketing.

The three major religions in the world include Christianity, Islam and Buddhism. The regions where these three major religions are believed are roughly distributed in: Christianity in Europe and the Americas, Islam in in Central Asia, West Asia, and North Africa, and Buddhism in Southeast Asia. For international marketers, if they are not aware of the local religion and the relevant religious requirements, regulations or taboos in countries with religious beliefs, they may not be able to carry out marketing activities at all, and may even easily offend others.

1. Religious Festivals

All religions and denominations have their religious festivals, with their ways of celebrating and taboos. It is necessary to be aware of the characteristics of religious festivals and their impact on marketing activities, such as whether religious festivals are legal holidays, whether businesses can operate in such holidays, what kind of holiday products are needed, or whether there are special regulations on such holidays, etc. For example, in Europe and the United States, shops are generally not allowed to open on Sunday, the Christian day of worship. In Muslim countries, the entire month of Ramadan (September in the Islamic calendar) is a religious holiday, during which the faithful need to fast during the day.

Religious festivals are also a good opportunity to develop markets. In many Christian countries, for example, people buy a lot of goods in the Christmas market before Christmas. The Hajj season in Muslim countries is an important religious holiday, which is also a good time for marketing.

2. Religious Taboos

International marketers need to avoid religious taboos or unnecessary offence. For example, Muslims do not eat pork and animal offal, and Chinese catering companies should pay attention to not selling relevant food when operating in Muslim countries. Hindus do not eat beef and thus McDonald's does not sell beef burgers in India, even though this product is a star product of McDonald's in the rest of the world. Still, there are opportunities for international marketers. For example, although alcohol is banned for Muslims, beverage sellers could have a wider market in Muslim countries.

3. Religious Practices

Marketing opportunities and markets can be created by exploiting the religious practices of local believers and their specific needs for certain goods. For example, the Japanese watch company Seiko introduced a multifunctional Muslim watch in Muslim countries to address the needs for religious practices. In addition to the general timing function, the watch also has some special functions designed for Muslims. For example, the local time can be converted to the time of Mecca, the holy place of Islam, at any time. The watch automatically beeps five times a day to remind believers to worship on time, and the direction of Mecca can be indicated in any area to ensure that believers can worship towards the holy place. As soon as the watch was launched, it immediately became popular with Muslims and won a market of hundreds of millions.

▶ Case 4-1

Japan Seiko Watch Company in the Islamic Countries

The Japanese watch company Seiko had a great success in Islamic countries. In the past, although Seiko watches were good in quality and cheap in price, due to the fierce international competition, it was difficult to open the market in Islamic countries. The company's marketing managers suddenly realized that the market they were facing was a market with a particular religious tradition. Muslims pray to Allah every day in the direction of the Holy Land of Mecca wherever they are in the world. Therefore, the company developed a watch with unique functions. The watch can convert local time into Muslim time, automatically reminding the person wearing the watch to pray at the time of prayer, and the "compass" on the watch always points to the direction of Mecca. When the watch was introduced on the market, it immediately gained the favor of Muslims, and Seiko Watch Company won a market of hundreds of millions.

4.3 Cross-cultural Communication

Cultural differences are not only reflected in consumption behaviors and decisions, but also in cross-cultural business communication. Communication is the process of transmission and feedback of thoughts and feelings between people or groups, and can take a variety of forms such as verbal, written, eye contact, gestures, etc. The communication styles of different cultures vary greatly.

4.3.1 High-context/Low-context Culture

Edward T. Hall, an American anthropologist, analyzed the style people communicate from the perspective of culture. Based on the accuracy and clarity of information transmission in the process of communication, he proposed an analytical framework of high-context and low-context culture to understand the communication styles of different cultures (Figure 4-2). According to Hall, content and context are two important elements that cannot be separated in the communication process. More specifically, the content is the information to be communicated (what to communicate), while the context is the background of communication (for example, when and where to communicate, how to communicate, etc.). The way in which content and context are related to each other reflects the communication style of a culture. Hall further divides culture into two categories according to different combinations of context and content: high-context culture and low-context culture.

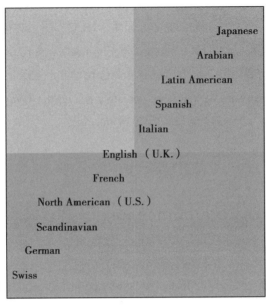

Figure 4-2 Hall's Model of High-context/Low-context Culture

1. High-context Culture

In the communication process of a high-context culture, more information is included in the context of communication, with only a little information being clearly transmitted through coding.

Verbal expressions in communication are often obscure, indirect and implicit, and people tend to expect others to understand non-verbal cues rather than explicitly inform the other party of their thoughts. It is characterized by linguistic indirectness, thus non-verbal communication plays an important role in the communication process by providing information through gestures, the use of space and even silence. Besides, high-context cultures are more sensitive to their surroundings and environment. The social status and familiarity of both parties as well as the social environment all provide additional information. Therefore, the high-context culture is more dependent on non-verbal communication. For example, words like "I love you" are rarely spoken out directly, since this information has already been transmitted through context.

In a high-context culture, the pace of negotiation is slow, and trust is the basis for people to fulfill the agreement. Thus, people prefer face-to-face communication rather than e-mails and other forms of communication.

Japanese culture, Latin American culture and Arab culture are typical high-context cultures.

2. Low-context Culture

In the communication process of a low-context culture, information is mainly conveyed through clear coding and explicit language. The low-context culture attaches importance to the content rather than the context.

In low-context cultures, people tend to express themselves directly, clearly, and frankly through language. The low-context culture is characterized by linguistic directness. The verbal expressions in communication carry a lot of information, and people are often confronted directly with the content of the message itself, with little information on the context and the participants. Hence, people in low-context cultures use e-mails more often than in high-context cultures.

In low-context cultures, people attach importance to time and efficiency in negotiations. An agreement with legal effects must be established in a written form, not in an oral form.

Cultures such as Switzerland, Germany, Scandinavia, the U.S., and Canada are more typical low-context cultures.

4.3.2 Perception of Time

The anthropologist Edward T. Hall divides the conception of time into two categories, polychronic time and monochrononic time, namely P-time and M-time.

1. P-time

P-time (Polychronic) is characterized by many things happening at the same time, a lot of involvement with people, and a tendency to accomplish goals and tasks in a more flexible way than following a set schedule.

In a P-time culture, people plan many things at the same time (multi-tasking) and may talk to many people simultaneously as well. When people undertake tasks, they pay attention to judging the situation, and each step of action is often determined randomly according to the surrounding environment in a more flexible way. People make fewer appointments in advance for social events, and often visit relatives and friends whenever and wherever they are available. Besides, the P-time culture assumes that dynamic and creative human activities should involve more interactions between individuals instead of proceeding like clockwork. People have a looser notion of being on time or late. Thus, interruptions are routine, and delays are expected. For example, in some Latin American countries, people are less concerned about being late for meetings.

P-time is usually more dominant in high-context cultures. For example, Arabs from a typical high-context culture do not like to rush in business, and they do not like deadlines either, so negotiations are likely to be prolonged. In such cultures, trust and friendship are the basis for establishing a business relationship. P-time allows for the time needed to develop such a relationship.

2. M-time

M-time (Monochrononic) uses a linear method to divide time into small units, focus on one thing at a time point, and care about punctuality.

In an M-time culture, people believe that time is very important as a scarce resource that needs to be managed and utilized. People are used to arranging their work and life according to a fixed and detailed schedule, emphasizing on promptness and efficiency. Time deeply restricts people's work and lifestyles. On the contrary, failure to comply with appointments on time is often seen as self-centered, disregardful for others or impolite. Most North Americans, Swiss, Germans and Scandinavians have a typical M-time perception of time.

Most low-context cultures operate on M-time. For example, Americans from a typical low-context culture tend to get straight to the point and get down to business immediately. This suggests that people from low-context cultures communicate with a focus on content, and value promptness and efficiency.

4.3.3 A Synthesis of Cultural Dimensions

The connotations, elements and influence of the cultural environment are profound and extensive, and the diversity and complexity of culture bring opportunities and challenges to international marketing activities. The research of cross-cultural scholars such as Hofstede and Edward T. Hall provides theoretical support and practical solutions for international marketers to understand and respond to cross-cultural issues. This section attempts to synthesize and summarize the various dimensions of culture explored in the previous section.

Relevant empirical experiences show that there is a close relationship between certain dimensions of Hofstede's theory. For example, the characteristic of individualism tends to be more obvious in cultures of lower power distance, while the feature of collectivism tends to be more obvious in cultures of higher power distance. Besides, there is a high correlation between Edward T. Hall's contextual theory and the concept of time. For example, people in low-context cultures tend to adopt a perception of Monochronic time, while people in high-context cultures tend to have a perception of Polychronic time. In addition, cultural dimensions of Hofstede's and Edward T. Hall's theories also have interactive effects. For example, British and American cultures are characterized by low power distance, individualism, low context and M-time. Alternatively, Arab and Latin American cultures are characterized by high power distance, collectivism, high context and P-time.

Based on Cateora et al. (2020), we synthesize and summarize the different dimensions of culture addressed in the previous sections. As shown in the table, according to the dimensions and characteristics of culture, Cateora et al. (2020) identifies two basic types of culture, which include information-oriented and relation-oriented culture. It should be noted that culture, due to its diversity and complexity, cannot be understood in a precise and absolute way. Nevertheless, this classification still provides implications for readers to further understand cultural diversity.

Table 4-1　A Synthesis of Cultural Dimensions

Dimensions	Characteristics of Information-oriented（IO）	Characteristics of Relationship-oriented（RO）
Cultural values	Low power distance	High power distance
	Individualism	Collectivism
Communication styles	Low-context	High-context
	Linguistic directness	Linguistic indirectness
	E-mails	Face-to-face
	Monochronic time	Polychronic time
Thought process	Focus on the foreground	whole picture（foreground and background）
Distance from English	Low distance from English	High distance from English
Examples	British, American, Swiss, German, Scandinavian cultures, etc.	Arab culture, Latin American culture, some Asian culture, etc.

As shown in the table, information-oriented (IO) cultures tend to show characteristics such as low power distance and individualism, low context, linguistic directness, e-mail communication, M-time, a focus on the foreground, low distance from English, etc. Typical examples of IO cultures are British, American, Swiss, German, Scandinavian cultures. Alternatively, the characteristics of relationship-oriented (RO) cultures include high power distance, collectivism, high context, linguistic indirectness, face-to-face communication, P-time, a view of whole picture, high distance from English, etc. Typical examples of RO cultures are Arab culture, Latin American culture, and some Asian cultures such as Japanese culture, etc.

4.4　Cultural Adaptation in International Marketing

Whether international marketing activities adapt to local culture determines the success or failure of the business. In this section, we will discuss the cultural adaptation of international marketing.

4.4.1　Obstacles to Cultural Adaptation

The two major obstacles in international marketing activities are ethnocentrism and self-reference criteria.

1. Ethnocentrism

Ethnocentrism, also known as "home-country centralism", is the idea that multinational corporations emphasize the superiority of the home country. It is characterized by taking the interests and cultural values of the home country and the parent company as the fundamental guidance. Product development, profit allocation, and personnel policy all reflect the "home country centered". The headquarter implements centralized decision-making by giving orders and instructions to subsidiaries. The technologies and strategies adopted abroad are largely the same as those in the home country.

2. Self-reference Criteria

Another obstacle associated with ethnocentrism is the self-reference criteria. Self-reference criteria (SRC) refers to the fact that once international marketers encounter a specific situation in their business, they unconsciously use their own cultural values, experience, and knowledge as the basis for understanding and dealing with the situation. In other words, managers with a tendency of SRC unconsciously adopt methods, approaches, practices, values, and personnel in the international market from their own company, culture, or home country. This happens generally at the initial stage of international marketing involvement. International marketing enterprises that have just entered the international market are not familiar with the specific situation of the local market and unconsciously refer to their past successful experience and practices in the domestic market as the basis for decision-making in the new situation.

In general, when managers from developed countries work in markets of developing or less developed countries, ethnocentrism and SRC may occur, impeding the ability to truly evaluate foreign markets. In fact, the international marketers who have succeeded in the host country are those who have taken great effort to overcome the barriers of cultural adaptation. On the other hand, however, in most cases, failures in the overseas market are related to the ignorance of such two obstacles. Especially when the cultural distance between the home country and the host country is significantly wide, efforts should be made to overcome these obstacles.

► Case 4-2

The Package of Changbai Mountain Ginseng

When the Changbai Mountain ginseng was exported, it was always shipped in wooden cases, each weighing up to 20 kg, and the packaging was very simple. Obviously, this is in line with our traditional values. However, the export price of this valuable mountain treasure was kept low by foreign businessmen. Later, after many studies, it is realized that in the Western concept, the more valuable things are, the more attention should be paid to their packaging, and that only cheap products have simple packaging. Later, the price of the Changbai Mountain ginseng rose tenfold when it was packaged in a single piece in an exquisitely-crafted box. From this example, we can see that to overcome the SRC tendency, we must learn to think and analyze problems from the other side's standpoint.

4.4.2 Global Awareness and Cultural Sensitivity

For international marketers, to overcome ethnocentrism and self-reference criteria requires a conscious effort to develop global awareness and cultural sensitivity, which is essential to international marketing success.

1. Global Awareness

International marketers need to develop global awareness, which refers to having the knowledge of global markets in aspects such as culture, economy, political and legal systems, etc., and especially having the tolerance of cultural differences and the willingness to learn about them.

To establish a global awareness, international marketers should first learn and understand the knowledge and information of countries around the world, especially the host country, in politics, economy, social culture, science and technology, and seek marketing opportunities from the environment. Besides, it is important for international marketers not only to respect the cultures of other countries, but also to pay attention to improving the ability, efficiency and effectiveness of cooperation.

2. Cultural Sensitivity

Being culturally sensitive is the starting point for successful international marketing. Cultural sensitivity means understanding the differences between the home and host cultures and the impact of such cultural differences. Being culturally sensitive enables international marketers to objectively understand and assess the differences between cultures and to appreciate and accept the host culture, thereby reducing conflicts, improving communication and making the partnership a success. Developing cultural sensitivity requires international marketers:

- To recognize that cultural differences exist objectively and that it is such differences that constitute the diversity and complexity of cultures.
- To understand that there are only differences between cultures, not right or wrong cultures. Don't make value judgment on other cultures.
- To appreciate such differences and view them in a proactive, positive and inclusive manner.
- To flexibly make use of cultural differences so that the differences can be a source or resource for solving problems.

4.4.3　Ways of Cultural Adaptation

1. Conduct Cultural Research in the International Market

Without adequate, complete and accurate market information, decisions on cross-border operations are impossible and may even result in huge losses for the company. When conducting cultural research in the international market, the enterprise should try to find a native who has lived in the target market country for a long time to participate in this work. That is to say, there must be a person under the influence of dual culture. In this way, the cultural research can save time, effort, and is relatively accurate and complete.

2. Strengthen the Training of International Marketing Talents

Specialized international marketing talents are urgently needed in managing international marketing activities. Such talents should not only have professional knowledge and skills in industry, understand basic knowledge of economics, marketing, consumer behavior, anthropology, psychology, linguistics, etc., but also be familiar with the cultural background and business practices of the host country. Most importantly, they are supposed to have global awareness and cultural sensitivity.

3. Design Products According to the Cultural Characteristics

When marketing internationally, it is important to design the characteristics of the culture to which the customers belong into the product, so that it can be adapted to the customers' cultural personality. For example, Transsion's TECNO mobile phone has achieved great success in the African market by developing their products according to the African cultural characteristics.

4. Establish International Management Systems in Accordance with Cultural Characteristics

Cultural differences also require enterprises to be adaptable in the formulation and implementation of international management systems, especially the compatibility of corporate culture and local culture. For example, in 1982, a Japanese manager of Honda Motor Factory in the United States asked American workers to wear factory uniforms, badges and sing factory songs before going to work, just as they did at the Honda factory in Japan. However, the initiative was rejected by American workers. The manager quickly realized that what worked in Japan might not work in the United States. The individualistic value of American culture is different from the collectivist value of Japanese culture.

Chapter Summary

- Culture has been defined as the human-made part of human environment—the sum total of knowledge, beliefs, art, morals, laws, customs, and any other capabilities and habits acquired by humans as members of society.
- Based on the iceberg model (or iceberg theory), culture can be divided into surface culture and deep culture.
- The characteristics of culture are historical, inherited, patterned, etc.
- Elements of culture include etiquette and customs, symbols, thought processes, values, religious beliefs, etc.
- Hofstede found that the cultural values differed along four primary dimensions: the Individualism/Collectivism Index (IDV), the Power Distance Index (PDI), the Uncertainty Avoidance Index (UAI), and the Masculinity/Femininity Index (MAS).
- Hall divides culture into two categories: high-context culture and low-context culture.
- Hall divides the conception of time into two categories, P-time and M-time.
- The two major obstacles in international marketing activities are ethnocentrism and self-reference criteria.
- Self-Reference Criteria (SRC) refers to the fact that once international marketers encounter a specific situation in their business, they unconsciously use their own cultural values, experience, and knowledge as the basis for understanding and dealing with the situation.

Main Concepts

culture, elements of culture, theory of Hofstede's cross-cultural dimensions, theory of Hall's high-context/low-context culture, Self-Reference Criterion (SRC)

Think and Practice

1. Define the concept of culture, and describe its characteristics.

2. How to understand the surface culture and deep culture in the cultural iceberg model? Give an example.

3. Outline the elements of culture. How can these cultural elements inspire international marketers?

4. What are the differences in thought processes between Chinese culture and Western culture, and can you illustrate with examples?

5. Explain the theory of Hofstede's Cross-cultural Dimensions.

6. Work in groups to investigate the characteristics of coffee consumption in China, South Korea, the United States and France, and analyze which characteristics are caused by cultural differences.

7. Explain the theory of Hall's High-context/Low-context culture.

8. Interview international students at your university to talk about the cultural differences they feel and analyze their communication styles.

9. Select a country that you are interested in and analyze its cultural characteristics from different dimensions of culture.

10. What are the obstacles to cultural adaption? Can you explain the concept of SRC and illustrate it with examples?

11. Why should an international marketer be concerned with the cultural environment of a host country?

Case Study

Lenovo's Cultural Adaption

Lenovo was founded in 1984 with just 11 researchers at the beginning. Up to now, Lenovo has been ranked among the world's top 500 companies, with 55,000 employees worldwide. The company operates in more than 160 countries around the globe.

Before 2000, Lenovo operated only in the Chinese market. At that time, Lenovo had developed into the No.1 in the Chinese PC market. When Lenovo put forward its vision of becoming an international company in 2000, the company did not have any international experience, nor did it have a strong M&A ability, so it was hard to imagine how Lenovo would go abroad. However, Lenovo has made many international efforts, opening offices in countries such as Germany, Thailand, etc. In 2003 and 2004, when IBM was selling its PC business, Lenovo realized its first step of globalization by acquiring IBM's PC business in 2005.

At the beginning of the M&A, the integration of language, culture and other aspects of the company's internal management and employees faced huge challenges. For example, in the beginning, most of the Chinese management did not speak English, so they held meetings with simultaneous interpretation earphones. On the other hand, Americans were very willing to speak and they kept talking in English. It was hard for the Chinese management team to speak at meetings, because first they had to understand the simultaneous translation, and later when they wanted to speak, they needed to organize the language, considering whether to speak in English or in Chinese. By the time they figured it out, the meeting was over. After the meeting, Americans always said that the Chinese often did not make it clear at the meeting, while Chinese people thought that the Americans kept talking all the time, but in fact, there was little content in their talking. There was actually a cultural difference.

For a domestic enterprise that aims to transform into a global company, the establishment of a globalized culture is the beginning of real globalization. Today, 40% of Lenovo's 100 global executives are from Chinese teams and 60% are teams from all over the world. Therefore, when holding an executives' meeting, everyone feels that it is like an U.N. meeting. In fact, when a company becomes a global company with managers coming from all over the world, it is very important for them to share common values.

Discuss the following questions.

1. Discuss the differences in cultural value between Chinese culture and American culture.
2. Discuss how Lenovo established a globalized culture instead of applying SRC.

Chapter 5

International Marketing Research

///////// *Learning Objectives* ///////////////////////////

- Be familiar with the process of international marketing research;

- Understand the importance of problem definition in international research;

- Be aware of the problems of availability and use of secondary data;

- Be able to apply quantitative and qualitative research methods;

- Understand the role of building an international marketing information system.

////////// *Key Terms* //////////////////////

marketing research　市场调研

research objective　调研目标

primary data　一手数据

secondary data　二手数据

qualitative research　定性分析

quantitative research　定量分析

data classification　数据分类

availability　可用性

reliability　可靠性

Marketing Information System(MIS)　市场信息系统

internal report system　内部报告系统

international marketing intelligence system　国际营销情报系统

international marketing research system　国际营销调研系统

international marketing decision support system　国际营销决策支持系统

▶ **Opening Case**

China Consumer Confidence Highest in the World

China holds the highest consumer confidence index score at 72.2 in December, and it is the only country with a score above 70, according to the global marketing research group Ipsos on Dec 22.

Moreover, China's scores in the expectations index, investment index and jobs index are also seeing a significant increase in December.

The global consumer confidence index reads at 45.9 in December, up 0.4 points compared with last month, according to the marketing research group.

The result is based on a monthly survey of more than 17,000 adults under the age of 75 from 23 countries.

China's consumer market is large, and the consumption growth is strong. Although the consumption demand has been temporarily suppressed in the past two years due to the epidemic impact, China still has huge consumption potential, said the Global Times, citing Yang Delong, chief economist of Shenzhen-based First Seafront Fund.

The investment index and jobs index increasing is indicative of the consumers becoming optimistic about their future financial situation, the local economy and the job environment, Yang added.

(Source: Adapted from *China Daily*)

5.1　The Introduction of International Marketing Research

5.1.1　The Concept of International Marketing Research

International marketing research refers to the activity in which marketers purposefully and systematically collect, record, and analyze information on international markets by using scientific methods. The aim is to gain a correct understanding of the market environment and evaluate companies' own behavior, providing a sufficient basis for making international marketing decisions.

The main tasks of international marketing research are:

1. To provide a scientific basis for determining the international target marketing plan;
2. To provide a scientific basis for timely solving the contradiction between supply and demand in international marketing;
3. To provide a scientific basis for the inspection and implementation of international marketing guidelines, policies and plans;
4. To provide a scientific basis for making effective marketing decisions to defeat competitors;
5. To provide a scientific basis for predicting the future development and changes of the international market.

5.1.2　Main Contents of International Marketing Research

1. The Market Needs

The market needs research mainly includes: the marketing maximum and minimum needs; the present and potential needs; the characteristics and scale of the needs of different goods; the survey of different marketing opportunities, corporate and competitors' current market shares.

2. The Controllable Factors

The study of controllable factors mainly includes research on factors such as products, prices, sales channels and promotion methods.

① Product research

Product research includes studying product performance, characteristics, customer opinions, and requirements. Additionally, it involves conducting Product Life Cycle research to understand the stage of the product's life cycle, and investigating product packaging, brand name, appearance, etc., to understand customers' impressions and whether these aspects align with consumers' customs or preferences.

② Price research

It includes the demand elasticity research of product prices, the effect research of new product price setting or old product price adjustment, the investigation of competitor price changes, and the timing of implementing price concession strategies and the implementation effects of this strategy.

③ Place research

It includes the status of the company's existing product distribution channels, the role of the middlemen in the distribution channels and their respective strengths, and the user's research on the contents of the middlemen, especially agents and retailers.

④ Promotion research

It mainly analyzes and compares the implementation effects of promotion methods such as personnel sales, advertising, and public relations.

3. The Uncontrollable Factors

① Politic environment research

This includes research on current government policies, decrees, and the stability of the political situation in the countries or regions where the major users of the company's products are located.

② Economic development research

It is mainly to investigate what kind of changes will be made in the macroeconomic development of the market faced by enterprises. The content of the survey has the level and degree of change of various comprehensive economic indicators.

③ Sociocultural factor research

This involves investigating sociocultural factors that can influence market demand changes, such as literacy, occupation, ethnic composition, religious beliefs, customs, social ethics and aesthetic awareness.

④ Technology development status and trend research

The primary focus is to understand the status and trends of the technology level related to the production of the enterprise. Additionally, it aims to grasp the improvement of the technical level of production enterprises manufacturing similar products in society.

⑤ Competitor research

To maintain the company's competitive edge, it is necessary to stay updated on various trends related to competitors. This research primarily focuses on aspects such as the number of competitors, their market share and trends, the marketing strategies they currently employ and plan to adopt, as well as research on potential competitors and other relevant aspects.

5.2 The Process of International Marketing Research

5.2.1 The Process of International Marketing Research

A marketing research study is always a compromise dictated by the limits of time, cost, and the present state of the art. A key to successful research is a systematic and orderly approach to the collection and analysis of data. Whether a research program is conducted in New York or New Delhi, the research process should follow these steps:

1. Define the research problem and establish research objectives.
2. Determine the sources of information to fulfill the research objectives.
3. Consider the costs and benefits of the research effort.
4. Gather the relevant data from secondary or primary sources, or both.
5. Analyze, interpret, and summarize the results.
6. Effectively communicate the results to decision makers.

Although the steps in a research program are similar for all countries, variations and problems in implementation occur because of differences in the cultural and economic development. Whereas the problems of research in England or Canada may be similar to those in the United States, research in Germany, South Africa, or Mexico may offer a multitude of unique challenges. These distinctions become apparent with the first step in the research process-formulation of the problem. The subsequent text sections illustrate some frequently encountered difficulties facing the international marketing researchers.

5.2.2 The Importance of Defining the Problem and Establishing Research Objectives

After examining the internal source of data, the research process should begin with a definition of the research problem and the establishment of specific research objectives. The major difficulty here is converting a series of common ambiguous business problems into tightly drawn and achievable research objectives. In this initial stage, researchers often embark on the research process with only a vague grasp of the total problem. A good example of such a loosely defined problem is that of the Russian airline Aeroflot. The company undertook a branding study to inform its marketing decisions regarding improving its long-standing reputation for poor safety standards and unreliable service. This goal is a tough challenge for international marketing researchers.

This first, most crucial step in research is more critical in foreign markets because an unfamiliar environment tends to cloud the problem definition. Researchers either fail to anticipate the influence of the local culture on the problem or fail to identify the self-reference criterion (SRC) and therefore treat the problem definition as if it were in the researcher's home environment. In assessing some foreign business failures, it becomes apparent that research was conducted, but the questions asked were more appropriate for the domestic market than for the foreign one. For example, all of Disney's years of research and experience in keeping people happily standing in long lines could not help Disney anticipate the scope of the problems it would run into with Disneyland Paris. The firm's experience had been that the relatively homogeneous clientele at both the American parks and Tokyo Disneyland were cooperative and orderly when it came to queuing up. Actually, so are most British and Germans. But the rules for queuing in other countries such as Spain and Italy are apparently quite different, creating the potential for a new kind of intra-European "warfare" in the lines. Understanding and managing this multinational customer service problem has required new ways of thinking. Isolating the SRC and asking the right questions are crucial steps in the problem formulation stage.

Other difficulties in foreign research stem from failures to establish problem limits broad enough to include all relevant variables. Information on a far greater range of factors is necessary to offset the unfamiliar cultural background of the foreign market. Consider proposed research about consumption patterns and attitudes toward hot milk-based drinks. In the United Kingdom, hot milk-based drinks are considered to have sleep-inducing, restful, and relaxing properties and are traditionally consumed prior to bedtime. People in

Thailand, however, drink the same hot milk-based drinks in the morning on the way to work and see them as invigorating, energy-giving, and stimulating. The market researcher must be certain that the problem definition is sufficiently broad to cover the whole range of response possibilities and not be clouded by his or her self-reference criterion.

Once the problem is adequately defined and research objectives established, the researcher must determine the availability of the information needed. If the data is available—that is, if it has been collected already by some other agency—the researcher should then consult these secondary data sources.

5.3 Primary Data and Secondary Data

The two major sources of information are primary data and secondary data:

1. Primary data. This can be defined as information that is collected first-hand, generated by original research tailor-made to answer specific current research questions. The major advantage of primary data is that the information is specific (fine-grained), relevant and up to date. The disadvantages of primary data, however, are the high costs and amount of time associated with its collection.

2. Secondary data. This can be defined as information that has already been collected for other purposes and is thus readily available. The major disadvantage is that the data is often more general and coarse-grained in nature. The advantages of secondary data are the low costs and amount of time associated with its collection. For those who are unclear about the terminology, secondary research is frequently referred to as desk research.

5.3.1 Gathering Primary Data: Quantitative and Qualitative Research

If a marketer's research questions are not adequately answered by secondary research, it may be necessary to search for additional information in primary data. These data can be collected through qualitative research and quantitative research.

In quantitative research, usually a large number of respondents are asked to reply either verbally or in writing to structured questions using a specific response format (such as yes/no) or to select a response from a set of choices. Questions are designed to obtain specific responses regarding aspects of the respondents' behavior, intentions, attitudes, motives, and demographic characteristics. Quantitative research provides the marketer with responses that can be presented with precise estimations. The structured responses received in a survey can be summarized in percentages, averages, or other statistics. For example, 76 percent of the respondents prefer product A over product B, and so on. Survey research is generally associated with quantitative research, and the typical instrument used is a questionnaire administered by personal interview, mail, or telephone or, most recently, over the Internet.

In qualitative research, questions are always open-ended and in-depth, and responses are usually unstructured. Consumers' first impressions about products may be useful. Direct observation of consumers in choice or product usage situations is another important qualitative approach to marketing research. Nissan Motors sent a researcher to live with an American family (renting a room in their house for six weeks) to directly observe how Americans use their cars. Most recently, the British retailer TESCO sent teams to live with American families to observe their shopping behaviors in advance of its new entry in the U. S. supermarket battleground with Walmart and others. Anderson Worldwide, Nynex, and Texas Commerce Bank have all employed anthropologists who specialize in observational and in-depth interviews in their marketing research. Qualitative research seeks to interpret what people in the sample are like—their outlooks, their feelings, the dynamic interplay of their feelings and ideas, their attitudes and opinions, and their resulting actions. The most often used form of qualitative questioning is the focus group interview.

Table 5-1 Quantitative Versus Qualitative Research

Differences between Qualitative and Quantitative Data	
Senior Class Survey: Qualitative Data Questions	Senior Class Survey: Quantitative Data Questions
Why do you think it is important to be community-minded?	Do you participate in community activities?
How do you show your school spirit?	Do you attend school events and functions?
What is the next step for you after graduation? Why would you choose that path?	After graduation, are you: A. heading to college? B. entering the workforce? C. enlisting in the military?

5.3.2 Using Secondary Data

1. Advantages of Secondary Research in Foreign Markets

Secondary research conducted from the home base is less expensive and less time-consuming than research conducted abroad. No contacts have to be made outside the home country, thus keeping commitment to possible future projects at a low level. Research undertaken in the home country about the foreign environment also has the benefit of objectivity. The researcher is not constrained by overseas customs. As a preliminary stage of a market-screening process, secondary research can quickly generate background information to eliminate many countries from the scope of enquiries.

2. Disadvantages of Secondary Research in Foreign Markets

Problems with secondary research in foreign countries are:

- Non-availability of data. In many developing countries, secondary data is very scarce. These weak economies have poor statistical services—many do not even carry out a census. Information on retail and wholesale trade is especially difficult to obtain. In such cases, primary data collection becomes vital.
- Reliability of data. Sometimes political considerations may affect the reliability of data. In some developing countries, governments may enhance the information to paint a rosy picture of the economic life in the country. In addition, due to the data collection procedures used, or the personnel who gathered the data, much data lacks statistical accuracy.
- Data classification. In many countries, the data reported is too broadly classified for use at the micro level.
- Comparability of data. International marketers often like to compare data from different countries. Unfortunately, the secondary data obtainable from different countries is not readily comparable because national definitions of statistical phenomena differ from one country to another. The term "supermarket", for example, has a variety of meanings around the world. In Japan, a supermarket is quite different from its U.K. counterpart. Japanese "supermarkets" usually have two- or three-storey structures; they sell daily necessities such as foodstuffs, but also clothing, furniture, electrical home appliances and sporting goods, and they have restaurants.

In general, the availability and accuracy of recorded secondary data increases as the level of economic development increases.

Although the possibility of obtaining secondary data has increased dramatically, the international community has grown increasingly sensitive to the issue of data privacy. Readily accessible large-scale databases contain information valuable to marketers, which is considered a privilege of the individuals who have provided the data. The international marketer must therefore also pay careful attention to the privacy laws in different nations and to the possible consumer response to using such data. Neglecting these concerns may result in research backfiring and the weakened position of the corporate.

Table 5-2   Primary Data Versus Secondary Data

Criteria	Primary Data	Secondary Data
Accuracy	A direct approach that starts from scratch. Data is highly accurate and zooms in on your research problem.	An indirect approach that hinges on existing data. May not be specific to your research problem.
Control	Researchers have a high degree of control.	Less control over data.
Relevancy	Very relevant to your research.	Negligible or less relevant to a new research.
Ownership	The researcher has ownership of the data.	No ownership of the data.
Cost and time	Expensive and time consuming.	Save you money and time.
Accessibility	Not freely or easily available to the public.	Available to the public and your competitors.
Bias	The data does not favor the researcher who collected it.	The data may lean toward the researcher who collected it.
Sampling errors	Errors in sampling arise by selecting the wrong sample size.	Errors arise by selecting outdated, irrelevant data that is no longer pertinent to the research problem.
Sources	Websites, journals, dissertations, literature reviews, balance sheets, and more.	Case studies, surveys, interviews question-naires, field observations, experiments, etc.

5.4 International Marketing Information System

Enterprise management information systems can usually be divided into marketing information systems, production information systems, financial information systems, human resources information systems and other subsystems. Marketing information system is an important part of enterprise management information system.

5.4.1 The Composition of the International Marketing Information System

The marketing information system refers to the organic combination of human, machine (computer-centric) and program. The marketing information system systematically collects, organizes, analyzes and evaluates the internal information related to marketing, and its purpose is to provide a reliable basis for marketing decisions.

From the perspective of information development, marketing information systems can generally be divided into:

- Internal Report System. The internal report system provides results data for managers.
- International Marketing Intelligence System. The International Marketing Intelligence System is a set of procedures and sources that give managers access to day-to-day information on the development of the international marketing environment.
- International Marketing Research System. The information on the internal reporting system and the international marketing intelligence system is generally routine.
- International Marketing Decision Support System. The International Marketing Decision Support System coordinates data collection, systems, tools and technologies through software and hardware support, interprets information about the internal and external environment of the enterprise, and transforms it into the basis of international marketing activities.

Figure 5-1   The Marketing Information Systems

5.4.2   The Role of International Marketing Information Systems

- It can meet the increasing demand of marketers for international marketing information.
- It can adapt to the increasing demands of customers.
- It can adapt to the ever-expanding needs of international marketing activities.
- It can adapt to the ever-increasing needs of international marketing activities.

▶ Case 5-1

Chinese Companies Are Accelerating
Their Efforts to Expand Overseas

Nearly 14% of companies reported that more than half of their 2020 revenue came from outside China. This indicates that China is continuing to open up its economy, and that Chinese companies are becoming increasingly global. Meanwhile, 75% of the companies surveyed generated most of their revenue from domestic businesses, with the overseas revenue accounting for less than a fifth of their total revenue. These results indicate that Chinese companies are focusing on the domestic market at the same time as expanding their presence overseas.

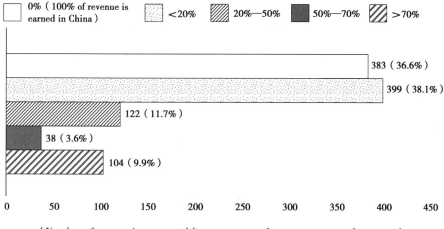

（ Number of companies surveyed by percentage of revenue generated overseas ）

Two-thirds of the companies we surveyed are engaged in overseas business activities, such as importing/exporting products and services, establishing overseas branch offices, serving as OEMs/ODMs, and engaging in cross-border e-commerce. 40.9% also export goods or services outside of China.

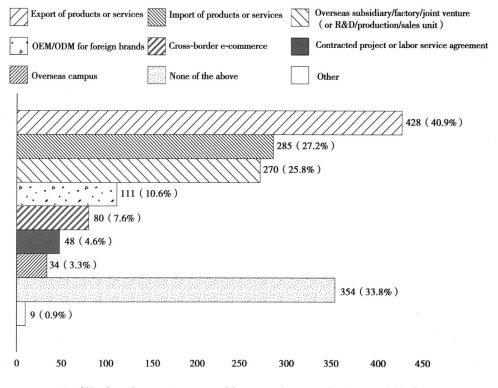

（ Number of companies surveyed by types of overseas business activities ）

Around 50% of the companies surveyed are engaged in overseas investment and financing activities, and have an extensive presence in overseas capital markets.

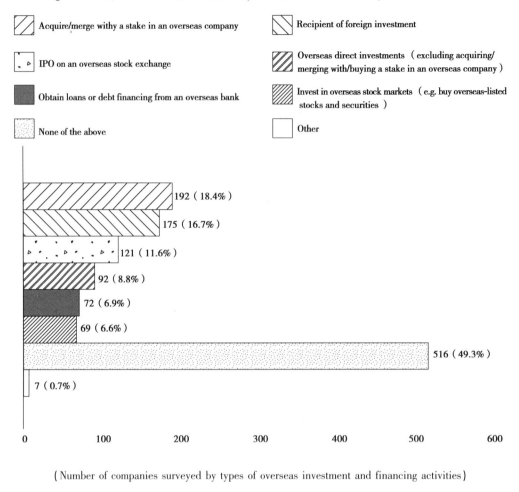

(Number of companies surveyed by types of overseas investment and financing activities)

Chapter Summary

- International marketing research refers to the systematic investigation, collection, collation, analysis and research of the information needed by enterprises in the whole process of international marketing activities. It enables companies to identify international marketing opportunities and open up potential international markets. It enables companies to have realistic and reliable objective evidence when making international marketing decisions and adapting marketing strategies and solutions.

- The contents of international marketing research mainly include researches on the international market demand capacity, product information, price information, distribution channel, promotion, political environment, economic development, social and cultural factors, the trend of technological development, as well as competition.

- The basic objective of the market research's function is to provide management with information for more accurate decision-making. This objective is the same for domestic and international marketing. In foreign marketing research, however, achieving the objective presents some problems that might not be encountered on the domestic front.

- An international marketer should initiate research by firstly searching for relevant secondary data. Typically, a great deal of information is already available, and the researcher needs to know how to identify and locate the international sources of secondary data.

- If it is necessary to gather primary data, the international marketer should be aware that it is simply not possible to replicate the methodology used in one country elsewhere. Some adaptation of the research method to different countries is usually necessary.

- International market information is a collective term for data, information, and intelligence about various economic (especially market factors) activities and related environments in the international market. Generally, the marketing information system can be divided into an internal reporting system; an international marketing intelligence system; an international marketing research system; and an international marketing decision support system.

Main Concepts

international marketing research; sampling survey; secondary data; primary data; survey method; internal reporting system; international marketing intelligence system; international marketing research system; international marketing decision support system

Think and Practice

1. What are the main tasks of international marketing research?
2. What does the research content of international marketing research mainly include?
3. What should be included in a complete international marketing research program?
4. How to choose the right international marketing research agency?
5. What are the main characteristics of the national markets such as the United States,

Japan, Western Europe, etc.?

6. What are the main differences in consumer behavior characteristics in countries around the world? Try to analyze the main causes of these differences.

> Case Study

KFC's Successful Marketing in China: Market Research Goes First

In the late 1980s, KFC began to consider how to break into the Chinese market with a large population and to explore the enormous potential in this huge market. Although the outlook was optimistic, KFC decision makers were facing many practical problems.

When the situation was uncertain, KFC conducted a thorough investigation of the Chinese market. Location is the number one factor in restaurant operations, as is the restaurant chain. The correct location of chain stores is the prerequisite and basis for standardization, simplification and specialization of chain operations. Therefore, KFC attaches great importance to site selection. The KFC site selection is carried out as follows.

1. Division and Selection of Business Districts

① Business district division. When KFC plans to enter a city, it first collects information about the area through relevant research companies. Some materials are free, and some need to pay. When the information is ready, the planning of business district begins. The company divides the business districts into several categories by scoring. Taking the commercial districts in Beijing as an example, there are high-end commercial areas, district-level commercial areas, community-level commercial areas, and tourism-oriented areas.

② Choose a business district. Choosing a business district means: Which business district is currently open for business? What are the main goals? In terms of the criteria of choosing the business district, on the one hand, the company should consider the market positioning of the restaurant itself; on the other hand, the stability and maturity of the business district should also be considered. The different market positioning of restaurants and the different targeted customer groups determine the choice of business districts.

2. Calculation of Customer Traffic and Restaurant Site Selection

① It is important to determine where the customer traffic is concentrated in this business district. The principle of KFC's site selection is to open a store in and around the place where the most customers are gathered. KFC collects data on customer traffic and uses specialized technology and software for analysis to determine the upper limit of investment in a certain location. If the upper limit is exceeded, opening a store will not be worth the loss.

② It is necessary to consider whether the flow of people will be intercepted by competitors. If a competitor's site is better than KFC's and intercepts the flow of people at the upper reaches of the moving line, then the address is not the best.

③ The selection of a commercial district also needs to consider whether there is a central point for customer flow in the district. One of the main indicators of the maturity of a commercial district is whether there is a concentration point for customer flow.

Discuss the following questions.

1. What are steps and processes for KFC to conduct a market research on site selection?
2. What data does KFC need to support when selecting a site?
3. Choose two KFC restaurants that are close to you and try to analyze the pros and cons of their location strategy.
4. Choose the adjacent KFC and McDonald's restaurants to compare the advantages and disadvantages of their location strategy.

Chapter 6

International Marketing Strategies

/////// **Learning Objectives** /////////////////////

- Understand the meaning and role of international market segmentation;

- Understand the principles and steps of international market segmentation;

- Understand the criteria for macro and micro segmentation of international markets;

- Understand the meaning of international target markets and strategies for selecting international target markets;

- Understand the meaning of positioning and strategies of positioning;

- Understand the international market entry strategies, and their respective advantages and disadvantages.

////// *Key Terms* ////////////////////

international market segmentation　国际市场细分

market competitiveness　市场竞争力

international target market selection　国际目标市场选择

international target market strategy　国际目标市场战略

narrow focus　有限集中策略

country focus　国家集中策略

country diversification　国家多角化策略

global diversification　全球多角化策略

market penetration　市场渗透策略

market development　市场开拓策略

product development　产品开发策略

diversification　经营多角化策略

vertical diversification　纵向多角化

horizontal diversification　横向多角化

concentric diversification　同心多角化

composite diversification　复合多角化

international target market positioning　国际目标市场定位策略

attribute positioning　功能属性定位

benefit positioning　利益定位

user positioning　使用者定位

brand personality　品牌个性定位

competitor positioning　竞争者定位

international market positioning strategy　国际市场定位策略

competitive positioning　对抗定位策略

niche positioning　避强定位策略

reverse positioning　反向定位策略

repositioning　重新定位策略

competitive repositioning　对竞争对手进行再定位

entry mode of international market　国际市场进入方式

indirect exporting　间接出口

direct export　直接出口

contract manufacturing　合同制造进入方式

management contract　管理合同进入方式

turnkey contracting　交钥匙承包进入

▶ Opening Case

Rebranding Chinese Manufacturers for the High-end Segment

According to the National Bureau of Statistics of China, the urban per capita disposable income (UPDI) has skyrocketed by 105 times (from 343.4 yuan per capita in 1978 to 36,396 yuan per capita in 2018) during the 40 years after China began its reform and opening-up.

Refrigerators, washing machines, ACs, and even cars, which were once seen as luxury goods, are now commonplace. In these 40 years, China encouraged multinational corporations to quickly solve the dilemma of domestic technology, management, and lack of productivity, and to promote the establishment of local supply chains. During this time, a large number of local private companies have grown rapidly. By providing spare parts and foundry services to foreign-funded enterprises, and even quickly imitating the design and technology of imported products, they have become the low-end product substitutes or high-end producers of imported brand products.

Under pressure from both low-end and high-end market segments in both domestic and international markets, Chinese manufacturers should redirect their strategic focus. They should maintain their competitive advantage in the mass market, and enter the high-end market segment by either creating sub-brands or acquiring a premium brand.

Firstly, high-end positioned brands will build brand awareness in developing and third world markets. With the advantage of brand stickiness in these markets, China can boost the segments' willingness to pay and become the incumbent as the first mover. Once Chinese brands are perceived as the premium, and once the UPDI in those markets catches up, China may start shipping high-end products to meet the potential booming demand, and maintain it as China's weapon to broaden its sources of income—the GDP export will boom alongside with the prominent markets.

Secondly, developing a high-end brand rests on a solid base of the sustainable capital inflow (for investment) and cutting-edge technology research and development (for product development). Once China owns the brand, high-end manufacturers will play an essential role in national research projects by leveraging their own capital and lab assets. They will become the shield to strengthen the Chinese brand's leading position. With sustainable weapons and shield, China will step up the global economic and technology pyramid, and China will win the eminent position as regards to her global presence.

Admittedly, it is extremely costly and time-consuming to reshape a brand. The key towards the high-end market segment relies not upon marketing or the power of politics, but upon true innovation, premium quality, and differentiated goods that match with consumers' needs and expectations. China has to establish a technology innovation incubator, launch a world-class quality system, maintain a rigorous proprietary regulation standard, and subsidize high-end entrepreneurship initial investment.

(Source: Adapted from CGTN)

Segmentation, targeting, and positioning are three of the powerful tools available to the marketer. A market segment is a subset of a larger market of people or organizations who will respond similarly to a marketing mix. Targeting is identifying a market segment and addressing that segment with a marketing mix tailored to meet the needs, wants, and resources of the segment. Positioning is establishing a place in the minds of the customers. Positioning defines the position of a product or company in the minds of customers.

Companies and organizations face a unique challenge in segmenting, targeting, and positioning products and services globally. The challenge is to ensure that segmentation, targeting, and positioning are correct globally and for each country or market.

6.1 International Market Segmentation

Meeting the needs of customers in the international market is the key to a company's international marketing activities. However, there are more than 200 countries and regions in the world, and the characteristics of consumer demand in different regions vary widely. In the case that it is difficult for enterprises to meet the needs of all consumers at the same time, many countries and regions must be divided according to certain standards. On the basis of international market segmentation, the company should conduct in-depth research and evaluation on each market segmentation and select the segment market in which the enterprise can meet its consumer demand as the target market. Since then, companies have chosen strategies for entering the international market. The three options of exporting mode, contracting mode and direct investment mode have their own advantages and disadvantages. When enterprises choose the entry mode, they must systematically and comprehensively analyze the target market environment and their own strength, so as to make correct decisions and ensure the realization of international marketing goals.

6.1.1　Bases of International Market Segmentation

1. The Meaning of International Market Segmentation

International market segmentation develops on the basis of market segmentation and is the application of the concept of market segmentation into international marketing.

In various markets, consumers usually have different needs due to the influence of many factors such as natural conditions, social-economic conditions and psychological conditions. The continuous development of productivity level not only provides material guarantee to meet the needs of consumers, but with the improvement of production level, new and higher demands will be put forward constantly. International market segmentation is the process of dividing the world market into subsets of customers that behave in the same way or have similar needs. Compared with the domestic market, the international market has more buyers and a wider distribution range. As an enterprise, it is often difficult for it to meet the needs of customers on a global scale due to the limitations of its own strength. To this end, the international market needs to be divided according to some standards.

International market segmentation is a necessary prerequisite for enterprises to determine the international target market and formulate international marketing strategies.

2. The Role of International Market Segmentation

Market segmentation makes it easier for marketing teams to develop highly targeted and effective marketing campaigns and plans. Below, we've outlined several benefits which exist with understanding and defining market segments.

① Greater company focuses

When a company has identified specific market segments, it helps them to focus on what segments they want to target with specific products/services/content/blogs and campaigns. When a company has a focus on specific segments, they ensure they are targeting the right segment with the right product which will see the greatest ROI.

② Better serve a customer's needs and wants

Having defined segments enables companies to satisfy a variety of customer needs by offering different bundles and incentives. Different forms and promotional activities will be used for different segments based on the segment needs/wants and characteristics.

③ Market competitiveness

When a company is focusing on a specific segment, their market competitiveness increases, which in turn will lead to a higher ROI. The company is focused on specific segments and learns everything it needs to know about these segments, to market its products to them.

④ Market expansion

With geographic segmentation as discussed earlier, market expansion is possible immediately. When a company understands their segments and how to market to a segment in a particular location, they can expand immediately into another nearby location. If segmentation is based on demographics, then once the company knows their demographic segment, they can expand into that segment with similar products.

⑤ Targeted communication

Even when product features and benefits are the same, it is important for companies to target segments with specific communication. For example, if your segment was senior engineers, they may respond better to technical information about a product in the form of white papers or infographics, but a project manager might respond better to information regarding cost savings, efficiencies, etc. in the form of a blog, case study or video. Messaging will be different for different segments. Platforms which are used to target different segments will also be different. The key is to understand your segments and target communication relevant to them on the relevant platforms.

▶ Case 6-1

Japanese Watches' Successful Entry into the United States

European watches have long dominated the world's market. Through international market segmentation, Japanese watch manufacturers have successfully entered the American market, which European watches once dominated, and created huge profits for Japanese enterprises. Japanese watchmakers first carried out a careful survey of the American market. According to the different demands of American consumers for watches, the market can be divided into three segments: The first category requires watches to be timed and low in price; Second, the requirements are accurate timing, durable, and moderately priced; The third category of requirements for the watch is that it should be from a world-famous brand, with elegant appearance, and rated timing. According to the survey results: ① The three segments are 23% , 46% and 31% . ② Swiss watch manufacturers, which had a large share of the American watch market at that time, always took the third category of consumers as the target market, specializing in expensive mechanical watches. ③ The needs of the first and second categories of consumers are not satisfied. After market segmentation and research, Japanese watchmakers found a marketing opportunity to offer American consumers electronic watches with accurate timing and low prices, which made a great success.

Implication: Japanese watches successfully entered into the United States, relying on scientific market segmentation and market positioning. Japanese watchmakers mainly used purchase behavior factors to segment the American market, and found that the demand for watches of medium and low prices in the United States had not been satisfied, so they seized the opportunity to occupy the middle and low-price watch market in the United States.

6.1.2　Principles of International Market Segmentation

International market segmentation is an effective means to identify opportunities in transnational business activities, but it is not always effective. Regardless of whether the segmentation analysis is performed at the country level or at the individual consumer level, several requirements must be met for market segmentation to be effective. The requirements, which apply equally to country and consumer segmentation, are shown in the follow.

① **Measurable**. Individual market segments should be easy to identify and measure, thus ensuring measurability. This means that the potential sales and purchasing power of the international target market must be measurable. Enterprises can measure the current sales status and the future sales trend of the international target market through various market research methods and sales forecasting methods. Otherwise, enterprises should not easily decide to choose their international target market.

② **Sustainable**. The market segments are large or profitable enough to serve. This refers to the international target market selected by the enterprise, which should have a large potential market, strong consumer demand, purchasing power and development potential. After entering this market, the enterprise is expected to obtain enough turnover and better economic benefits. For example, in developed countries where the population growth is slow and the problem of aging age structure is becoming increasingly prominent, the elderly market has considerable potential for enterprises. All kinds of elderly health care, elderly hospitals, elderly entertainment, leisure and other industries will develop into a sufficient market. On the contrary, for those markets with insufficient demand, segmentation will not be satisfactory.

③ **Accessible**. The ability to communicate with the target market, determining the market's accessibility, is essential as well. Internationally, the differences in language in individual countries may pose obstacles, greatly increasing the cost of advertising and other promotions. Marketing in large emerging markets, such as China, could present challenges for different reasons: Communicating with Chinese consumers in the countryside may be difficult because the large rural population has only limited access to technology. The ability to serve the market is also essential. Companies should be able to freely access the market; the market must be open to international companies and reachable (i.e. local governments and local media should permit access to the target market).

④ **Actionable**. Actionability refers to the idea that the should respond to the marketing strategies used, assuming that the company is targeting the market with the appropriate marketing mix. Effective programs can be designed to attract and serve the segments. This means that the international target market selected by enterprises can enable enterprises to effectively formulate international marketing plans, strategies and strategies, and effectively implement them. At the same time, enterprises should be able to adjust their marketing strategies conveniently in the international target market to cope with various possible market changes.

6.1.3 Macro Segmentation of the International Market

There are many countries in the world. Which market (or markets) is the most advantageous for enterprises to enter? This requires dividing the entire market into several sub-markets according to certain criteria (such as economy, culture, geography, etc.). In the same marketing environment, companies can choose a certain group or several countries as the target market. International market segmentation in this sense is called macro segmentation.

Macro international market segmentation is the first step of the process of international market segmentation. Based on the macro segmentation, companies first determine which country or countries to enter, and then carry out further micro-segmentation within the country.

There are two main issues in international market segmentation: One is to determine the criteria for international market segmentation. The other is to determine the process or basic steps of macro-segmentation.

The criteria of macro international market segmentation basically include geographic factors, cultural factors, economy factors and a combination of these criteria.

1. Geography

Geographic segmentation is dividing the world into geographic subsets. The advantage of this segmentation is proximity: markets in geographic segments are closer to each other and easier to visit on the same trip. The countries in the same geographical region have similar natural conditions, cultural backgrounds and consumption habits, which can be developed as a market. In particular, after the Second World War, regional trade and economic integration developed rapidly, making it more likely that geographically close markets would be homogeneous. Regional groups such as the European Union, the North American Free Trade Agreement and the Asia-pacific Economic Cooperation have a strong influence on international marketing, and sometimes entering one country in a regional group equals entering all the other countries in the group.

However, the application of geographical standards also has major limitations: the mere fact that markets are in the same geographic region does not mean that they are similar. For example, Canada, the United States, and Mexico in North America are geographically adjacent, but their economic development levels are quite different, especially Mexico's economic level is not comparable to that of the United States, and these regions are difficult to form a common market.

2. Culture

Culture affects every part of our lives, every day, from birth to death, and everything in between. It affects how we spend money and how we consume in general. Therefore, it is very beneficial to segment the international market according to cultural standards for marketing decisions. There are many ways to think about culture. One of the important influences of culture on international marketing decisions is that all cultural factors (such as language, education, religion, race, aesthetics, values and social groups) can constitute the segmentation criteria of the international market. However, since there are so many cultural types in the world, it is very difficult to classify all the cultural types in different countries of the world and develop a strategy for each cultural type. An alternative approach would be to reclassify the world's many different cultural types into the following five elements: ① material culture (technology, economy); ② social system (social organization, education, political structure); ③ belief system (religion, nationality, race); ④ aesthetic; ⑤ language.

Simply using culture as a standard for market segments is not feasible in many cases. Taking religion as an example, it is often not enough to divide countries by religion in order to implement a joint marketing strategy for a group of countries. Pakistan and Saudi Arabia are both strongly Islamic, but their economic differences make it hard to link them up for the same marketing strategy. Saudi Arabia, with a per capita GDP of $12,000, is a big buyer of consumer and industrial goods, while Pakistan, with a per capita GDP of $390, has little market potential for international marketers. Therefore, some other segmentation variables should be taken into account when applying cultural standards for international market macro segmentation, so as to avoid one-sidedness caused by single variable segmentation.

3. Economy

Economic criteria are used to classify countries according to economic development indicators, such as Gross National Product, per capita national income, Economic Growth Rate and Infrastructure Development Level. For most consumer and industrial products, national income is the single most important segmentation variable and indicator of market potential. The World Bank segments countries into high income (more than per capita GNP of $12,536), upper-middle income (per capita GNP of $4,046 to $12,535), lower-middle income (per capita GNP of $1,036 to $4,045), and low income (below per capita GNP of 1,035 dollars).

The advantage of international marketing segmentation of economic standards is that it makes countries of the same sub-market more similar in terms of the economic development level or the economic environment, and helps to select target markets and formulate different marketing strategies according to the market size and quality. For example, Unilever carries out targeted marketing activities according to the economic development characteristics of different countries. It launches soap in low-income countries, hand washing detergent in low to middle income countries, machine washing detergent in middle to upper income countries and fiber softener in high income countries. However, countries at the same level of economic development may be located around the world, and the target markets available for selection may be scattered, which is not conducive to improving marketing efficiency and strengthening international marketing management.

4. Combination Method

The international market combination method simultaneously analyzes the international market from three major factors: national potential, degree of competition, and degree of risk, thereby dividing each submarket of the international market into 18 types of market segments. In this method, national potential refers to the sales potential of a company's products or services in the country's market. It includes population, economic growth, real gross national product, per capita national income, population distribution, industrial production, consumption pattern, etc. The degree of competition depends on both internal and external factors. Internal factors include the share of the enterprise in the market, the enterprise resources and facilities, and the enterprise's ability and advantage to adapt to the characteristics of the country. External factors include the competitiveness of competitors in the industry, competition from alternative product industries, and industry structure at home and abroad. Risk refers to the political risk, financial risk and business risk (such as the shift of consumer preference) faced by enterprises in the country, as well as various factors affecting profits, capital flows and other business results.

The combination method is a useful method for enterprises to carry out macro segmentation of the international market and can be used as the basis for enterprises to analyze foreign market opportunities. However, it requires a lot of information, both internal and external, which may not be easy to collect and analyze. In addition, this approach applies at the market level of a product rather than the company level. As a result, a company marketing multiple products or services overseas will have to make many segmentation plans for this. Doing so creates strategic significance and helps analyze opportunities for potential product markets.

6.1.4 Micro-segmentation of International Market

The purpose of micro-segmentation is to identify clusters of consumers that respond in a similar fashion to a company's marketing strategies. Identifying individual market segments enables the company to develop products that meet the precise needs of target consumers with a marketing mix that is appropriately tailored for those segments.

In the international consumer market, different consumer groups have different desires and needs and form different buying habits and behaviors due to the influence of various factors such as the geographical region, age, gender, religious belief, income level, lifestyle and psychology of consumers. According to these factors, enterprises can divide the consumer market of a country or region into several different market segments or sub-markets. The differences in consumer needs determined by these factors are the basis of consumer market segmentation. In international marketing, they are generally summarized into four categories: geographical factors, demographic factors, psychological factors and behavioral factors.

1. Geographic Factors

Geographic segmentation can be performed at the macro-segmentation level—country analysis, regional blocks, and so on—as well as within the country. Consumers differ within countries with regard to demographics and psychographics, such as ethnicity, religion, and the language spoken.

In the application of geographical segmentation, it should be noted that the geographical factor is a static factor, the classification of consumers is relatively general, and consumers in the same geographical region also have obvious differences in demand, so market segmentation must be combined with other factors.

2. Demographic Factors

Demographic segmentation is based on measurable characteristics of populations such as age, gender, income, education, and occupation. Demographics are easy to measure and to compare across countries. Among the variables of population segmentation, the four most valuable ones are per capita income, total population, age characteristics and religious belief.

① Per capita income

The level of national income and per capita income of residents directly affect the size of the international market. According to the level of per capita income, consumers' income can be divided into three levels: high income, middle income and low income. Over 70 percent of the world income is located in the triad. Thus, by segmenting in terms of a single demographic variable—income—a company could reach the most affluent markets by targeting three regions: the European Union, North America, and Japan.

② Population

In the international market, for many low-value and consumable consumer goods, the total population is often a more important segmentation variable than per capita income, such as China and India. However, it is worth noting that countries such as China and India with large populations and low per capita incomes still have a small but significant number of high-income people. From the perspective of consumption level, these consumers have approached or reached consumers in middle-developed countries. From the perspective of total consumption, it is also equivalent to a small, medium-sized developed country. Therefore, this situation should also be considered when carrying out population segmentation.

③ Age

Age is another useful demographic variable. Consumers at different ages have different demands for commodities due to their different physiological conditions and interests. With the development of the social economy and the improvement of residents' income, the demand of consumers has undergone great changes in various stages, which is a factor that cannot be ignored in international market segmentation.

④ Religious belief

There are three major religions in the world: Christianity, Islam and Buddhism, as well as many regional religions. Consumers with different religious beliefs also show differences in demand characteristics. In Pakistan, for example, Islam is the national religion, with more than 95% of the population. The sale of alcohol in the country is a fault for believers who adhere strictly to Muslim traditions that prohibit drinking.

3. Psychographic Factors

Psychographic segmentation involves grouping people in terms of their attitudes, values, and lifestyles. With the development of the social economy and the continuous improvement of people's living standard, the demand of consumers changes from physiological demand to psychological demand. People from the same subculture, social class and occupation may have different lifestyles and personalities, and have different needs for commodities. That is to say, psychological factors are an important factor influencing consumers' desires and needs.

More and more enterprises segment the consumer market according to the different lifestyles of consumers. For example, automobile manufacturers design and produce economical, safe and less polluting cars for "law-abiding" consumers, and design and produce gorgeous and highly sensitive cars for "car players". Clothing manufacturers design and produce different styles of women's clothing, such as plain, fashionable, manly, etc. For these consumers with different lifestyles, not only the product design is different, but also the product price, distribution shop and advertising are different.

In order to conduct lifestyle segmentation, enterprises can generally use the following three scales to measure consumers' lifestyles:

① **Activities**, such as the consumer's work, leisure, vacation, shopping, sports, hospitality and other activities;

② **Interests**, such as consumer interest in family, fashion of clothing, food, entertainment, etc.;

③ **Opinions**, i. e. consumers' opinions on themselves, social problems, politics, economy, products, culture, education and the future.

According to the different personalities of consumers, enterprises can endure their products with a "brand personality" similar to that of some consumers and establish a "brand image" through advertising. In the late 1950s, for example, Ford buyers were once thought to be independent, impulsive, ambitious, change-oriented and confident consumers. Buyers of GM Chevrolet cars were once considered conservative, frugal, creditworthy, less macho and less extreme. These consumers with different personalities are interested in the products of these companies, and thus sales are promoted.

4. Behavioral Factors

Behavior segmentation focuses on whether people buy or use a product, as well as how often and how much they use it. Consumers can be categorized in terms of usage rates—for example, heavy, medium, light, and nonuser.

Segmentation variables are based on when consumers buy or use a product, which is based on the fact that many consumptions or services are specifically adapted to a particular occasion, such as China's Spring Festival, the Mid-Autumn Festival, Western Valentine's

Day, Christmas, etc. Marketers launching timely products to meet the special needs of this opportunity will be a great success. In the United States, consumers usually drink orange juice at breakfast. An orange juice company promoted the consumption of orange juice at lunch or dinner to promote the sales of orange juice.

Consumers often buy different products and brands because they have different purchasing motives and pursue different interests. Take buying toothpaste as an example. Some consumers buy Jieyin toothpaste mainly to keep their teeth white. Some consumers buy Fangcao toothpaste, mainly to prevent dental caries and periodontitis. According to the different interest that consumers pursue, the overall market can be divided into seeking practicality, seeking safety, seeking economical, seeking novelty, seeking beauty and seeking luxury and other market segments. Enterprises can weigh the advantages and disadvantages according to their own conditions, select a certain market as the target market, design and produce products suitable for the needs of the target market, and convey the information of such products to consumers pursuing such interests with appropriate advertising media and advertising phrases. The practical experience of business management in western countries proves that profit segmentation is an effective segmentation strategy.

Consumers can also be segmented according to users' status: potential users, nonusers, ex-users, regulars, first-timers, and users of competitors' products. Large Western companies with abundant resources and high market share are generally interested in consumer groups such as potential users. They focus on attracting potential users to expand their market position. Small businesses have weak resources and tend to focus on attracting regular users. Tobacco companies are targeting China because the Chinese are heavy smokers.

It should be noted that the characteristics of consumers' purchasing behaviors are relatively abstract, and it is difficult to collect specific data. In order to effectively use the segmentation method to provide a basis for decision-making for the enterprise's international marketing, on the one hand, enterprises should make in-depth market research and statistical analysis of the characteristics of consumer behavior quantitatively. On the other hand, enterprises should also combine other segmentation methods of double or multiple segmentation to ensure the effectiveness of market segmentation.

▶ Case 6-2

Chinese Phones Get Africans Talking

Chinese smartphone brands have been steadily winning over young Africans with feature-packed models that are also helping to spur the digital transformation of the continent. With offerings aimed at the young, manufacturers such as Xiaomi, Huawei and Tecno have garnered plaudits for their models enabling high-definition videos and gaming while boasting quality speakers.

By opening online and offline stores, Xiaomi has managed to increase the range of products it offers. Customers can now pick up TV boxes, smart switches, smart lights and a host of Wi-Fi accessories. Focusing on innovation to cater to the diverse needs of customers has driven the increased popularity of the brand with young people. Some of the products, such as the Xiaomi 12 series, cater to the upper end of the market while others hold sway at the entry and midrange levels. The average selling price for Xiaomi phones is up to 75 percent cheaper than its rivals' offerings.

The Chinese companies in Africa are making a headway because they appeal to trends followed by young people. Young Africans are hungry for technological connectivity and digital inclusion. Chinese companies like Huawei and Xiaomi have become major partners for Africa in modernizing infrastructure related to digital connectivity.

Chinese companies have been at the heart of Africa's technological advancement by constructing data centers, laying fiber optic cables and piloting 5G technologies. This is widely appreciated by young people in Africa who yearn for lower connectivity costs, he said.

6.2　International Target Market Selection

6.2.1　The Meaning of the International Target Market

As we discussed, segmentation is the process by which marketers identify groups of consumers with similar wants and needs. Targeting is the act of evaluating and comparing the identified groups and then selecting one or more of them as the prospect with the highest potential.

6.2.2 Criteria for Assessing International Target Markets

The three basic criteria for assessing opportunity in global target markets are the same as in single-country targeting.

1. Current Segment Size and Growth Potential

Is the market segment currently large enough that it presents a company with the opportunity to make a profit? If it is not large enough or profitable enough today, does it have the high growth potential so that it is attractive in terms of a company's long-term strategy?

China represents an individual geographic market that offers attractive opportunities in many industries. Consider the growth opportunity in cross-border E-commerce, for example, a survey released recently by the International Post Corporation (IPC) indicated that purchases made through Amazon, eBay and Alibaba occupy two-thirds of global cross-border e-commerce. IPC sent questionnaires to over 24,000 consumers in 26 markets across North America, the Asia-Pacific and Europe. Statistics shows that, compared with consumers in other countries, Chinese people are more likely to shop online, with 36 percent buying something online at least once a week. China is the most popular market for online consumers, followed by the U.S., Germany and the U.K. The U.S. and China are the main markets for cross-border e-commerce in the Asia-Pacific and Canada. China is a tremendously large and potential market.

2. Attractiveness of Segment Market Structure

The company also needs to examine major structural factors that affect long-run segment attractiveness. Porter believes that there are five forces that determine the long-term intrinsic appeal of the entire market or any of its segments, and companies should assess the impact of these five groups on long-term profitability. The five groups are: competitors in the same industry, potential new competitors, alternative products, buyers and suppliers. They have the following threats:

① The threat of fierce competition in segmented markets

If there are many powerful or competitive competitors in a segment market, the segment market will lose its attractiveness. If the market segment is stable or declining, the production capacity continues to expand substantially, fixed costs are too high, barriers to withdraw from the market are too high, and competitors invest heavily, the situation will be even worse. These conditions will lead to frequent price wars, advertising battles, and new product introductions and will make it expensive to compete.

② The threat of new competitors

If a particular market segment is likely to attract new competitors, they will increase new production capacity and resources, and compete for market share, making this market segment unattractive. The key issue is whether new competitors can easily enter this market segment. If new competitors encounter strict barriers when entering this market segment and suffer strong retaliation from the original companies in the market segment, it is very difficult for them to enter. The lowering of barriers to protecting market segments, the weaker the revenge of companies that originally occupied the market segment, and the less attractive this segment will be.

③ The threat of substitutes

The existence of many actual or potential substitute products may limit prices and profits. Companies should pay close attention to the price trend of substitute products. If technology develops in these alternative products industries, or the competition becomes increasingly fierce, the price and profit of this market segment may decline.

④ The threat of increased bargaining power of buyers

The relative power of buyers also affects segment attractiveness. Buyers with strong bargaining power relative to sellers will try to force prices down, demand more services, and set competitors against one another—all at the expense of sellers' profitability.

⑤ The threat of increased bargaining power of suppliers

Finally, a segment may be less attractive if it contains powerful suppliers that can control prices or reduce the quality or quantity of ordered goods and services. If suppliers are concentrated or organized, or there are few alternative products, or the supplied products are important input factors, or the conversion cost is high, or suppliers can move forward, then the bargaining power of the suppliers will be stronger. Therefore, it is the best defense strategy to establish good relationships with suppliers and develop multiple supply channels.

3. Company Objectives and Resources

Even if a segment has the right size and growth and is structurally attractive, the company must consider its own objectives and resources. Some attractive segments can be dismissed quickly because they do not mesh with the company's long-run objectives. Or the company may lack the skills and resources needed to succeed in an attractive segment.

6.2.3　International Target Market Strategy

The international target market strategy is a comprehensive plan for the development of an enterprise in the international market. It includes the purpose, goal, resource and policy of entering the international market and is to guide the enterprise to develop continuously and carry out international business activities in the world market. Generally, the planning period for the entry strategy is three to five years.

The international target market strategy is actually a combination of several separate products and market plans. Each enterprise needs to plan the entry strategy for each product to enter each international market, and then centralize and coordinate these plans to form its overall strategy.

The strategy for each individual product to enter the international market specifically includes the following decisions:

- The choice of the target product or the target market;
- The purpose and goal of entering the target market;
- The choice of the entry mode of the target market;
- The formulation of a marketing plan for the target market;
- The control system for monitoring the operation activities of the target market.

The planning process of the international target market strategy is a continuous and endless process, from selecting the target products and markets to determining the target market's operating objectives, selecting the market entry modes, formulating the marketing plan, and finally, correcting the strategic factors through the control system according to the existing problems. This continuous cycle ensures the success of enterprises' entry strategy.

As the world market is more extensive and complex, enterprises can choose four types of international target market strategies: Narrow Focus, Country Focus, Country Diversification and Global Diversification.

1. Narrow Focus

In this strategy, choices are concentrated in a few countries and a few markets, serving only a certain group of consumers. Enterprises may choose this strategy with limited funds and can only operate in a segment market. There may be no competitors in this segment market; This segment market may become the beginning of promoting the continued development of the segment market. Through intensive marketing, the company can better understand the needs of this market segment and establish a special reputation, so it can establish a consolidated market position in this market segment. In addition, through the specialization of production, sales and promotion, the company has also obtained many economic benefits. If the market segments are selected properly, the company's investment can be highly rewarded. However, intensive marketing is riskier than the general situation. Individual market segments may suffer a setback. Or a competitor decides to enter the same market segment. For these reasons, many companies prefer to diversify their marketing into several market segments.

2. Country Focus

In this strategy, choices are concentrated in a few countries, but to enter a number of different markets.

3. Country Diversification

In this strategy, companies enter many different countries at the same time, but only concentrate on a few markets. For example, BENZ, BMW and other premium RVS enter many different countries at the same time, but they are concentrated in a few high-end consumer groups.

4. Global Diversification

That is to say, access to multiple different countries and markets at the same time. Large enterprises can realize the global diversification strategy and cover the whole international market according to their own powerful resources. There are two ways to achieve this: Undifferentiated Marketing or Differential Marketing.

Undifferentiated Marketing refers to that enterprises ignore the differences between market segments and only provide one product for sale throughout the market. The focus of the enterprise is to produce products that buyers generally need, not to produce different products that they need. Enterprises only design one product and make only one marketing plan that arouses the interest of the widest range of customers. It adopts the method of large-scale distribution and large-scale advertisement, in order to establish the best image of products in people's minds. This strategy was adopted by Coca-Cola before the 1960s when it aimed its products at all customers with a single flavor, a uniform price and bottles, and the same advertising theme. Undifferentiated marketing can reduce enterprises' marketing investment in market research, product development, and formulation of various marketing mix schemes. This strategy is more suitable for products with wide demand, high homogeneity of market, mass production and mass sale.

Differential marketing refers to enterprises operating in most market segments, but carefully designing different marketing schemes for each distinct market segment. General Motors, for example, has adopted this marketing strategy when it claims that it will produce a car for everyone with different "wealth, goals and personalities". International Business Machines (IBM) also supplies different hardware and software to different segments of the computer market. The advantage of a differentiated marketing strategy is that the production is flexible and targeted, so that consumer needs are better met. In addition, because the company operates in multiple market segments, it can reduce operating risks to a certain extent. Success in several market segments can help to improve the image of the company and increase market share. However, the corresponding marketing and management costs will also increase, which may make the resource allocation of the enterprise unable to be effectively concentrated, so that it is difficult to form advantages for the fist products.

6.3　International Target Market Positioning

After the global market has been segmented and one or more segments have been targeted, it is essential to plan a way to reach the targets. To achieve this task, marketers use positioning.

6.3.1　The Meaning of Market Positioning

Positioning is the location of your product in the mind of your customer. Thus, one of the most powerful tools of marketing is not something that a marketer can do to the product or to any element of the marketing mix: positioning is what happens in the mind of the customer. The position that a product occupies in the mind of a customer depends on a host of variables, many of which are controlled by the marketer.

Positioning determines a vivid impression or image of the product, and vividly conveys this image to the customer, so that the product reaches the appropriate position in the market. If the company's product positioning is accurate and the image is clear, it will be easy to succeed in the market, otherwise it will often lead to failure. For example, the brand Tide is positioned as a powerful, multi-purpose household detergent; the brand Sole is positioned as a fluffing agent and liquid detergent; the brand Cheer has achieved great success in adapting to various temperatures.

The most effective way of positioning a company/product is to know your customer segment and concentrate on understanding this target group, and create an image that matches with their needs/wants. Advertising is only one way to communicate with customers; companies communicate with their markets in many ways. Positioning is thus considered a systematic way to find a window into the customer's mind. It has to be done at the right time and under the right circumstances. Moreover, it has to be done constantly and consistently. Companies such as Apple and Gillette try to position themselves as the most innovative and leaders in their industries, and they have consistently tried to do that through communication.

▶ Case 6-3

Apple's Run to the Top

In the 15 years between 1996 and 2011, Apple has gone from a quirky, small PC competitor near bankruptcy to the world's most valuable company. This remarkable change of fortunes required daring strategies, intuitive innovation and well-executed commercialization, but also for the established players to miss new market opportunities and the changes in demand in their markets.

Apple was able to leverage its business assets (such as its supply chain in digital goods and software capabilities) to develop the iPod and iPhone. The physical product would have been imitable, but the brilliance of the strategy was that the plethora of third-party application providers and media content owners connected through a single marketplace (iTunes). Apple has repeated the successful formula of filling unoccupied differentiated product spaces by innovating, the results being the iPhone and its killer app, mobile Internet, iTab, and now the latest rumored venture, the iTV. Each innovation was able to uncover a large market whose needs had not been previously met, and, through the combination of being an early mover and skillful marketing/commercialization, to realize high prices and above-average profitability. Ironically, Microsoft, by not protecting the consumer markets, has allowed Apple to grow strong and now, through young employees exerting pressure on IT departments, Apple is able to make inroads into Microsoft's heartland, the corporate market, as well.

Can Apple maintain its leadership?

1. The Positioning of Competitors and Analysis of Their Competitive Advantages

To build profitable relationships with target customers, marketers must understand customer needs and deliver more customer values better than competitors do. To the extent that a company can differentiate and position itself as providing superior customer value, it gains a competitive advantage.

To form their own competitive advantage, companies must investigate and analyze competitors' positioning strategies, including competitors' products, prices, packaging, technology levels, new product development, and product costs, to confirm their competitive potential and competitive advantage. Core competitiveness is based on the existing resources and comparative advantages of the enterprise, and the combination of knowledge, skills and experience rooted in the internal organization and operation of the enterprise body.

To find points of differentiation, marketers must think through the customer's entire experience with the company's product or service. An alert company can find ways to differentiate itself at every customer contact point. In what specific ways can a company differentiate itself or its market offer? It can differentiate along the lines of product, services, people, or image.

① **Product differences**. Through product differentiation, brands can be differentiated by features, performance, or style and design. Consumers are willing to pay a high price for Jaguar cars because of their special and beautiful style.

② **Service differences**. The fierce competition and technological advancement make it more and more difficult to establish and maintain differentiation in physical products. Therefore, the key points of competition are gradually shifting to value-added services, with service differentiation through speedy, convenient, or careful delivery. For example, General Electric not only sells expensive X-ray equipment to hospitals, but also installs them, and also provides serious training for users of the equipment and long-term service support. Others differentiate their service based on high-quality customer care. In an age where customer satisfaction with airline service is in constant decline, Singapore Airlines sets itself apart through extraordinary customer care and the grace of its flight attendants. "Everyone expects excellence from us," says the international airline. "So even in the smallest details of flight, we rise to each occasion and deliver the Singapore Airlines experience."

③ **Personnel differences**. Companies can gain a competitive advantage by hiring and training people who are better than their competitors. People differentiation requires that a company select its customer-contact people carefully and train them well. For example, Disney World people are known to be friendly and upbeat. Disney trains its theme park people thoroughly to ensure that they are competent, courteous, and friendly. Each employee is carefully trained to understand customers and to "make people happy".

④ **Image differences**. Even when competing offers look similar, buyers may perceive a difference based on company or brand image differentiation. Therefore, the company or brand image should convey a product's distinctive benefits and positioning. Effective image differentiation requires the following aspects: establish a product's characteristics and value plan, communicate this characteristic through a distinctive channel, use all available communication methods to promote the brand (such as logos, text, media, atmosphere, events, and employee behavior, etc.) , and convey a message that touches the inner feelings of customers. For example, Nike has always maintained its appeal in the vagaries of the youth market because of its superior image.

2. Understand the Target Customers' Demand Characteristics and Evaluation Criteria

On the basis of investigating the competitors' situation, the company should also understand the customers' maximum preferences and wishes for the products and services they purchase, and clarify their judgments on the quality of the products to provide the basis for business analysis and identification of a competitive advantage.

3. Analysis of Potential Competitive Advantages in the Target Market

The potential competitive advantage of the target market refers to what is the most attractive product among all competitors' products and services in the target market. For example, what is the key competitive advantage to win in the target market, or what is the competitive advantage of ensuring that the company wins? Only when the competitive advantage of the company matches the competitive advantage gained in a particular market can the company win in the market competition.

Companies need to avoid three major market positioning errors. The first is that the positioning is too low, that is, there is no real position for the enterprise. The second type of error is too high a positioning, that is, the image passed to the buyer is too narrow. The third type is the chaos of enterprise positioning, giving buyers a vague and chaotic corporate image.

4. Choose a Competitive Advantage and Positioning Strategy

The choice of a competitive advantage is to analyze the competitive advantages available to enterprises, determine the priority, and select the most competitive advantage. On the basis of understanding and analyzing the needs of customers in the target market and the competitive advantages of competitors, and determining and selecting the comparative competitive advantages of enterprises, enterprises can choose the positioning strategy and market positioning.

Enterprises can position their products based on the following aspects.

① **Attribute positioning**. Product attributes refer to some performance characteristics of the product itself or what the product can do, or product features such as price, quality, luxury, and trendy. For example, Honda's promotion of its Civic model in advertising is cheap. In the premium RV, Toyota's Lexus and Nissan's Infiniti are positioned in the minds of consumers to be of high quality and fuel efficient, Mercedes-Benz are positioned in luxury and honor, Volvo positioned in safety, and BMW positioned in youth and excellent performance.

② **Benefit positioning**. Product benefits refer to what benefits consumers will receive after purchasing a product. International marketers can use product benefits as a basis for product positioning and emphasize what consumers can do to solve this problem. The toothpaste of the Aim brand emphasizes excellent taste because its positioning of children's product and opens up a 10% share of the U.S. toothpaste market.

③ **User positioning**. This refers to the user-based product positioning, emphasizing who is suitable and should use the product. For example, La New develops and manufactures shoes suitable for Taiwanese feet and customized special insoles, so that more consumers with special foot shapes or who need to stand for a long time can find fit and comfortable shoes. Virginia Slims created the positioning of women's cigarettes and swept the large female market.

④ **Brand personality**. Everyone has a different personality, and the brand has a unique personality. International marketers can use the brand personality to build product positioning. For example, in 2006, INFINITI introduced the new FX45, abandoning the already rigid SUV silhouette. This model, with its 18-inch aluminum rim, is full of fashion curves and sexy sports car design. It provides a sense of speed on the road, with greater trustworthy stability than other SUVs.

⑤ **Competitor positioning**. When a firm compares its brand with those of competitors, it uses a competitor positioning strategy. For example, the U.S. "Avis Car Rental" (Avis) took a roundabout attack tactic and positioned itself as: "In the car rental industry, Avis is just No. 2. Why go with us? Because we try harder than anyone else." Avis used this strategy to attack the market leader "Hertz", and thus successfully compared the company with the industry leader Hertz.

5. Accurately Disseminate the Positioning Concept of the Enterprise

After making market positioning decisions, enterprises can conduct positioning publicity through advertisements, public relations and other means, so that the public can accurately understand the positioning concept of enterprises, and avoid the deviation between the market positioning of enterprises and the public understanding caused by improper publicity. Enterprises should reflect the exclusivity of their market positioning and highlight the characteristics and individuality of their products and services through positioning publicity.

6.3.2 International Market Positioning Strategy

The market positioning strategy is actually a competitive strategy that reflects the competitive relationship between a product or a business and similar products or peer companies. In the international market, after comparing their products with international competitors' brand products, companies must consider what products to use to meet the needs of target consumers or target consumer markets. Under normal circumstances, the company's original products have formed a certain image in the minds of customers and occupy a certain position, such as: Coca-Cola in the cola market, Gillette in the razor market, Mercedes-Benz and BMW in the automotive market, Disneyland in theme parks,

Montblanc in the pen market, etc. In the market for these products, it is quite difficult for participating companies to gain a foothold. Therefore, companies must choose an appropriate market positioning strategy in order to gain a place in the fierce market competition. In marketing practice, the market positioning strategies that are often used include confrontation positioning, niche positioning, reverse positioning and repositioning.

1. Competitive Positioning

Competitive positioning is a way of positioning against competitors that dominate the market. That is to say, in order to occupy a better market position, the company will compete face-to-face with the most dominant or strong competitors in the market, and make its products enter the same market position as its competitors. In the world beverage market, Pepsi adopted this method when it entered the market as a rising star, and face-to-face compete with Coca-Cola. This kind of approach may lead to fierce market competition and there exists a high risk, so enterprises should know each other well and strive to do better than their competitors.

2. Niche Positioning

This is when a company adopts a roundabout way to avoid the market positioning of strong competitors. When an enterprise realizes that it is unable to compete with powerful competitors and obtain an absolute advantage, it can develop special products not in the target market according to its own conditions, open up new market areas, and fill market vacancies. The niche positioning strategy enables enterprises to gain a foothold in the market faster, and establish an image among consumers or users with low risks and a high success rate, which is adopted by most enterprises. Hedy company's market positioning of "Non-Coke" soda successfully avoided competition with Coca-Cola and Pepsi, and its sales soared 10% in the first year after the implementation of "non-cola" positioning.

3. Reverse Positioning

In a highly competitive market, sometimes the image of a competitor may be similar to or better than oneself. In this case, reverse positioning is an ideal positioning method. "Avis" is the second place in the U.S. car rental industry. Its slogan is: "In the car rental industry, Avis is just No. 2. Why go with us? Because we try harder than anyone else." In the past 13 years, Avis lost money every year. When the company fully understood the facts of his second position, the company suddenly realized that they had to work harder to reverse the deteriorating trend. After changing the position of Avis, the operation immediately improved, and gradually turned into a profit.

4. Repositioning

After selecting the positioning of a market target, if the positioning is not accurate or if the positioning is correct, but the market situation changes, or for some reason, consumers' or users' preferences change, companies should consider repositioning. Repositioning is the process of changing consumer perceptions of a brand relative to competitors.

5. Competitive Repositioning

In order to accurately determine the product's or brand's position, it is sometimes possible to reposition the competitor. Beck's had trouble getting into the U.S. market. In the United States, it is unlikely to be the No.1 imported beer (Heineken) in America or the first imported beer (Lowenbrau) from Germany. The competitive repositioning strategy solved this problem, "You have tried the most popular German beer in the U.S., so let's try the best beer in Germany—Beck's." Today, Beck's Beer is the second-largest European beer in the United States. This approach is not a direct positioning of the company's own product or brand, but it can achieve this indirectly.

▶ Case 6-4

The Positioning of Yiwu: The World's Capital of Small Commodities

Yiwu, subordinate to Jinhua City of Zhejiang Province, is located in the central part of Zhejiang Province. It is 55 kilometers (34 miles) from urban Jinhua and 158 kilometers (98 miles) from Hangzhou, the capital of Zhejiang Province. Known as the world's capital of small commodities, Yiwu is the world's largest wholesale market of small commodities which has 236 categories and more than 1.8 million kinds of commodities. They are exported to more than 210 countries and regions. So most of the people from abroad you see in Yiwu are businessmen rather than tourists. And the place where they will visit is Yiwu Commodity City, which consists of the Yiwu International Trade City, the Huangyuan Clothing Market and the Binwang Market. All kinds of goods, such as clothes, toys, accessories, furniture and electronic products, can be found there. To cater to the city's prosperous economy and accelerate its urbanization, the city has developed a number of public facilities, including star-rated hotels, convenient transportation and amusement places.

6.4 Entry Modes of the International Market

When a company decides to expand internationally, it faces a host of decisions for the best interest of the company. This is followed by a series of considerations. Which countries should it enter and in what sequence? What criteria should be used to select entry markets? The entry mode of the international market refers to the systematic planning of the products, technologies, skills, management know-how or other resources that enter the foreign market. The choice of an entry mode is one of the most critical strategic decisions of an enterprise, because it will directly affect its business activities and a certain amount of resource input after it enters a foreign market.

Enterprises can enter foreign markets in a variety of ways, including: Exporting entry, which includes indirect export and direct export; Contracting entry, which includes licensing, franchising, management contract, contract manufacturing and turnkey project; Investment entry, which includes joint ventures and sole proprietorships. The choice of a specific entry mode reflects the strategic intention, such as what interests the enterprise wants to obtain and how to obtain such interests in the target market. Therefore, for enterprises engaged in international marketing, understanding the characteristics of various entry modes is conducive to the correct choice.

6.4.1 Exporting Entry Mode

For a long time, exporting has been regarded as an important way for enterprises to enter the international market. From a macro perspective, exporting has been encouraged by governments of various countries because it is conducive to increasing domestic employment, enhancing national foreign exchange income and improving the international competitiveness of domestic enterprises. At the same time, from the perspective of enterprises, in order to reduce the risks brought by domestic competition and expanding, enterprises in various countries will also expand exports as an important way to enter the international market.

The export model has many advantages. ① Because exporting faces the least political risk, it is often used as an initial way for companies to enter international markets. ② When the market potential of the home country is not accurately explored, the export mode can play the role of asking the way. ③ When enterprises find the target market attractive, they can use exports to accumulate experience for future direct investment. ④ When the political and economic conditions of the target market deteriorate, the business relationship with this market can be terminated at a very low cost.

The export model also has some disadvantages. For example, the fluctuation of the exchange rate and the change of the government's trade policy will bring negative effects to the earnings of export enterprises. In addition, exporters often find it difficult to respond quickly to changes in target markets and have poor control over marketing activities.

Exporting can be divided into indirect export and direct export.

1. Indirect Exporting

Indirect exporting means that the company sells its products to intermediaries in the company's home country who, in turn, sell the product overseas. Through indirect exporting, enterprises can start to export products without increasing fixed asset investment, with low operating costs, low risk, and no impact on the current sales profit. Moreover, enterprises can use this way to gradually accumulate experience and lay a foundation for later transformation into direct export.

2. Direct Exporting

Companies engaging in direct exporting have their own in-house exporting expertise, usually in the form of an exporting department. Such companies have more control over the marketing mix in the target market.

In the direct export mode, a company itself performs a series of important activities. These activities include: investigating the target market, finding buyers, contacting distributors, preparing customs documents, arranging transportation and insurance, etc. Direct export gives enterprises partial or total control over foreign marketing programs; They can quickly get more information from the target market, and modify the marketing plan according to the market needs.

6.4.2　Investment Entry Mode

With the development of economic globalization and the opening up of the economies of various countries, more and more enterprises are using foreign direct investment as the main mode of entering foreign markets. Foreign investment can be divided into two forms: joint venture and sole proprietorship.

1. Joint Venture

Joint ventures involve a foreign company joining with a local company, sharing capital, equity, and labor, among others, to set up a new corporate entity. Joint ventures are a preferred international entry mode for emerging markets. In developing countries, joint ventures typically take place between an international firm and a state-owned enterprise.

Many developing countries welcome this type of investment as a way to encourage the development of local expertise, of the local market, and of the country's balance of trade, assuming the resultant production will be exported abroad. In most developing countries, an international firm typically provides expertise, know-how, most of the capital, a brand name reputation, and a trade-mark that is internationally protected, among others. The local partner provides the labor, the physical infrastructure, local market expertise and relationships, as well as connections to government decision-making bodies. However, joint ventures also have limitations. For example, the two sides often have disputes over investment decisions, or marketing and financial control, which hinders multinational companies from implementing a unified and coordinated global strategy.

2. Sole Proprietorship

A sole proprietorship—also referred to as a sole trader or a proprietorship—is an unincorporated business that has just one owner who pays personal income tax on profits earned from the business. Many sole proprietors do business under their own names because creating a separate business or trade name isn't necessary.

This type of business is the easiest and cheapest form to start. For this reason, it is common among small businesses, freelancers, and other self-employed individuals.

Advantages of sole proprietorships:

① The easiest and cheapest way to start a business

Though the process varies depending on the jurisdiction, establishing a sole proprietorship is generally an easy and inexpensive process, unlike forming a partnership or a corporation.

② Few government rules and laws

There are very few government rules and regulations that are specific to proprietors. Sole proprietors must keep proper records, file, and pay taxes on business income and other personal income sources.

③ Full management control

Proprietors control all aspects of their business, including production, sales, finance, personnel, etc. This degree of freedom is attractive to many entrepreneurs, as the venture's success also means personal success.

④ Flow-through of business profit

There is no legal separation between the owner and the business, so the owner gets 100% of the profits. Although all profits go to the owner, taxes are paid once, and proprietors pay taxes individually.

Disadvantages of sole proprietorships:

① Unlimited legal liability

There is no legal separation between the owner and the business. Similar to how all profits flow to the owner, all debts and obligations rest with the proprietor.

② Limit to available capital

Owners put their own resources to bear when going into business for themselves. There are limits to their financial resources and the amount of credit they get when they seek out lending relationships.

③ Skills and experience

The proprietor must make "good enough" decisions in all business areas. If an owner does not have enough knowledge or skills, their decisions may be flawed. There is a finite amount of time to do things correctly or learn to do everything adequately.

6.4.3　Contracting Entry Mode

Contracting entry is a long-term non-equity relationship between an international enterprise and a legal entity in the target country, in which the former transfers technology or skills to the latter.

1. Licensing

With the in-depth development of international marketing activities, licensing has become a widely adopted entry mode. Licensing is a contractual arrangement where one company (the licensor) provides technology, know-how, patents, or a successful brand to another company (the licensee) in exchange for a licensing fee and an ongoing royalty stream that is based upon a negotiated percentage of the licensee's sales that use the licensed technology. Licensing can be an appealing form of global market entry. A company can use licensing agreements with a foreign firm to supplement its domestic bottom line with almost no capital or marketing costs. For example, under the licensing system, Coca-Cola and Pepsi are globally produced and sold, by local bottlers in different countries.

Benefits and limitations:

In licensing, the licensor gets the advantage of entering the international market at little risk. However, the licensor has little or no control over the licensee, in terms of the production, distribution and sales of the product. In addition to this, if the licensee gets success, the firm has given up profits, and whenever the licensing agreement expires, the firm might find that it has given birth to a competitor.

As a prevention measure, there are certain proprietary product components supplied by the licensor itself. Although, innovation is considered as the appropriate strategy, so that the licensee will have to depend on the licensor.

On the other hand, the licensee acquires expertise in production or a renowned brand name. It expects that the arrangement will increase the overall sales, which might open the doors to a new market and help in achieving the business objectives. However, it requires considerable capital investment and, to start the operations, the developmental cost is also borne by the licensee.

2. Franchising

Franchising is an arrangement in which the franchisor gives the franchisee the right to distribute and sell the franchisor's goods or services and use its business name and business model for a specified period of time, possibly covering a geographical area. The franchisor is the owner of the business that provides the product/service, while the franchisee is the person who receives the rights to use the franchisor's business name, model, etc. Franchising exists in several forms. According to the Franchising Council of Australia, the most common way of franchising identified is in the "business format franchising".

In a business format franchising, the franchisee has the right to sell the franchisor's goods or services, but also uses the franchisor's designs, quality control, training, and also benefits from his/her advertising and promotions, accounting systems, and operating procedures.

There are three main types of franchises.

- Most franchises fall under the business format type where the franchisor licenses a business format, operating system, and trademark rights to its franchisees.

- The second type of franchise is product distribution, which is more of a supplier-dealer setup. The franchisor grants the franchisee permission to sell or distribute a product using their logo, trademarks and trade name, but typically does not provide an operating system to run the business with.

- The third is manufacturing, where the franchisor permits the franchisee to manufacture their products (e.g. clothing) and sell them under its trademarks.

3. Contract Manufacturing

Contract manufacturing is defined as the production of goods by a company for a brand or label of another company. This is an outsourcing process that is conducted by a contract manufacturer who offers such services for several firms. The products that are manufactured are customized as per the specifications and design of the customer and sometimes even their own.

Contract manufacturing is the organization that creates or manufactures a product for another company. The concept is also used to refer to the companies that offer special services to several organizations about the manufacturing process. The role of a manufacturing company can also act as a mutually beneficial liaison between two companies, one that wants a certain product and the other that can deliver that product.

In the international scenario, contract manufacturing is applicable when one firm asks another company located in a different country to manufacture its products. The contract manufacturing mentions a set of requirements concerning the quality, delivery dates, quantities, and certification. It also mentions strict guidelines for testing and inspection of the goods, modifications to orders, compensation, and guarantees in case of the breach of a contract.

4. Management Contract

Management contracts are legal agreements that enable one company to have control over another business's operations. Business owners often sign these written agreements directly with the management company. This typically gives the management company operational control for an established period of time, usually for two to five years. Most management contracts are task-specific and focused on the work itself, not established outcomes. For example, the British Airport Authority (BAA) has contracts to manage airports in Indianapolis (U.S.), Naples (Italy) and Melbourne (Australia) because it has developed successful airport management skills.

Advantages of management contracts:

① It enables a firm to exploit an international business opportunity without having to place a great deal of its own physical assets at risk;

② The government can award companies management contracts to operate and upgrade public utilities;

③ The government uses the management contract to develop skills of local workers and managers.

Disadvantages of management contracts:

① International management in countries that are undergoing political or social unrest can place a threat before the managers of the company to manage its operations;

② Suppliers of expertise may put a threat of new competitor in the local market.

5. Turnkey Contracting

Turnkey contracting refers to the way that an enterprise enters the foreign market by signing a contract with a foreign enterprise and completing a large project, and then delivering the project to the other party. The responsibilities of the enterprise generally include the design and construction of the project, and the provision of services after the delivery of the project, such as providing management and training of workers, to prepare the other party for the operation of the project. In addition to inter-company turnkey contracts, many are with foreign governments for some large public infrastructure such as hospitals, roads and ports.

The most attractive aspect of turnkey entry is that the contracts are often for large, long-term projects and lucrative. However, due to its long-term nature, such projects are more uncertain, such as encountering political risks. It is often difficult for companies to anticipate the impact of changes in foreign governments on project results.

There are several key benefits to turnkey contracts.

- The first benefit to a turnkey contract for the client is that the client leaves the important decisions to the service provider.
- As a result, clients who do not have the right skills and experience can rely on the service provider's expertise to get the job done properly.

- Another benefit for the client is that in turnkey contracts, the service provider remains responsible for the project risk for the entire duration of the project.
- The client will get the title to the final work product once it's been delivered by the service provider in accordance with the contract specifications.
- For the service provider, a turnkey contract is easier to manage as it does not have to deal with the ever-changing needs and requests of the client.
- The service provider is responsible to deliver the project in accordance with the contract, nothing more, and nothing less.
- Another benefit for the service provider is that its responsibilities are clearly called out in the contract.

❯ Chapter Summary

- International market segmentation refers to the process in which an enterprise divides the entire international market into several sub-markets of products and marketing mix with significantly different demands according to the needs of consumers and certain segmentation criteria, so as to select one or more of these sub-markets as its international target market.
- The macro segmentation criteria of the international market are geographical criteria, economic criteria, cultural criteria and portfolio criteria. The international market is divided into consumer market and industrial market.
- The micro segmentation of the international consumer market is mainly based on geographical factors, demographic factors, psychological factors, behavioral factors, etc., while international industrial product market segmentation is mainly based on end users, customer size and purchasing power, purchasing organization characteristics, etc.
- International market segmentation must follow the principles of being measurable, substantial, accessible and actionable.
- The international target market is part of the market that the enterprise decides to enter, that is, the buyer group that the enterprise chooses to meet its needs with corresponding products and services.
- The strategy of the international target market includes the selection of the target market, the purpose and objectives of entering the target market, the choice of the target market's

entry method, the formulation of the marketing plan for the target market, and the control system for monitoring business activities in target markets.

- International target market selection strategies generally include strategies of narrow focus, country focus, country diversification and global diversification. The development of the international target market includes market penetration, market development, product development and diversification.

- The steps of international target market positioning include the positioning of competitors and analysis of their competitive advantages, understanding the demand characteristics and evaluation criteria of target customers for products, analyzing the potential competitive advantages of the target market, selecting the competitive advantages and positioning strategies, and accurately spreading the positioning concept of enterprises.

- International market positioning strategies include confrontational positioning, niche positioning, reverse positioning, repositioning, and competitive repositioning.

- The entry mode of the international market refers to the systematic planning of the products, technologies, skills, management know-how or other resources when companies enter into the foreign market.

- Enterprises usually have three ways to enter into foreign markets: exporting entry, including indirect export and direct export; contracting entry, including licensing, franchising, management contracts, contract manufacturing, and turnkey engineering; investment entry mode, including joint venture and sole proprietorship.

Main Concepts

international market segmentation, international market targeting, target market positioning, undifferentiated marketing, differentiated marketing, confrontational positioning, niche positioning, reverse positioning, repositioning, competitive repositioning, licensing, franchising

Think and Practice

1. Why do companies need to segment the international market before entering the international market?

2. What are the principles and steps of international market segmentation?

3. What is the difference between international market macro segmentation and international market micro segmentation?

4. What factors should be considered when positioning the international market?

5. How does an enterprise position itself in the international target market? What are the positioning strategies?

6. What are the ways to enter the international market?

7. What is the contracting entry mode? What are the specific methods?

8. What common problems do Chinese enterprises face when entering the international market? Try to analyze how to resolve these problems.

⊙ Case Study

How Huawei's Global Experience Creates Global Leadership

A primary belief of Ren Zhengfei, the founder of Huawei Technologies Co., is that if a company wants to go global, it needs to ensure that its people think with a global mindset. Building on the founder's philosophy, Huawei has moved to an employee performance system that measures "global experience", an important criterium for identifying future leaders. As Zhengfei noted: "You need to get down and manage at the front lines to get a true taste of things. To qualify for greater responsibility, you need successful experience in the field."

A belief exists in Huawei that leaders of global (and virtual) teams need to be able to diagnose and interpret potential cultural tripwires in the group. In other words, one needs to be able to understand and deal with how cultural differences might impact team functioning to take up leadership within Huawei.

Leaders are expected to go out there and gain experience in their field offices around the world to improve work situations and efficiency in serving customers from diverse cultural backgrounds. In this sense, global mobility of Huawei's high potentials is systematic. In other words, to Huawei leaders, the notion of global means integrating Chinese and western perspectives—not simply being Chinese in a global world. In fact, Zhengfei noted that "the management teams in our research centers in China must be world-class and have a global perspective. They must not operate like a local team, because a Chinese style will lead to complacency".

Discuss the following questions.

1. From this material, how does Huawei position itself in the world market?

2. How does Huawei achieve its positioning?

3. Search for information on products of Huawei and its main overseas markets, and choose one product and one overseas market to analyze the strategies of segmentation, targeting, positioning of the chosen product in the chosen market, and the mode of entry into that market.

Chapter 7

Product Strategy of International Marketing

//////// **Learning Objectives** //////////////////////

- Describe the whole product concept and the content of each level;

- Understand the basic basis of international product " standardization " and the " differentiation " strategy;

- Understand the theory of the international product life cycle;

- Understand the procedure of international new product development;

- Distinguish product brand and trademark.

////////// *Key Terms* //////////////////////

whole product concept 产品整体概念

International Product Life Cycle(IPLC)
国际产品生命周期

core product 核心产品

actual product 实际产品

augmented product 延伸产品

introduction stage 引入期

growth stage 成长期

maturity stage 成熟期

decline stage 衰退期

New Product Development (NPD) 新产
品开发

idea generation 构思产生

idea screening 构思筛选

concept development and testing 概念开
发与测试

marketing strategy development 营销战
略制定

business analysis 商业分析

test marketing 营销测试

commercialization 商业化

products standardization 产品标准化

products differentiation 产品差异化

product line 产品线

brand 品牌

brand equity 品牌资产

packaging 包装

service 服务

▶ Opening Case

Galanz Sees an Export Increase as Demand Grows

Galanz Group, a leading Chinese household electrical appliance maker, realized a year-on-year increase of 9.8 percent in exports for the first half of 2022 thanks to diversified products specially tailored for overseas customers, according to the company.

The company's products being shipped overseas include a full range of environmentally friendly smart appliances ranging from microwave ovens, refrigerators, steam ovens, air fryers, dishwashers and washing machines to clothes dryers.

Of the shipments, 30 percent were exported to countries and regions related to the Belt and Road Initiative.

Development of high value-added products in combination with real overseas market demand contributed to the company's export growth.

For example, the company, based in Guangdong province, has developed small liter microwave ovens and refrigerators in the North American market, where such appliances are promoted to recreational vehicle customers.

Noting the RV market was a new channel for Galanz's products in North America, the company has also organized special teams of engineers to assist local customers in improving the RV structural space and installation.

Galanz has designated its sales teams to visit major overseas markets since July, aiming to expand its shipments in the second half of the year, usually a peak season for home appliance sales.

(Galanz's independent appliances enter mainstream channels in Vietnam)

(Source: Adapted from *China Daily*)

7.1 Products and Whole Product Concept

7.1.1 Product Concept

The concept of product can be divided into a narrow sense and a broad sense. In a narrow sense, the concept of product is confined to the form and specific use of a certain substance. It is generally understood or expressed as a tangible object created by labor with value and use value that can meet human needs. The broad concept of product has a very broad extension and profound connotation, which is generally expressed as: all tangible goods and intangible services that can satisfy the specific needs and desires of consumers or users through exchange. Tangible goods include product entity and its quality, style, characteristics, brand, and packaging; Intangible services include psychological satisfaction, trust and various after-sales support and service assurance.

7.1.2 Whole Product Concept

The continuous expansion and change of consumer demand have expanded the connotation and extension of products. Products expand from tangible goods to services, personnel, places, organizations, and concepts. To this end, the product composition is studied in connection with consumer demand and product composition among enterprises.

Concerning product composition, academia has expressed it on three levels: core product, actual product and augmented product.

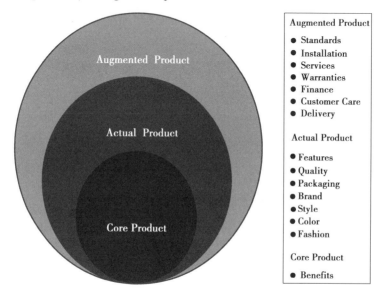

Figure 7-1 Whole Product Concept

1. Core Product

The core product refers to the basic utility or benefits provided to consumers. They are what consumers really want to buy. They are the most basic and main content of the overall concept of products. Consumers buy products not for the sake of obtaining the products themselves, but for the sake of satisfying the utility and benefit of their specific needs. For example, people buy washing machines instead of large iron boxes with motors and switch buttons, so as to replace manual laundry and reduce housework and facilitate daily life. Consumers are willing to pay a certain fee to buy a product for the basic utility of the product and benefit from it. Therefore, the production and operation activities of enterprises' products should first consider what utility or benefits can be provided to consumers and focus on these basic utility or benefits of products.

2. Actual Product

The actual product refers to the specific product form of the core product, which is the appearance of the product entity provided to the market. Formal products are composed of five tangible factors: product quality, characteristics, style, brand, and packaging. Products with the same utility may have differences in their existing forms. To purchase a product, consumers should consider many factors, such as quality, shape, style, color and brand reputation, besides requiring the product to have some basic functions and to provide some core interests. The basic utility of a product must be realized in some specific form. Therefore, when designing products, enterprises should focus on the core interests pursued by consumers, and at the same time pay attention to how to present such interests to consumers in a unique form.

3. Augmented Products

Augmented products refer to the sum of various additional services and benefits that consumers acquire when purchasing formal products and expected products. They include product specifications, credit, free delivery, guarantee, installation, maintenance, technical training, etc. Similar products provided by different enterprises are getting closer and closer at the core and formal product levels. Therefore, in order to win the competitive advantage, enterprises should focus on providing more extended products than their competitors, because extended products are conducive to guiding, inspiring, stimulating consumers to buy, repeating and increasing the purchases.

7.2 Product Life Cycle in the International Market

7.2.1 Product Life Cycle and Its Marketing Strategy

Product life cycle theory is an important basis for enterprises to formulate the product strategy and the marketing mix strategy. Because products are in different stages of life cycle, there are great differences in market demand and competitiveness. The formulation of the product strategy, the marketing mix strategy and other strategies of enterprises must adapt to the changes of product life cycle. This is the survival and development of enterprises in a dynamic market environment, and a key issue to win a favorable market position.

1. The Concept of Product Life Cycle

From introducing products into the market to withdrawing from the market, there is a process of birth, growth, maturity and decline. Marketing describes the process of products in the market with product life cycle. Product life cycle refers to the whole marketing period from the successful development of products into the market, through the growth and maturity stage, to the end of the recession from the market. The length of a marketing period of products in the market is influenced by many factors, such as the change of consumers' demand and the speed of product renewal. Therefore, different products have completely different life cycles.

2. The Stages and Characteristics of Product Life Cycle

Because of the influence of market factors, the sales and profits of products in their life cycle are not uniformly changed. In different periods or stages, products have different sales and profits. From this point of view, the life cycle of products can be measured by the changes of sales and profits. According to the change of sales volume, the typical product life cycle includes four stages: introduction period, growth period, maturity period and decline period, showing a "S" curve, as shown in Figure 7-2.

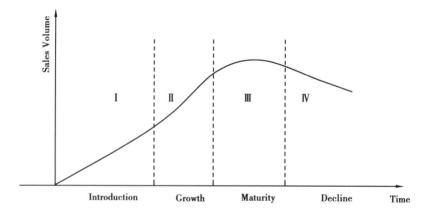

Figure 7-2　Product Life Cycle Curve

The four stages of typical product life cycle show different characteristics:

① **Introduction stage**. The introduction period, also known as the introduction period and the trial period, refers to the initial sales stage of the new product just introduced into the market. Its main features are:

- Product design has not been finalized. There are few designs and varieties, small production batches, high unit production costs, and high advertising and promotional costs;

- Consumers are not familiar with the product. Only a few customers pursuing novelty may purchase. Sales volume is small;
- The sales network has not yet been fully and effectively established. Sales channels are not smooth and the sales growth is slow;
- Because of a low sales volume and a high cost, enterprises usually make little profit or even lose money;
- There are few producers and few competitors for similar products.

② **Growth stage**. The growth period, also known as the best-selling period, refers to the period when products are rapidly accepted by customers in the market and the sales volume and profits are rapidly increasing. Its main features are:

- Products have been finalized. Varieties of designs and colors increase, and production batches increase;
- Consumers have become familiar with new products. The sales volume increases rapidly;
- Relatively ideal sales channels are established;
- Because of the sales growth and decreased cost, profits rise rapidly;
- Producers of similar products see profitability, enter the market to participate in competition, and market competition begins to intensify.

③ **Maturity stage**. The maturity period, also known as the saturation period, refers to the period when product sales tend to be saturated and begin to decline slowly and the market competition is very fierce. Maturity usually lasts the longest in the product life cycle. According to the sales characteristics of this stage, the maturity period can be divided into three periods: the growth maturity period, the stable maturity period and the recession maturity period. The main characteristics of the three periods are as follows:

- Sales channels are saturated in the mature period. The growth rate rises slowly, and a few consumers continue to enter the market;
- In the stable mature period, the market is saturated, sales are stable, and the growth rate of sales is only proportional to the number of purchasers. If there are no new buyers, the growth rate will stagnate or decline;
- Sales began to decline slowly in the mature period of the recession, and consumer interest began to shift to other products and substitutes.

[Box 7-1]

Innovation of New Products Postpones the Time of Total

The figure demonstrates how the continuous development of new uses for the basic material constantly produced new waves of sales. The exhibit shows that in spite of the growth of the women's stocking market, the cumulative result of the military, circular knit, and miscellaneous grouping would have been a flattened sales curve by 1958. (Nylon's entry into the broadwoven market in 1944 substantially raised sales above what they would have been. Even so, the sales of broadwoven, circular knit, and military and miscellaneous groupings peaked in 1957.)

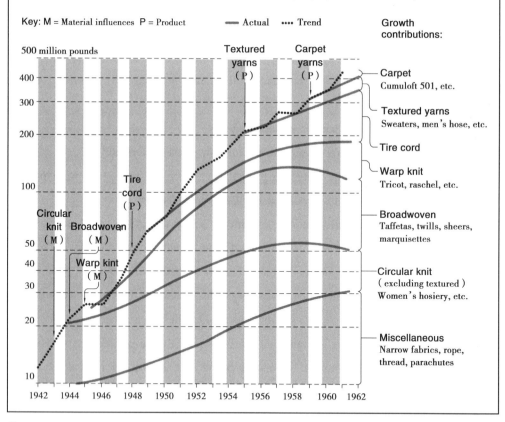

④ **Decline stage**. The decline period, also known as the unsalable period, refers to the period when the sales of products have dropped sharply, and the products have gradually been eliminated by the market. Its main features are:

- The demand, sales and profits of products are rapidly declining, and prices are the lowest;

- New products or substitutes have appeared in the market, and consumers' interests completely shifted;

- Most competitors have been forced to withdraw from the market, enterprises that remain in the market are forced to reduce services and drastically reduce promotions. Expenses maintain a minimum level of operation.

3. Marketing Strategies at Various Stages of the Product Life Cycle

① Marketing strategies at the introduction stage

During the period of introduction, the focus of enterprise marketing is to make correct judgment, seize the opportunity, and adopt effective marketing strategies in order to occupy the market, form a batch scale, and enter the growth period quickly. In the introduction period, there are four marketing strategies for enterprises to choose.

- The quick skimming strategy. This strategy is to launch new products with a high price and a high promotion cost in order to rapidly expand sales, gain a higher market share and recover investment quickly.

- The slow skimming strategy. The slow skimming strategy is to launch new products with a high price and a low promotion cost in order to gain more profits.

- The rapid-penetration strategy. This strategy is to launch new products with a low price and a high promotion cost, so as to quickly occupy the market and obtain the highest market share.

- The slow-penetration strategy. The slow-penetration strategy is to launch new products with a low price and a low promotion cost. Low prices can prompt the market to accept the new products quickly, while low promotion costs can reduce marketing costs and achieve more profits.

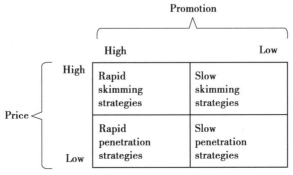

Figure 7-3　Marketing Strategies at the Introduction Stage

② Marketing strategies at the growth stage

The growth period of strong market demand and high profits will attract the participation of competitors. Therefore, the focus of enterprise marketing in this stage is to expand market share and consolidate market position. Enterprises can adopt the following marketing strategies.

- **The product strategy**. At this stage, consumers have a certain amount of choice when buying. In order to expand sales, companies make buyers increase their purchases and enable potential buyers to implement purchases. They should adopt brand-name product strategies. Enterprises can improve and perfect products, provide excellent after-sales service and other measures to improve the competitiveness of products, so that consumers have a sense of trust.

- **The price strategy**. Enterprises are flexible in pricing according to market competition and their own characteristics. Choosing the right time to lower the price of the product can not only win over the customers who are more sensitive to the price, but also impact the competitors.

- **The channel strategy**. Companies consolidate the original sales channels, increase new sales channels, open up new markets and expand the sales scope of products.

- **The promotion strategy**. Companies strengthen the promotion links and establish a strong product image. The focus of promotion should be shifted from the establishment of product popularity in the introduction period to the promotion of special performance and characteristics of products and the improvement of the image and reputation of products and enterprises. The main goal is to establish brand preference, maintain old customers and win new customers.

③ Marketing strategies at the maturity stage

In the maturity stage, as long as enterprises maintain market share, they can obtain stable income and profits. The marketing emphasis in the mature period is to stabilize the market share, maintain the existing market position, and extend the product life cycle through various improvement measures, in order to obtain the highest yield. To this end, enterprises can adopt the following three strategies.

- **The market improvement strategy**. This strategy does not need to change the product itself, but achieves the purpose of expanding product sales by discovering new uses of the product, changing sales methods and opening new markets.

- **The product improvement strategy**. This strategy is to meet the different needs of consumers by improving the products themselves, so as to expand the sales of products. Any level of improvement in the overall product concept can be regarded as product improvement.

- **The marketing mix improvement strategy**. This strategy is to stimulate sales by changing the factors of marketing mix, so as to prolong the growth and maturity of products. Commonly used methods are special price, early purchase discounts, subsidized freight, deferred payment and so on, to attract consumers and improve the competitiveness of products.

④ Marketing strategies at the decline stage

During this period, companies should not abandon old products when new products do not keep up so that they completely lose their existing markets and customers, nor should they hold onto old products and miss opportunities, leaving the company in a difficult position.

7.2.2   Product Life Cycle in the International Market

When expanding the concept of the PLC to international markets, two different approaches appear.

1. International Product Life Cycle (IPLC)—a Macroeconomic Approach

The IPLC theory (originally Vernon, 1966) describes the diffusion process of an innovation across national boundaries. Each curve in the IPLC represents net exports or net imports for a particular country. When the curve is above the horizontal line, net export results, and when it is below, net import results.

Typically, demand first grows in the innovating country. In the beginning, the innovating country exports its excess production (greater than domestic demand) to other advanced countries, where demand is also increasing. Only later does demand start to grow in less developed countries. Consequently, production primarily takes place in the innovating country during the initial stages. As the product matures and technology is diffused, production expands to other industrialized countries and eventually to less developed countries. The shift of efficiency and comparative advantages moves from developed countries to developing countries. Eventually, advanced countries, no longer cost-effective, import products from their former customers.

Examples of typical IPLCs can be found in the textile industry and the computer/software industry. For example, many software programs today are made in Bangalore, India.

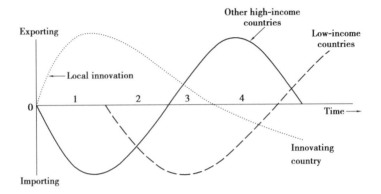

Figure 7-4   International Product Life Cycle—a Macroeconomic Approach

2. Product Life Cycles across Countries—a Microeconomic Approach

In foreign markets, the time span for a product to pass through a stage may vary from market to market. In addition, due to different economic levels in different countries, a specific product can be in different PLC stages in different countries. Figure 7-5 shows that the product (at a certain time) is at the decline stage in the home market while it is at the maturity stage in Country X and at the introduction stage in Country Y.

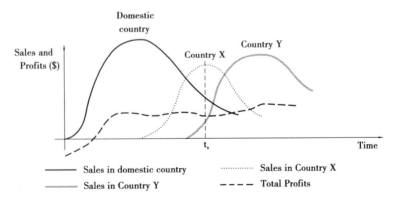

Figure 7-5   International Product Life Cycle—a Microeconomic Approach

7.3　New Product Development in the International Market

7.3.1　The Concept of New Product

In marketing, a new product has a different meaning from that created by a new invention in the process of technological development. The content of a new product in marketing is more extensive. Products that appear for the first time in the market, or products that an enterprise produces and sells for the first time, all belong to the category of new products. New products are generally divided into the following four categories:

1. Brandy New Product

Brand new products refer to new products developed by applying modern scientific and technological achievements, and featuring new principles, new technologies and new materials.

2. Innovative New Product

Innovative new products refer to products that make significant innovations by incorporating science and new technology into existing products. These innovations lead to a notable improvement in product performance and meet new consumer demands.

3. Improved New Product

Improved new products refer to products of which the uses and performances remain unchanged, but improvements are made to the quality, design, style, or packaging of existing products.

4. Imitation of New Products

Imitation of new products refers to products that are produced by copying existing products.

For enterprises, brand-new products cost a lot of manpower, financial resources and material resources, from theory to technology, from laboratory to production. Therefore, it is difficult for enterprises to develop such new products. However, the development process of innovative new products is relatively short. For innovative new products, consumers already know the original products, so they are easy to be accepted, and enterprises are trying their best to develop such new products. It is easier to improve new products and copy new ones, so most companies do this. These kinds of products are often seen in the international market.

7.3.2 New Product Development Procedures

New Product Development (NPD) refers to the complete process of bringing a new product to market. Developing new products is a complicated task that involves high investment and high risk. To minimize mistakes and risks, enterprises must adhere to scientific and systematic development procedures when creating new products. The development process of new products encompasses the entire journey from generating ideas, evaluating and developing concepts, to the final product. The new product development process includes 8 main steps: idea generation, screening concept, concept development and testing, marketing strategy development, business analysis, product development, test marketing, and commercialization.

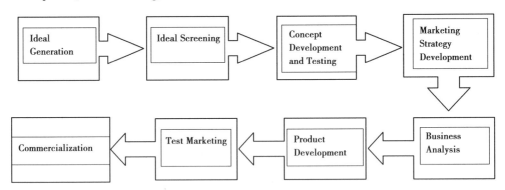

Figure 7-6 New Product Development Procedures

1. Idea Generation

The development of a new product begins with the idea of developing it. The successful development of a new product starts with a creative and valuable idea. Although not all ideas are likely to become new products, seeking as many ideas as possible can provide more opportunities to develop new products.

There are many sources of new product ideas, mainly from customers, competitors, middlemen, technical personnel, sales personnel and so on. In addition, new product ideas can be sought from inventors, patent agents, universities, research institutes, consulting firms, advertising agencies, trade associations and related publications. Because ideas come from many sources, the chance for ideas to receive serious attention depends on the organization responsible for new product development. To this end, marketing personnel of enterprises must actively and orderly seek, collect and accept all kinds of new product ideas.

2. Idea Screening

Idea screening is about evaluating new product ideas, studying their feasibility, and picking out those that are creative and valuable. The purpose of screening ideas is to select those product ideas that are in line with the development goals and long-term interests of the enterprise and are in harmony with the enterprise resources, and to find those ideas that are not very viable and have no future prospects early.

Enterprises generally need to consider the following factors when screening ideas: first, environmental conditions, which involve the scale and composition of the market, the degree and prospect of product competition, national policies, etc. Second, the enterprise's strategic tasks, development goals and long-term interests, which involve the enterprise's strategic tasks, profit goals, sales goals and image goals. Third, the development and implementation ability of the enterprise, including business management ability, human resources, financial ability, technical ability and sales ability. In the process of screening ideas, companies should avoid two types of mistakes: one is to erroneously give up those feasible new product ideas; the other is to misuse them to develop some dead-end new product. In either way, it will cause significant losses to the enterprise. Therefore, enterprises must start from their own actual situation and decide the product idea according to the specific circumstances.

3. Concept Development and Testing

Product ideas retained after screening must evolve into product concepts. A product concept is a detailed version of the idea stated in meaningful consumer terms. A product image is the way consumers perceive an actual or potential product. Product concept refers to the product idea or a potential product image that has been formed in the minds of consumers with clear elaboration of text, image, model, etc. The product concept is detailed in meaningful consumer language.

A product idea can translate into several product concepts. For example, a dairy company has an idea to develop a nutritious milk product. From this idea, the following three product concepts were developed:

Concept 1: an instant milk powder for breakfast, so that adults can quickly supplement nutrition without the need to prepare breakfast;

Concept 2: a delicious snack drink for children to drink at noon to refresh themselves;

Concept 3: a healthy drink, suitable for the elderly to drink at night.

Each product concept should be positioned to understand the competitive situation of similar products and optimize the best product concept. This requires product concepts to be tested and evaluated by representative consumers in the target market. Through the product concept test, enterprises can better choose and improve the product concept.

4. Marketing Strategy Development

A marketing plan is drawn up for a product concept after being tested and validated. The initial marketing plan should include three parts:

① Explain the size, structure, behavior of the target market, market positioning of new products, recent sales, market share, profit rate, etc.;

② Outline the planned price, distribution channels, promotion methods and the marketing budget of the new product;

③ Explain the long-term development of new products and put forward ideas, such as long-term sales and profit targets, marketing mix strategies at each stage of the product lifecycle, etc.

5. Business Analysis

Business analysis is the economic benefit analysis of the new product concept, which involves making a further assessment of the new product's sales, costs, and profits to determine whether it is in line with the enterprise's goals and whether to enter the formal development stage of new products.

Business analysis involves forecasting sales and calculating costs and profits. When estimating sales of new products, it's necessary to investigate the sale of similar products in the past and target market circumstances in depth and to calculate the minimum and maximum sale quantity in order to estimate the risk size. Then the staff should discuss and analyze together with the relevant departments, and estimate the cost and calculate the profit. Based on these cost and profit data, the financial attractiveness of new products can be analyzed.

6. Product Development

Product concepts that successfully pass business analysis can enter the product development phase. In this phase, product concepts described in words, graphics or models are transformed into product models or samples in a physical form. A lot of investment is spent in this phase, and the question is whether the product concept can be translated into a technically and commercially viable product.

It takes days, weeks, months, even years to develop a successful product. The engineering and technical department will carry out material selection and processing design, structural modeling design and value engineering analysis. The marketing department will carry out appearance design, packaging design and brand planning. After the sample is manufactured, rigorous functional and consumer testing must be carried out. Functional testing is conducted in the laboratory or on the site, mainly to check whether the product conforms to relevant safety and technical requirements, whether it conforms to national, industrial or enterprise standards, whether the technological process is reasonable and advanced, and whether the quality of parts or finished products is reliable. Consumer testing involves giving some samples to consumers to try out, so as to get their opinions on new products.

7. Test Marketing

If the business is satisfied with the results of the product test, then it will enter the market testing stage. Market testing is a process of combining new products with the brand, package, price and initial marketing plan, and then putting new products into the market in small quantities to test whether the new products are really popular in the market. The goal is to understand how customers and sellers will react to handling, using and repurchasing of the product, and how big the potential market is.

8. Commercialization

After the successful test marketing of the new product, it can be formally mass-produced and formally introduced to the market. At this point, the company faces the biggest investment decision: firstly, the company needs to build or rent equipment needed for full production, of which the scale of production will be the most critical. For safety reasons, many companies keep their production capacity within forecast sales. Secondly, enterprises need to invest a lot of marketing costs, and many new products often need high advertising and promotion budget support at the initial stage of listing.

7.4 Products Standardization and Differentiation Strategy in the International Market

7.4.1 Product Standardization Strategy in International Markets

1. The Standardization Strategy of International Products

The standardization strategy for international products means that enterprises offer the same products to all markets in different countries or regions around the world. The premise of implementing the strategy of product standardization is market globalization. Since the 1960s, with the development of society, economy and technology, international communication has become more and more frequent, countries and regions around the world are more and more dependent on each other, and more and more common in consumer demand. Similar needs have formed a unified world market. As a result, enterprises can produce globally standardized products to achieve economies of scale. For example, in North America, Europe and Japan, there has emerged a new customer group with similar levels of education, income, lifestyle and leisure pursuits. An enterprise may offer a standardized product or service to a similar market segment in different countries as an overall market segment, such as Coca-Cola, McDonald's fast food, Kodak film, Hollywood movies, Sony Walkman and other products of consumers all over the world.

2. The Significance of the Product Standardization Strategy in the International Market

With the rapid pace of economic globalization, it is undoubtedly of great significance for enterprises to carry out the product standardization strategy in order to gain global competitive advantages.

- The product standardization strategy can enable enterprises to implement economies of scale, significantly reducing the cost of research, development, production and sales to increase profits.

- Selling standardized products on a global scale is conducive to building a unified image of products in the world, strengthening the reputation of enterprises, and helping consumers to identify the products of enterprises, so that the products of the enterprise enjoy a high reputation in the world.

- Product standardization also enables enterprises to effectively control global marketing. The geographical scope of international marketing is larger than that of domestic marketing. If there are many types of products, the marketing resources for each product are relatively small, and it is difficult to control effectively. On the one hand, product standardization reduces the difficulty of marketing management. On the other hand, it concentrates on marketing resources. The enterprise can invest relatively abundant resources on a small number of products and have stronger control over marketing activities.

3. Conditions of the Standardization Strategy for International Products

Enterprises should decide whether to choose a product standardization strategy according to the following aspects:

① Product demand characteristics

From the perspective of global consumers, demand can be divided into two categories: the common and country-neutral needs of the global consumer and the individual needs of the environment-related national consumers. A standardized product sold on a global basis must be one with similar requirements worldwide. The consumer's demand for any kind of international product includes two components: The general demand for the product without difference and the individual demand for difference. International marketers should identify whether the consumers' undifferentiated common demand dominates or the differentiated individual demand dominates in product demand. It is advisable to adopt the strategy of product standardization for the products whose common demand is dominant.

The demand characteristics of the following products are manifested as the undifferentiated common demand is greater. A large number of industrial products, such as various raw materials, production equipment, parts and components, etc. Some daily consumer goods, such as soft drinks, film, washing products, cosmetics, health products, sports equipment, etc. Products with local and national characteristics, such as Chinese silk, French perfume, Cuban cigars and so on.

② Product production characteristics

From the perspective of product production, the product categories suitable for product standardization are products that can obtain large-scale economic benefits in terms of procurement, manufacturing, and distribution. In particular, technically standardized products, such as televisions, video recorders, stereos, etc.; Technology-intensive products with high research and development costs, which must be standardized globally to compensate for the huge investment in product research and development research costs, such as aircrafts, supercomputers and pharmaceuticals.

③ Competitive conditions

If there are no competitors in the international target market, or if the market is not competitive, the enterprise can adopt a standardized strategy. If the market is competitive, but the company has unique production skills and cannot be emulated by other companies, the enterprise can adopt a standardization product strategy.

④ A cost-revenue analysis

Make decisions strictly on the basis of revenues. The standardization of products, packaging, brand names and promotional campaigns can undoubtedly reduce costs significantly, but it only makes sense if there is a large demand for standardized products.

In addition, consideration should be given to national technical standards, legal requirements and national marketing support systems, that is, national institutions and functions that provide services and assistance to enterprises in their marketing activities. For example, if some national retailers do not have preservation facilities, fresh food is difficult to sell in the country. Although the product standardization strategy has many advantages for enterprises engaged in international marketing, the defect is also very obvious. That is, it is difficult to meet the different needs of consumers in different markets.

7.4.2　The product Differentiation Strategy in the International Market

1. The Meaning of the Product Differentiation Strategy

The international product differentiation strategy means that an enterprise offers different products to different markets in different countries and regions around the world, to meet the special needs of each market. If the product standardization strategy is driven by common consumer demand among international consumers, the product differentiation strategy, then, aims to meet the diverse individual needs of consumers in different countries and regions due to the varying geographical, economic, political, cultural, and legal environments, especially the cultural environment.

Although there are some common human needs, the differences in consumer demand in the international market in different countries or regions are dominant. In some product areas, especially those with strong sociocultural relevance, the differences in international consumer demand for products are more prominent. Enterprises must adapt certain aspects of their original products according to the specific conditions of consumers in the international market to meet different consumer needs.

2. Pros and Cons of the Product Differentiation Strategy

Implementing the product differentiation strategy is that the enterprises produce and sell products that meet the characteristics of local consumers according to the different objectives of the marketing environment and demand characteristics. This product strategy is more about producing and selling products from the perspective of the personality of international consumer needs, which can better meet the individual needs of consumers, help to open up international markets, and help establish a good international image for the company. It is the mainstream product strategy of the enterprise in the international market marketing. However, the product differentiation strategy also puts forward higher requirements for enterprises. First of all, it is necessary to identify the demand characteristics of consumers in each target market country, which puts forward high requirements for the market research ability of enterprises. Secondly, it is necessary to develop and design different products for different international markets, which requires the research and development capabilities of enterprises to keep up. Thirdly, as the variety of products produced and sold by enterprises increases, the cost of production and marketing will be higher than that of standardized products, and the management difficulty of enterprises will also increase. Therefore, when choosing the product differentiation strategy, enterprises should analyze their own strength and input-output ratio, and then make judgment based on the situation of various aspects.

7.4.3 Selection of the Standardization and Differentiation Strategies

With the development of the economy and the improvement of people's living standard, the individualization of consumer demand is becoming more and more prominent. The product differentiation strategy should be the main product strategy of enterprises engaged in international marketing. In marketing practice, however, companies often combine product differentiation and product standardization strategies. The differentiation and diversification of many products are mainly reflected in the form, such as product form, packaging, brand and so on, and the core part of the product is often the same. It can be seen that the differentiation and standardization strategies of international products are not independent, but complement each other. Some products of the country of origin do not need to change much, but only need to change the packaging or brand name to enter the international market. Some of the country-of-origin products will require major changes if they are to be accepted by the world's consumers. This shows that a company's product strategy is usually a combination of product differentiation and product standardization, in which sometimes the degree of product differentiation is higher, while sometimes the degree of product standardization is higher. The Enterprise should choose the combination of product differentiation and product standardization according to the specific situation.

▶ Case 7-1

Chinatown Business Serves as a Bridge

A historic business in Chinatown in India's eastern Kolkata city is serving as a culinary bridge by making popular Chinese sauces and other food products for more than 70 years.

Owned by an Indian of Chinese origin, the iconic Pou Chong is known for making and selling a wide array of sauces such as garlic chili and Szechwan. Pou Chong, which means "a harmonious and safe journey in life", was founded by Lee Shih Chuan in the late 1950s. His granddaughter Janice Lee said Pou Chong produces more than 40 varieties of sauces and now caters to restaurants and locals. Its products are supplied to five-star restaurants and major hotels, among other clients. And they are also popular among households in Kolkata.

"When he first began making the green chili sauce, he would literally sell it for very little," Janice Lee said. "Roadside cucumber sellers would use this sauce as a dressing. Eventually, there was a growing demand for it and the green chili sauce became a staple for Kolkata-style Chinese noodles, kathi rolls (paratha wraps with fillings) and most importantly, the chili chicken. It became almost indispensable to Kolkata Chinese food."

Hunan sauce and oyster sauce, which are produced using ancient techniques, are extremely popular sauces to make Hunan chicken and Hunan fried rice. Hunan sauce, originating from Hunan province, has a distinctive taste.

"We use Indian spices and mix it in a traditional way of making chili sauce, which was learned by my ancestors from China," she said.

After Lee Shih Chuan founded Pou Chong and grew the business, it evolved from being just a sauce company to making many more Chinese food products like dumplings, spring rolls and Chinese sausages. In 2017, the company launched its KIM range of products, establishing a premium brand for authentic Hakka products. Kim in Chinese means "gold". The Lee family's ancestors came from a Hakka Chinese village called Meixin. "We carry the same language and customs," Janice said.

7.5 Brand, Packaging and Service Strategies of International Products

7.5.1 The Concept of Brand and Trademark

Establishing brand position in the market and corporate image through brand and trademark is an effective means of competition for enterprises.

The main concepts related to brands and trademarks are:

① **Brand**. A brand is a name given to a product by an enterprise or an intermediary. The definition of branding in western marketing is: A brand is a name, term, symbol, logo, pattern, or combination thereof that identifies a product or service of a seller or group of sellers. Brands can be mainly divided into producer brands and middleman brands.

② **Brand name**. It refers to the part of the brand that can be called by language. Such as Huawei, Haier, Lenovo, Xiaomi, etc.

③ **Brand mark**. It refers to the part of the brand that can be recognized, but not directly expressed in words. Brand logos are often symbols, patterns, or specially designed colors, fonts, and the like. For example, the American Metro-Goldwyn-Mayer Film Company uses a roaring lion as its brand logo; "Coca-Cola" is a special pattern designed with English letters, and Forever Brand Bicycle is a bicycle pattern that is a combination of two characters: "永久".

④ **Trademark**. The brand name or brand logo of a brand is called a trademark after being registered with the relevant government department. A registered trademark is an industrial property right that is protected by national laws and can prevent others from using it.

7.5.2 Branding and Trademark Strategy

1. Basic Strategy of Branding

In order to make the brand play a better role in marketing, we should adopt an appropriate brand strategy. There are several brand strategies to choose from:

① Branding strategy

A branding strategy is a strategy for companies to decide whether to use a brand. The use of a brand undoubtedly has many benefits for the company. For most companies, in order to develop the reputation of the product, the brand should be used. But from another perspective, the use of the brand means that the company has to bear the corresponding responsibilities, such as maintaining the stability of the product quality, promoting the brand, and fulfilling the obligations stipulated by the law. If the company is unable to take on these responsibilities, it is not necessary to use the brand. For example, some new ventures whose products have not yet been finalized sometimes do not necessarily use brands in light of their own actual conditions. In addition, some homogeneous products classified by specifications (e.g. coal), small commodities without certain technical standards, or products that are not customarily purchased by the brand but purchased by physical objects and samples (e.g. cloth, toys, etc.), do not necessarily use the brand, either.

② Brand user strategy

The brand user strategy is the strategy by which the company decides whose brand to use. Once a company decides to use a brand, it must consider which brand it uses. There are generally three options: The first is to use the brand of the company (i.e. the manufacturer's brand); The second is to use the brand of the middleman (i.e. the dealer's brand); The third is to use the hybrid brand, that is, some products use the manufacturer's brand, and some products use the dealer's brand. For companies with relatively strong financial resources and high production technology and management level, they generally strive to use their own brands. But in a highly competitive market, it is not easy to create an influential brand in a short time. Therefore, in some cases, companies may also consider using other brands that have a certain market reputation. The advantage of using other people's brands is that they can use the licensor's brand reputation to quickly open the market; Obtain licensor technology and management assistance; Use the licensor's sales channels and maintenance service network to alleviate the pressure on enterprises; Take no or a little responsibility for product advertising. There are also some risks and worries about using other people's brands: The enterprise loses control over the selling price of the product; After the expiration of the agreement between the two parties, if the licensor is unwilling to renew the agreement, the enterprise may fall into a sales dilemma; The biggest loss may be the loss of the opportunity to create its own brand image. In short, enterprises should consider the advantages and disadvantages of using their own brands and using other brands according to their own conditions, and weigh them again and make decisions.

③ Brand quantity strategy

The brand quantity strategy is a strategy for companies to decide how many brands to use. After deciding to use the brand of the company, enterprises also have to decide how many brands to use. There are four strategies to choose from for different product lines or different product lines under the same product line:

• Individual brand strategy

The individual brand strategy is that companies use different brands for different products they produce. For example, the Shanghai Toothpaste Factory uses brands such as Maxam, Chung Hwa, Black and White, and Qingfeng. The advantage of this strategy is that the company can carry out targeted marketing activities according to the needs of different market segments; While producing high-quality and high-grade products, enterprises can also produce low-end products without being affected, creating conditions for enterprises to comprehensively utilize resources; With this strategy, the relationship between brands is loose and will not affect other products of enterprises because of the problems and bad reputation of individual products. The disadvantage of this strategy is that too many brands will affect the effectiveness of advertising and are easily forgotten. This kind of strategy needs strong financial support, so it is generally suitable for large enterprises with strong strength.

• Unified brand strategy

The unified brand strategy is that all products of the company use the same brand. For example, GE's products all use the "GE" brand. The advantage of adopting this strategy is that it can reduce the brand design fee and the promotion cost. At the same time, if the brand reputation is high, it will also help the new product launch. The shortcoming is that if a product has a problem, it will affect the image of the entire brand and endanger the reputation of the company.

- Category brand strategy

The category brand strategy is that companies classify their products according to certain criteria and use different brands. In this way, the same category of products implements a unified brand strategy, and different categories of products implement individual brand strategies, which combine the benefits of a unified brand and individual brand strategies. For example, Jian Libao Group, the brand used in beverages is "Jian Libao", and the brand used in the sportswear category is "Li Ning".

- Corporate name plus individual brand strategy

The corporate name plus an individual brand strategy is that enterprises use different brands for different products, and each brand is given the name of the enterprise before. For example, the General Motors Corporation (GM) produces a variety of cars, each with its own individual brands, such as "Cadillac" "Chevrolet", etc., plus "GM" in the front to show the products of General Motors. This strategy can make new products serialized and expand brand influence with corporate reputation.

④ Brand-extension strategy

A brand-extension strategy is that enterprises use the reputation of their successful brands to launch improved products or new products. Brand-extension strategies usually have two approaches:

- Vertical extension. It refers to that the enterprise launches a brand first, and after the success launches a new and improved brand product, and then launches the updated brand product. For example, in the Chinese market, Procter & Gamble launched the "Rejoice" shampoo and then launched a new generation of "Rejoice" shampoo.
- Horizontal extension. Under this strategy, enterprises use successful brands on different products that are newly developed. For example, the Giant Group has launched a series of products such as computer software, biological products and pharmaceuticals under the "Giant" brand.

Brand-extension can greatly reduce the promotion costs such as advertising, so that new products can enter the market quickly and smoothly. This strategy, if used properly, is conducive to the development and growth of the company. However, brand-extension may not necessarily succeed. In addition, brand-extension may also weaken or even damage the image of the original brand, making the original brand's uniqueness gradually forgotten. Therefore, enterprises should be cautious in brand extension decision-making, analyze and evaluate the impact of brand extension on the basis of investigation and research. In the process of brand extension, various measures should be taken to reduce the impact on the original brand as much as possible.

⑤ Multi-brand strategy

A strategy under which a seller develops three or more brands in the same product category. Although the multi-brand strategy will reduce the sales of the original brand, the total sales of several brands may be more than that of the original brand. For example, P&G's shampoo in the Chinese market has three brands: "Head & Shoulders" "Rejoice" and "Pantene". Each brand has its own distinct personality and has its own development space. The feature of "Head & Shoulders" is anti-dandruff, the feature of "Rejoice" is to make the hair smooth and supple, and the feature of "Pantene" lies in the nutrition and health care of the hair. The total market share of the three brands in the Chinese market is as high as 60%.

Brands are not the more the better. When a company launches multiple brands, if each brand has a small market share, and no one is particularly profitable, then adopting a multi-brand strategy is a waste of resources for the enterprise. At this time, companies must abolish weaker brands and concentrate on a few favorable brands. When developing new brands, companies should focus on competing with competitive brands outside the company, but not the self-competition of internal brands.

⑥ Brand repositioning strategy

The brand repositioning strategy refers to the repositioning of product brands by enterprises due to changes in certain market conditions. When companies reposition their brands, they should consider two factors. First, the cost of moving a product brand from one market segment to another. The further the gap between repositioning and original positioning, the higher the cost of repositioning. Second, the benefits of repositioning the brand. The amount of revenue depends on the number of consumers in the market segment, the average purchase rate, the strength and quantity of competitors, and so on. Enterprises should analyze the various options for repositioning the brand, weigh the pros and cons, and choose the best.

2. Trademark Expansion Strategy

The main strategies for trademark expansion are as follows:

① Joint strategy

It refers to the applicant registering two or more similar trademarks on the same or similar products, the purpose of which is to prevent his trademark from being counterfeited by others. For example, Dragon Tiger Brand King Oil registers dozens of trademarks of animals, such as cats, bears, leopards, and cows. Joint trademarks are not necessarily used. Their purpose is to prevent others from infringing.

② Defensive trademark

It means that the applicant applies a registered trademark for other products. For example, Sony Corporation of Japan (SONY) registered the "Sony" trademark on bicycles, foodstuffs and other products that are not similar with electrical appliances, in order to prevent others from using it and damaging Sony's image.

③ Group trademark

For the sake of common interests, a number of enterprises voluntarily form industrial and commercial organizations with legal personality, such as group companies and joint stock companies, and apply for the registration of trademarks for common use. This trademark is called a group trademark. This requires a constitution to be followed by all members.

④ Certification trademark

A commodity that has been certified by certification trademark can be a certified commodity. Certification trademark can distinguish the characteristics of the product origin, raw materials, manufacturing methods, quality, etc., such as the pure wool logo of the International Wool Bureau and the green food logo of China.

7.5.3 Packaging and the Packaging Strategy

1. The Concept of Packaging

Packaging refers to the activities of designing and producing the container or wrapper for a product. It is an important part of the product entity, with the function of protecting and beautifying the product, facilitating operation, and promoting consumption and sales.

Product packaging generally includes three levels. First, primary package, which is the direct container of the product; Second, secondary package, which is used to protect the product and promote sales; Third, shipping package, which is also known as the outer package for easy storage, transport and products indentification. In addition, it also includes labeling which consists of the words and patterns of the manufacturer, country of origin, weight, product description and ingredients attached to the package.

2. Packaging Strategy

The main packaging strategies are:

① **The similar packaging strategy**. A variety of products produced by an enterprise use the same pattern, color, text or other common features on the packaging to make consumers notice that they are the products of the same enterprise. Photographic materials such as Kodak's color film, color paper, sets of potions and others are similarly packaged.

② **The combined packaging strategy**. Combine several kinds of related products together according to people's consumption habits to facilitate the consumer to carry and use, such as the combination of tea and tea set, clothing and personalized jewelry, so that consumers will have a chain reaction and steric effect in use.

③ **The multi-purpose packaging strategy**. When designing the packaging, it is considered that the use of the product can make the consumer use it for other purposes, such as a beautiful wine bottle can be used as a vase, which will induce consumers' desire to buy it again.

④ **The attached package strategy**. In the commodity packaging, a small toy or gadget is included to attract consumers to buy and repeat purchases. For example, American Mac's coffee has a coffee spoon or coffee cup in its gift box, which is more effective in promotion.

7.5.4　Service and the Service Strategy

1. The Concept of Service

Service is an activity or benefit provided by a market that meets a customer's needs. In the marketing process, the service occupies the pivotal status, and the tangible products must be combined with services to constitute a complete product and satisfy the customer's needs systematically. With the continuous improvement of the technical means, the production technology and the management level, the production of physical products is becoming more and more quantitative and standardized. The products have the characteristics of multi-function, high technology and so on. The quality differences between tangible products have gradually narrowed, while the differences between services have become increasingly prominent. In modern marketing activities, service has become a powerful means of competition and has a great impact on increasing market share. For example, the CT scanner introduced to the market by Toshiba of Japan has the tangible characteristics of reliability and high quality. However, Toshiba sells "products" far beyond the product entity itself, which provides a series of superior services, such as transportation, installation, commissioning, maintenance assurance, operator training, technical advice and helping users to broaden their application areas. A series of effective services have made the overall product more efficient, and that is why users are willing to accept although their products are at a high price.

2. Service Strategy

The service strategy mainly includes:

① The Service Mix Strategy

To determine the service mix, marketers need to consider what services the enterprise can provide, investigate customer requirements for service items, and rank them in order of importance. Such as the Canadian industrial instrument manufacturers proposed service items: reliable delivery, easy contact, free warranty, wide-ranging business, to provide design and loans. When making a service mix strategy, enterprises should also understand the service mix provided by competitors, and then make the best use of the advantages to avoid the disadvantages.

② The Service Level Strategy

In general, a higher service level will give customers greater satisfaction. Customers' repurchases will be more frequent, but there may be other situations where a service item is irrelevant or less relevant to sales. Therefore, when making a service level strategy, it should be classified and analyzed according to the needs of consumers and the achievements of each service item, in order to clarify the items that should focus on improving the service level of the project. In general, enterprises can strengthen communication with consumers through regular questionnaire survey, collect consumers' evaluations of the importance of service items and service achievements, and then formulate feasible service level strategies.

③ The Service Form Strategy

In the service form, the enterprise must first determine the form of service provision.

There are generally three forms: First, the enterprise can organize and train a service team which is composed of various service personnel in charge of each market segment. Second, sales services should be handled by intermediaries (wholesalers and retailers). Third, the enterprise can entrust the service to a specialized service company. Each of the above three forms has its advantages and disadvantages. Enterprises should choose appropriate forms according to the social environment, service cost and service demand. Secondly, the choice of the service network location is generally determined by whether it is convenient, close to customers, and can offer more service items. The proximity of the network to the customer is an important condition for high-level service.

Chapter Summary

- The whole product concept includes three levels: core product, actual product and augmented product.
- The typical product life cycle involves four stages: introduction, growth, maturity and decline, which is a curve of "s" shape, and the four stages reflect different characteristics and different marketing strategies.
- There are four kinds of new products: brand-new products, innovative new products, improved new products and imitative new products. A new product development process includes 8 main steps: idea generation, idea screening, concept development and testing, marketing strategy development, business analysis, product development, test marketing, commercialization.
- The standardization strategy of international products means that enterprises provide the same products to all markets in different countries or regions of the world. The product differentiation strategy is to supply different products to different markets in different countries and regions in order to adapt to the special needs of different markets. The selection of a product series refers to all kinds of the marketing mix strategy which combines the standardization and differentiation strategy of international products with the promotion strategy of international products.
- Brand and the trademark strategy are an important part of the product strategy. Packaging is an important part of the product entity which has the function of protecting and beautifying products, facilitating business and consumption, and promoting sales.

Main Concepts

whole product concept, product life cycle, new product development, brand, packaging, service

Think and Practice

1. Explain the conditions of the standardization strategy and the differentiation strategy.
2. Briefly describe the characteristics of each stage of the product life cycle and the marketing strategies.
3. Outline the new product development process.
4. What are the characteristics of each stage of the international product life cycle?
5. What are the brand strategies for products in the international market?

Case Study

Cutting-edge Technology Transforms "Made-in-China" Image

Due to the unremitting efforts of Chinese industries to move up the global value chain, more consumers around the world are recognizing the higher quality and cutting-edge technology of "Made-in-China" products.

Thanks to the country's innovation drive, high-tech products made in China and domestic Chinese brands have in recent years entered the daily lives of worldwide consumers and taken a growing share of the international market.

More and more users and observers have come to agree that "Made-in-China" is now more about high technology and quality and less about large quantities at low prices.

From "Made-in-China" to "Created-in-China"

In many countries, "Made-in-China" once meant cheap commodities. Nowadays, this impression has begun to change. Those Chinese products, once peddled at low prices, now have been replaced by quality products with high innovation value.

According to a report published by the World Intellectual Property Organization (WIPO) last November, China surpassed the U.S., Japan and South Korea to rank top in the world for patent applications, receiving over one million applications in 2015.

In August 2017, China also joined the ranks of the world's top 25 innovative economies in the Global Innovation Index released by Cornell University, international graduate university INSEAD, and the WIPO.

"This is in keeping with all the developments that we have seen in China in recent years, including the use of innovation as a major component in the transition of the Chinese economy from 'made-in-China' to 'created-in-China'," said Francis Gurry, director general of the WIPO.

Quality & Cost-effective

Take Fiji, an island country in the South Pacific Ocean, as an example. Low-end products from China, such as textiles and petty commodities for daily use, still take up a significant market share. However, products such as personal computers and mobile phones are quickly making their presence felt.

In electronics stores across Fiji, Chinese mobile phone brands such as Huawei, ZTE, Xiaomi, OPPO and OnePlus are popular and seen by many locals as being more cost-effective, and now compete with Apple and Samsung.

In the realm of personal computers, Chinese brands, led by Lenovo, take up a considerable market share, while in the home appliances sector, TV sets, air conditioners, washing machines and microwave ovens manufactured by Chinese companies such as Haier, Hisense and Gree are widely seen on the Fijian market.

For a developing country with humble purchasing power, cost performance is one of the key concerns for local customers, and Chinese electronic products are typically seen to better address those concerns.

Chinese drones tend to be more affordable, Tiale Vuiyasawa, a senior official with Fiji's Ministry of Defense, told Xinhua.

Liao Xiaoping, secretary general of the Fiji-China Business Council, said that in recent years Chinese products no longer feature large quantities supported by low prices, and the change reflects the progress of Chinese technology.

Discuss the following questions.

1. Think about one product from one of the Chinese brands mentioned in the text, and use the whole product concept to analyze the different levels of the product.

2. Collect information on the oversea markets of the Chinese brand you selected. Analyze the standardization strategy or the differentiation strategy adopted by the product in its overseas market, and explain the reason for choosing such a strategy.

3. Innovation, quality and price, which factor do you think is most important for international marketing of Chinese products?

Chapter 8

Pricing Strategy in the International Market

////////// **Learning Objectives** //////////////////////

- Choose pricing methods according to the characteristics of different inter-national markets;
- Flexibly use pricing strategies to motivate consumers;
- Learn to respond to price changes in different markets;
- Use price strategies to respond to competitors in different countries.

////// **Key Terms** /////////////////////

pricing basis 定价依据

pricing objective 定价目标

inflation 通货膨胀

exchange rate fluctuation 汇率波动

profit-oriented 以利润为导向

sales-oriented 以销售为导向

statue quo pricing 现状定价

cost-oriented pricing method 成本导向定价法

cost-plus pricing method 成本加成定价法

incremental analysis pricing method 增量分析定价法

target profit pricing method 目标利润定价法

demand-oriented pricing method 需求导向定价法

perceived-value pricing 感知价值定价

backwards pricing 向后定价

competition-oriented pricing method 竞争导向定价法

going-rate pricing 现行定价

sealed-bid pricing 密封投标定价

skim pricing 脱脂定价

natural pricing 自然定价

penetration pricing 渗透定价

mantissa pricing 尾数定价

integer pricing 整数定价

prestige pricing 声望定价

fetch-in pricing 进货定价

discrimination pricing 歧视定价

discount pricing 折扣定价

product portfolio pricing 产品组合定价

international transfer pricing 国际转让定价

quotation control 报价控制

price escalation control 涨价控制

parallel input control 并行输入控制

price standardization 价格标准化

price differentiation 价格差异化

headquarter pricing 总部定价

subsidiary pricing 公司定价

dumping 倾销

▶ **Opening Case**

BYD Expects Quadrupled 2022 Net Profit

China's leading new energy vehicle manufacturer BYD Company Limited expects to see drastic rises in both revenue growth and net profit in 2022.

The company's 2022 net profit is expected to range from 16 billion yuan ($2.37 billion) to 17 billion yuan, an increase of 425.42 percent to 458.26 percent year-on-year, according to a company report on performance forecast released on Monday.

Its revenue is expected to exceed 420 billion yuan, said the report.

Sales of new energy vehicles recorded a strong year-on-year growth in 2022, driving a significant improvement in earnings, while effectively easing cost pressure caused by rising upstream raw material prices, according to the company.

In 2022, BYD sold over 1.86 million new energy vehicles, an increase of 208.64 percent over the previous year, ranking first in global NEV sales.

(People experience a BYD Han electric car during a media preview of

the 100th Brussels Motor Show in Brussels, Belgium, Jan 13, 2023)

(Source: Adapted from *China Daily*)

8.1 Pricing Basis and Pricing Objectives in the International Market

There are many factors that affect product pricing, including pricing objectives, costs, market demand, competitors' products and prices. In general, the maximum level of product pricing usually depends on market demand, and the minimum level of product pricing depends on the cost. The determination of the upper and lower limits of products depends on a company's pricing target, government policies, regulations, and the price of competitors' among similar products.

8.1.1　Pricing Basis in the International Market

Pricing is an essential factor in the marketing mix. The product pricing directly determines the income of the company and also affects the competitiveness of the products in the international market. Domestic pricing is inherently complicated. When products are sold to the international market, factors such as freight, tariffs, exchange rate fluctuations, and political situations increase the difficulty of international pricing. Therefore, companies must make great efforts to make pricing strategy in international marketing. Basic pricing issues shall take into consideration such as pricing methods, pricing strategies, price adjustment strategies, and pricing trends.

1. Cost Factors

The price can't be decided by companies as they like. In the long run, the selling price of any product must be higher than the cost, so that production costs and operating expenses can be offset by sales revenue. Therefore, in the process of setting prices, companies must estimate the associated costs. For existing products, the related costs refer to the direct costs associated with production and distribution and the indirect costs of transportation. And for new products, the related costs contain direct costs over the entire life cycle and indirect costs of transportation.

Cost accounting is a significant part of pricing. The cost composition will change with different regional sales. Even if both export and domestic products are produced domestically, their costs will not be exactly the same. If the export product has been modified on the basis of foreign measurement regulations, power systems and other aspects, the cost may increase. Conversely, if the functions of the export product are simplified or removed, the cost may decrease.

Some of the same cost items for international marketing and domestic marketing may have very different importance for the two. For example, freight, insurance, and packaging fees account for a large proportion in the cost of international marketing. Other cost items are unique to international marketing, such as customs duties, customs clearance, and document processing. Now we will explain the cost items that have special significance for international marketing.

① **Tariffs**. A tariff is a fee paid when goods enter another country from one country. It is a special form of taxation. Tariffs are one of the most common features of international trade, and they have a direct impact on the price of imported and exported goods. Tariffs can increase the government's fiscal revenue and protect the domestic market. Tariffs are generally expressed in terms of tariff rates and can be levied on the basis of a quantitative, ad valorem or mixed. In fact, other administrative expenses such as import visa fees and quota management fees are also a large amount, which is actually another kind of tariff. In addition, countries may also impose transaction taxes, value-added taxes, and retail taxes, which also affect the final sale price of the product. However, generally, these taxes are not just for imported products.

② **Cost of intermediaries and transportation**. The system and structure of market distribution vary among nations. In some countries, companies can supply products in target markets through relatively direct channels to reduce the burden of brokers with lower cost of storage, transportation, and promotion. In other countries, intermediaries have to bear higher costs due to the ineffective distribution system.

③ **Cost of risk**. In international marketing practice, risk costs mainly include financing, inflation and exchange rate risk. Due to the long period of payment, the risks of financing, inflation and exchange rate fluctuations are increased. In addition, the intervention of bank credit is necessary to reduce the risk and trading obstacles for buyers and sellers with an increasing cost burden. These factors should be taken into consideration in international marketing pricing.

- **Inflation**. In international marketing practice, the estimate of cost should consider the impact of inflation. In countries with high inflation or exchange rate fluctuations, the selling price must reflect the product cost as well as the replacement cost. The selling price of goods is often lower than the sum of replacement costs and overheads, even lower than the replacement cost in some circumstance. In this case, no selling is better. Therefore, when the contract is a long-term contract or with delayed payment for several months, the inflation factor must be taken into account. Heinz launched a new type of fruit drink in Brazil, which was sold to retailers by consignment in one word sold first and paid second. Because of the up to 300% inflation, even a one-week extension will greatly reduce profits. The new product was withdrawn from the market in just two years. High inflation rates in many developing countries, especially in Latin America, have resulted in widespread government price controls as a constant threat to companies.

- **Exchange rate fluctuations**. In the past, international trade contracts were easy to make, and payments could be made in a relatively stable currency. The U.S. dollar used to be the standard currency for various transactions. Now, the floating relations among all major currencies are free, and no one can accurately predict the exact value of a currency's exchange rate. Enterprises are increasingly emphasizing the pricing in trade contracts with the currency of the seller's country. And long-term hedging has become more common. In long-term contracts, it is even more necessary to lock in an exchange rate that fluctuates daily to prevent increased costs, especially when there is a long time between signing and delivery. The difference in the exchange rate cannot be underestimated, and Nestlé lost $1 million in six months. Some companies have even greater losses due to exchange rate changes.

2. Market Demand

Market demand is affected by the changes of price and income. The corresponding rate of change in demand due to factors such as price or income is demand elasticity. The price elasticity of demand reflects the sensitivity of demand to price, calculated as the ratio of the percentage change in demand to the percentage change in price. For example, a one percent change in price may cause a certain percentage change in demand. There are no substitutes or competitors in the market. Buyers do not care about higher prices and change their buying habits slowly for less willingness to look for substitutes. Buyers believe that quality has improved, or that there is currency expansion, etc. In all cases where the product lacks elasticity of demand, the product can be set at a higher price.

The lowest price of a product depends on the cost of the product, and the highest price depends on the market demand for the product. The cultural background, natural environment and economic conditions in different countries determine the different consumption preferences of consumers. The number of consumers interested in a product and their income will determine the final price of a product. Even for low-income consumers, the urgent need for a product can cause the product to sell at a high price. But demand alone is not enough. It needs to be backed up by the ability to pay. Therefore, the ability of foreign consumers to pay has a great impact on the pricing of export products. To understand the demands and consumption capacity in detail, it is necessary to study the customs and income distribution of the target market in depth.

3. Market Competition Structure

The lowest price of a product depends on the cost of the product, and the highest price depends on the market demand. How high a company can set the price of a product in the limit depends on the price level of the same product offered by the competitor. Different from the domestic market, companies face different competitive situations and competitors in different foreign markets, and the pricing strategies of competitors vary widely. Therefore, companies have to formulate corresponding price strategies for different competition situations. Competition imposes restrictions on the freedom of pricing of companies, and companies have to adapt to the price of the market. Unless the company's products are unique and protected by patents, it is not possible to implement a high-price strategy. When the quality is generally the same, the price should generally be the same or slightly lower to guarantee sales volume. When the quality of the product is higher, the price can be set higher. In contrast, the price should be lower.

Companies should also know that competitors may adjust their prices to the company's pricing strategy. Competitors may not adjust prices but compete with the company for customers by adjusting other variables in the marketing mix. For the price changes of competitors, it is necessary to grasp the relevant information in time and make appropriate responses.

4. Government's Price Control Policy

With the development of globalization, on the one hand, the openness of markets in various countries has further expanded; On the other hand, in order to protect the domestic market, governments have strengthened control and diversified forms of control. The government's regulation of corporate pricing is multifaceted from macro to micro through law to administrative orders.

The pricing in international marketing must be influenced by the domestic government and the foreign government simultaneously. Most domestic governments use price subsidies to reduce the prices of export products and enhance their competitive strength. The domestic government imposes price subsidies on export products, which can lower the prices of export products and enhance the international competitiveness of products. For example, if the U.S. government imposes price subsidies on agricultural products, it can improve the competitiveness of its agricultural products in the international market. China's export product tax rebate system is also to enhance the competitiveness of export products.

The host government controls the price mainly through the legislative form or administrative means to stipulate the upper and lower price limits of the product. The anti-dumping law is used to oppose the dumping policy. The government restricts the consumption of imported goods and protects the domestic market through direct pricing. For example, the Japanese government once priced U. S. wheat entering the Japanese market at twice the price of Japanese domestic wheat. The government often freezes all prices for a certain period of time during the period of domestic economic stagflation. In addition, governments have played an increasingly important role in pricing certain products on the international market, such as the International Coffee Agreement, the Cocoa International Agreement, the White Sugar International Agreement, and some wheat prices through intergovernmental negotiation.

The host government can also influence the pricing strategies in many aspects, such as tariffs, taxes, exchange rates, interest, competition policies, and industry development plans. Tariffs and other restrictions imposed by some countries to protect national industries have increased the cost of imported goods. As an export enterprise, it is inevitable to encounter restrictions on the price regulations of various governments. For example, the government's minimum and maximum price limits for imported goods constrain the freedom of pricing. In the face of strengthening price control, enterprises must not only follow the legislation of the host country, but also be good at using the "big marketing" strategy, especially the use of political power, to win a favorable pricing environment.

8.1.2   Pricing Objectives in the International Market

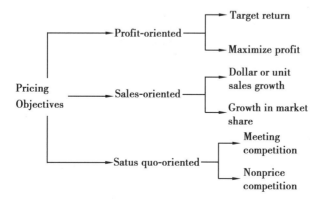

Figure 8-1   Pricing Objectives in the International Market

1. Profit-oriented Objectives

Over the long term, and often over the short term, marketing managers should set objectives oriented toward making a profit. A target return objective sets a specific level of profit as an objective. Often this amount is stated as a percentage of sales or of capital investment.

A target return objective has administrative advantages in a large company. Performance can be compared against the target. Some companies eliminate divisions, or drop products that aren't yielding the target rate of return.

Some managers aim for only satisfactory returns. They just want returns that ensure the firm's survival and convince stockholders they're doing a good job. Similarly, some small family-run businesses aim for a profit that will provide a comfortable lifestyle.

Many private and public nonprofit organizations set a price level that will just recover costs. In other words, their target return figure is zero. For example, a government agency may charge motorists a toll for using a bridge but then drop the toll when the cost of the bridge is paid.

Similarly, firms that provide critical public services—including many utilities, insurance companies, and defense contractors—sometimes pursue only satisfactory long-run targets. They are well aware that the public expects them to set prices that are in the public's interest. They may also have to face the public or government agencies that review and approve prices.

A profit maximization objective seeks to get as much profit as possible. It might be stated as a desire to earn a rapid return on investment.

Pricing to achieve profit maximization doesn't always lead to high prices. Low prices may expand the size of the market and result in greater sales and profits. For example, when prices of cell phones were very high, only businesses and wealthy people bought them. When producers lowered prices, nearly everyone bought one.

If a firm is earning a very large profit, other firms will try to copy or improve on what the company offers. Frequently, this leads to lower prices.

2. Sales-oriented Objectives

A sales-oriented objective seeks some level of unit sales, dollar sales, or share of the market—without referring to profit.

Some managers are more concerned about the sales growth than profits. They think the sales growth always leads to more profits. This sometimes makes sense in the short term. For example, many Procter Gamble brands in product categories such as shampoo, soap, and diapers lost market share during the recent recession. When the economy began to recover. P&G kept prices low and sacrificed profits in order to grow with the recovering economy. It might also work well when products are in the introductory or early growth stages of the product life cycle. However, over the long term, this kind of thinking causes problems when a firm's costs are growing faster than sales. Although some firms have periods of declining profits in spite of the growth in sales, business managers should usually pay more attention to profits, not just sales.

Some nonprofit organizations set prices to increase market share-precisely because they are not trying to earn a profit. For example, many cities set low fares to fill up their buses, reduce traffic, and help the environment. Buses cost the same to run empty or full, and there are more benefits when they're full even if the total revenue is no greater.

Many firms seek to gain a specified share (percentage) of a market. If a company has a large market share, it may have better economies of scale than its competitors. In addition, it's usually easier to measure a firm's market share than to determine if profits are being maximized.

A company with a longer-run view may aim for an increased market share when the market is growing. The hope is that the future volume will justify sacrificing some profit in the short run. HP, Dell, and Acer have waged pricing battles in an effort to gain market share in the personal computer market. A high market share offers economies of scale and negotiating power with suppliers. Companies as diverse as 3M and Coca-Cola look at opportunities in Eastern Europe and Southeast Asia this way.

Of course, market share objectives have the same limitations as straight sales growth objectives. A larger market share, if gained at too low a price, may lead to profitless "success".

3. Statue Quo Pricing Objectives

Managers satisfied with their current market share and profits sometimes adopt status quo objectives—don't-rock-the-pricing-boat objectives. Managers may say that they want to stabilize prices, or meet competition, or even avoid competition. This don't-rock-the-boat thinking is most common when the total market is not growing.

Sometimes firms in an industry make price changes very carefully—and only if others follow their lead. This tends to prevent price wars, which can drag down all firms' profits. For example, the airline industry typically raises prices collectively. One airline might add a fuel surcharge—if the others do not follow, that airline backs off and all maintain the status quo.

A status quo pricing objective may be part of an aggressive overall marketing strategy focusing on non-price competition-aggressive action on one or more of the Ps other than price. Some companies that sell products through the Internet originally thought that they'd compete with low prices and still earn high profits from volume. However, when they didn't get the sales volume they hoped for, they realized that there were also some non-price ways to compete.

8.2   International Market Pricing Methods

[Box 8-1]

The Price of Starbucks in Every Country

Starbucks' intimidating mission statement is to "inspire and nurture the human spirit—one person, one cup, and one neighborhood at a time".

Since opening its first international unit in Tokyo, Starbucks has spilled out into 80 nations in just a quarter-century. It now boasts over 32,000 stores across the world. In the fast-food ranks, Starbucks is the second largest fast-food chain after McDonald's, and it depends on its store-to-store consistency even more.

But whether you purchase a Tall Latte in an unusual Indian Starbucks or one of the 600 new Chinese stores that Starbucks has scheduled this year, there is one significant distinction to expect—cost. Starbucks prices its menu variously from country to country.

Pricing work is complex, enterprises must consider all aspects of factors, and take a series of steps and measures. There are six steps in pricing decision: selecting pricing targets, estimating costs, measuring price elasticity of demand, analyzing competitive products and prices, selecting an appropriate pricing method and selecting final prices.

The price of enterprise products is affected and restricted by market demand, cost, and competition, which should be considered in an all-round way when setting the price. However, in practical work, enterprises often only focus on one aspect. Generally speaking, there are three orientations in enterprise pricing: cost orientation, demand orientation and competition orientation.

8.2.1 Cost-oriented Pricing Method

The cost-oriented pricing method is a cost-based pricing method, including the cost-plus pricing method and the target pricing method, and is characterized by being simple and easy to use.

1. Cost-plus Pricing Method

The so-called cost-plus pricing refers to the unit cost plus a certain percentage of the sales price. Therefore, the pricing formula of cost-plus is as follows:

$$P = C * (1 + R)$$

Among them, P is the unit product price; C is the unit product cost; R is the cost addition rate.

Like cost-plus pricing, retailers often base their mark-ups on retail price. There are two ways to measure the margin rate: ① measured by the retail price, that is, the margin rate = gross profit/price. ② measured by the purchase cost, that is, the margin rate = gross profit/purchase cost.

Does it make logical sense to add a fixed margin to the cost? The answer is no. In the process of setting the price, any pricing method that ignores the current price elasticity is difficult to ensure that the enterprise realizes the maximum profit, whether it is long-term profit or short-term profit. Demand elasticity is always in constant change, so the optimal margin should be adjusted accordingly.

The reason why the cost-plus pricing method is popular with the business community is mainly due to:

- The uncertainty of cost is generally smaller than that of demand. Placing prices to unit costs can greatly simplify the enterprise's pricing procedures without adjusting to changes in demand.
- As long as all enterprises in the industry adopt this pricing method, the price is

similar when the cost is similar to the margin, and the price competition will be reduced to a minimum as a result.

- Many people feel that the cost-plus method is fair to both the buyer and the seller. When the buyer's demand is strong, the seller can get a fair return on investment without taking advantage of this favorable condition to obtain additional benefits.

Companies based on cost need to consider whether to use the full cost pricing method or the variable cost pricing method. Companies that use variable cost pricing only consider the marginal cost of export products. These companies view overseas sales as additional revenue and that earnings after deducting variable costs are contributions to total profits. These companies may offer the most competitive prices in foreign markets, but are likely to be charged with dumping because they sell products abroad at a net price below the domestic market price. In this way, they are subject to anti-dumping duties or fines, which offset their original competitive advantage. But, in any case, the variable cost or marginal cost pricing method is equivalent to profits for fixed costs.

2. Incremental Analysis Pricing Method

The incremental analysis pricing method is mainly to analyze whether there is incremental profit after accepting the new task. Incremental profit is equal to accepting the incremental income caused by the new task minus the incremental cost. The common denominator between this pricing method and the cost addition pricing method is that the former is based on the total cost, while the latter is based on the incremental cost (or variable cost). This price is acceptable if incremental income is greater than incremental cost (or the price is higher than the variable cost).

In enterprise operation, the incremental analysis pricing method is applicable to the following three cases:

① **Whether the business should accept new tasks at a lower price**. To further exploit the surplus production capacity, it is necessary to decide whether to accept the new task at a lower price. Accepting a new task does not require additional fixed costs, so the pricing of the new task is based on the cost of change if the cost of change is increased. The condition is that the acceptance of the new task does not affect the normal sales of the original task.

② **To reduce losses, companies can fight for more tasks by reducing prices**. The market is depressed, and the task of the enterprise is very few. At this time, the main contradiction of the enterprise is to survive, that is, to try to lose less. It can strive for more tasks by cutting prices, so that it can lose less. In this case, the incremental analysis pricing method should be used to make pricing decisions.

③ **Enterprises produce several products that are substituted or complementary to each other**. One of these price changes will affect the demand for other related products, so the price decision should not only consider the benefits of one product in isolation, but also consider the comprehensive benefits of several products. At this time, it is also appropriate to use the incremental analysis pricing method.

3. Target Profit Pricing Method

The target pricing method refers to the price based on the estimated total sales revenue (sales) and the estimated output (sales volume). One of the main defects of this pricing method is that the enterprise calculates the price with the estimated sales volume, and the price is precisely an important factor that affects the sales volume.

8.2.2 Demand-oriented Pricing Method

The demand-oriented pricing method is a kind of pricing method based on market demand intensity and consumer feeling, including cognitive value pricing, reverse pricing, and demand differential pricing. Among them, the demand difference pricing method (also known as differential pricing) is not only a pricing method, but also involves the flexible pricing strategy.

1. Perceived-value Pricing

It refers to cognitive value pricing, which is based on the buyer's cognitive value of the product. Cognitive value pricing is consistent with the concept of modern market positioning. When enterprises develop new products for the target market, they need to reflect specific market positioning in quality, price, service and so on. Therefore, the enterprise must first determine the value and price provided. Secondly, estimate the quantity of sales according to this price, then determine the required production capacity, investment and unit cost according to the sales volume. Finally, calculate whether a satisfactory profit can be obtained according to the price and cost. If the company can get a satisfactory profit, then continue to develop the new product, otherwise give up the concept of this product.

The key to cognitive value pricing is to accurately calculate all the market cognitive values provided by products. If the company overestimates the cognitive value, it will set a higher price. If the price is much higher than the cognitive value, consumers will find it difficult to accept. If the price is much lower than the cognitive value, it will also affect the image of the product in the hearts of consumers.

2. Backwards Pricing

It refers to the reverse calculation of the wholesale price and the retail price of the product according to the final price acceptable to the consumer after calculating the cost and profit of their own operation. This method is not based on the actual cost, but on the market demand as the starting point, and strives to make the price acceptable to consumers. In the distribution channel, wholesalers and retailers adopt this pricing method.

8.2.3 Competition-oriented Pricing Method

There are usually two methods, the going-rate pricing method and the bid pricing method.

1. Going-rate Pricing

Going-rate pricing refers to the pricing of enterprises according to the average current price level of the industry. Companies often adopt this pricing method when product costs are difficult to estimate, or when companies want to live peacefully with their peers, or if they have difficulty understanding the buyer's and competitor's reaction to corporate prices.

Whether in a perfectly competitive market or an oligopolistic market, this is the usual pricing method for homogeneous product markets.

In a perfectly competitive market, companies that sell similar products do not actually have much choice on pricing. They can only be priced according to the current price of the industry. Under the conditions of oligopoly, companies also tend to be the same price as their competitors. Because under this condition, there are only a few large companies on the market, and they know each other very well. Buyers are familiar with the market, and if the price is slightly different, they will turn to low-priced companies.

In the product differentiation market, companies have greater freedom to determine their prices. Product differentiation makes buyers less sensitive to price differences.

Enterprises must always determine their proper positions relative to competitors, or act as a high-priced enterprise, or act as a medium-priced enterprise, or act as a low-cost enterprise. Enterprises should be different from competitors in pricing, and their product strategies and marketing plans should be adapted to match the price competition of competitors.

2. Sealed-bid Pricing

The procurement agency advertises or sends a letter explaining the specific requirements of the proposed variety, specifications, quantity, etc., and invites the supplier to bid within the prescribed time limit. The procurement agency opens the bid on the specified date, generally chooses the lowest quotation and the most favorable supplier to complete the transaction, and signs the purchase contract. If the supplier wants to do this business, it must fill out the form within the specified time limit, and fill in information of the available goods such as the name, variety, specification, price, quantity, delivery date, etc., and seal it to the tenderer. The bid price is based on an estimate of the competitor's quotation, not the cost of the supplier's own cost. The purpose is to win the contract, so it is generally lower than the opponent's quotation.

However, companies cannot set the offer too low. To be precise, the quotation cannot be set lower than the marginal cost to avoid deteriorating business conditions. However, the quotation is much higher than the marginal cost, although the potential profit may increase, which will reduce the chance of obtaining a contract.

8.3   International Market Pricing Strategy

The pricing basis, pricing target and basic pricing method have pointed out the direction for the international companies to set the price, but the market competition is very fierce. When determining the final price, the enterprise needs to consider the influence of various other factors and adopt various flexibility. The ever-changing pricing strategy combines price and other factors in the marketing mix to promote and expand sales and improve overall business efficiency. There are several types of pricing strategies for enterprises.

8.3.1　New Product Pricing Strategy

When enterprises introduce new products to the market, the first thing to consider is the pricing of new products. Whether the pricing strategy of new products is chosen correctly or not, it is directly related to whether new products can smoothly open and occupy the market. There are three main pricing strategies for new products: skim pricing, penetration pricing, and neutral pricing.

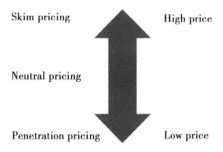

Figure 8-2　Strategies for Pricing a New Product

1. Skim Pricing

Skim pricing, also known as get fat pricing and skimming pricing, is a high price strategy, which refers to setting the price of new products at a higher price at the beginning of the new product listing, in order to make rich profits in a relatively short period of time, and to recover investment as soon as possible and reduce investment risk. This pricing strategy, named for its similarity to skimming cream from milk, is more commonly used in commodities where demand is inflexible.

The advantage of skim pricing is very obvious. In the market where customers are more psychologically motivated, high prices will help to open up the market. The initiative is large, and after the product matures, the price can be gradually reduced in stages, which is conducive to attracting new buyers. The price is high, and the demand is too fast to increase, so that it is compatible with the production capacity.

Of course, there are certain risks in using this strategy. Although high prices are profitable, it is not conducive to expanding the market and increasing sales. It is also not conducive to occupation and stability of the market. The price is much higher than the value, which hurts consumption to some extent. It is easy to attract competitors, forcing companies to lower prices, and the good times are not long.

When the purpose of the company is to enter a market segment that is relatively insensitive to price and willing to pay a high price for the parents of the product, the skim pricing method can be used. If supply is limited, companies can also use the skim pricing method to maximize sales revenue and align supply and demand. If the company is the sole supplier of a new product, the skim pricing method can maximize the profit of the company before competition and forced price cuts. This kind of pricing method is often used in the market where there are only two income classes—the rich and the poor. Because the cost of the product is too high, it is not allowed to set a price that can attract low-income people, so the company simply sets a high price, so that the product is oriented to the market segment with high income and low-price flexibility. Prior to the advent of Procter & Gamble, Johnson & Johnson used this pricing method to sell baby diapers in Brazil. With the rise of the middle-income market, this opportunity is gradually disappearing, and the large market capacity will inevitably attract competitors. As a result, the supply of goods will increase and price competition will emerge.

2. Penetration Pricing

Penetration pricing is the opposite of the skim pricing strategy. It is a low-price strategy. It is also a strategy of small profits but quick turnover. It refers to the consumer psychology of using consumers to seek cheapness when new products are put into the market, and intends to set prices lower. In order to attract customers, companies will rapidly expand sales and increase market share. This pricing strategy is applicable to products where the new product has no significant features, the product has economies of scale, the market is fiercely competitive, the price elasticity of demand is large, and the market potential is large. Low prices can effectively stimulate consumer demand, prevent competitors from intervening to maintain a high market share, expand sales and reduce production costs and sales expenses. For example, Seiko's watch adopts an infiltration pricing strategy and competes with Swiss watches in the international market at a low price, eventually capturing most of the market share of Swiss watches.

For enterprises, adopting a skim pricing strategy or a penetration pricing strategy requires comprehensive consideration of market demand, competition, supply, market potential, price elasticity, product characteristics, and corporate development strategies, etc., through extensive research and scientific analysis of the target market to set the price.

The penetration pricing strategy is a pricing method that deliberately sells products at lower prices to stimulate the market and increase market share. Penetration pricing is used the most when competing and maintaining market share as a competitive strategy. However, in a country where the economy continues to develop rapidly and a large number of people enter the middle-income class, penetration pricing can be used to stimulate the market growth with minimal competition. If penetration pricing maximizes sales revenue and gains a competitive advantage in terms of market share, then the strategy may be more profitable than skim pricing.

3. Neutral Pricing

Neutral pricing, also called the appropriate pricing strategy, is a price strategy between the skim pricing and the penetration pricing. The strategy refers to the fact that enterprises set the price of new products to be moderate, so as to take care of all aspects of interests and make all parties satisfied. Because the skim pricing is too high, it is unfavorable to consumers, it may be rejected by consumers, and it has certain risks. The penetration pricing is too low. Although it is beneficial to consumers, it is easy to cause a price war. Besides, because of the low price, the payback period of funds is also long, and enterprises with weak strength will be unbearable. While the satisfactory price strategy adopts moderate prices, basically both supply and demand are satisfactory, so many companies adopt satisfactory pricing strategies. Sometimes companies will adopt a neutral pricing strategy in order to maintain the consistency of the product line pricing strategy.

Because the neutral pricing strategy obtains the average profit, it can not only attract consumers, but also avoid price competition, so that enterprises can gain a firm foothold in the market and obtain long-term development. However, it is difficult to determine the price that both the enterprise and the customer are satisfied with.

▶ Case 8-1

Develop an Appropriate Price Strategy Based on Local Conditions

Regardless of the formal pricing policies and strategies used, companies must be aware that the market may set the right price for the product. In other words, the price must be in the right place so that consumers can feel the value of the product, and the price must be acceptable to the target market. Therefore, in some markets, products are sold in small units so that the price per unit is acceptable to the target market. Warner-

Lambert sells five boxes of bubble gum in Brazil. Although bubble gum accounts for 72% of the entire chewing gum market, it has not been successful because the price exceeds the target market. Later, it was packaged in a single piece, and the price quickly became a target market, resulting in a rapid market share.

Mattel has been very successful in selling Barbie to high-income people in most parts of the world, but its new extensions such as "Holiday Barbie" have been successful in the U.S., but not as good as in foreign markets. Simply exporting U.S. products to overseas markets has led to excessive prices in some markets. Mattel estimates that Barbie's sales potential is $2 billion in low-cost segments. In order to capture this market, Mattel will introduce a lower-priced Barbie doll called "Global Friends".

Implications: The price must be acceptable to the target market so that consumers can feel the value of the product.

8.3.2 Psychological Pricing Strategy

The psychological pricing strategy is a strategy for enterprises to formulate corresponding commodity prices according to different consumer psychology to meet the needs of different types of consumers.

Commonly used psychological pricing strategies include the following:

1. Mantissa Pricing

Mantissa pricing, also known as "non-integer pricing", refers to the intentional use of the consumer's low-cost, realistic psychology to bring the price of goods with tail, in order to encourage customers to buy goods. This pricing method is mostly used in low- and middle-grade goods. Psychologists have shown that small differences in price tails can significantly affect consumers' buying behavior. For instance, the retail price of washing powder is set at 4.9 yuan instead of 5.1 yuan. Although the difference is only 20 cents, it will give consumers the illusion that the former is much cheaper. Sometimes the last price makes consumers feel real, such as 68.98 yuan for a bottle of wine, so that consumers feel that the price is carefully calculated by the enterprise, giving people a real feeling. Sometimes the tail number is chosen solely to satisfy certain customs and preferences of consumers, such as the "13" taboo of consumers in Western countries, the "4" taboo of Japanese consumers. Consumers in the United States, Canada and other countries generally think that singular numbers are less than double numbers, and odd numbers are cheaper than even numbers. Consumers in China like the numbers "6" and "8".

2. Integer Pricing

Integer pricing refers to the psychology of seeking the name and convenience of consumers, and the commodity price is defined as an integer ending with "0". In daily life, consumers often like to judge the quality of goods by price, which makes them appear high-grade and caters to consumers' psychology. If a diamond necklace is priced at $100,000 instead of $99,999, the actual price is within $100,000, not $90,000. Therefore, the use of integer pricing can improve the image of high-end brand goods or goods that consumers do not know much about. In addition, setting the price as an integer also saves the trouble of change and improves the efficiency of exchanges.

3. Prestige Pricing

Prestige pricing refers to the intention of enterprises to set the price of famous brand products higher than that of similar products in the market according to the psychology of consumers seeking names. Famous brand goods can not only alleviate buyers' concerns about the quality of goods, but also satisfy some consumers' special desires, such as status, identity, wealth, fame and self-image, so consumers are often willing to pay high prices to buy them.

Prestige pricing often uses integer pricing, which makes it easier to show the high-end goods. Of course, the reputation pricing strategy must not be abused. It is generally applicable to famous and high-quality goods. If the enterprise itself has a bad reputation and the quality of the goods is not good enough, it is easy to lose the market by adopting this strategy. In addition, in order to maintain prestige prices, it is sometimes necessary to properly control the market ownership. One of the operating principles of luxury products is that things are scarce and precious. The watches produced by the Count of Jewelry Watches are usually sold in limited quantities. What's more, customers need to wait for one and a half years to get watches made by famous craftsmen, which can fully show their customers' dignity and status.

4. Fetch-in Pricing

Fetch-in pricing is a pricing method that intentionally reduces the price of a few commodities to attract customers. Enterprises set the prices of certain commodities below the market price in a certain period of time, which can generally attract the attention of consumers and attract them to come shopping. It is suitable for consumers' psychology of seeking cheapness. When choosing and purchasing these commodities, customers often patronize other commodities with normal or high prices. In fact, the loss of a few commodity prices leads to the expansion of sales of other commodities and increases the overall profits of enterprises. For example, when Japan's "creative pharmacy" sells a bottle of 200 yuan tonic at a super-low price of 80 yuan, a large number of people rush into the store every day to buy the tonic. It is said that if it goes on like this, it will surely lose money, but the financial accounts show that the surplus increases sharply every month. The reason is that no one comes to the store to buy only one kind of medicine. When people see that tonics are inexpensive, they will associate with the idea that "other drugs must be inexpensive", which contributes to the blind buying behavior.

This strategy should pay attention to the following points: the price reduction of goods should be large, generally close to or below the cost. Only in this way can the attention and interest of consumers be aroused, and the purchase motivation of consumers be stimulated. The quantity of discounted goods should be appropriate. Too many stores are losing too much money and too few can easily arouse consumers' disgust. Price reductions used for solicitation should be distinguished from areas where inferior and obsolete goods are evident. The price reduction products that attract the price must be marketable products with new varieties and high quality, but not processed products. Otherwise, it not only fails to attract customers, but also may damage the reputation of enterprises.

8.3.3 Discrimination Pricing

Discrimination pricing refers to the establishment of two or more prices for the same product or service to adapt to the differences in customers, locations and time, but this difference does not reflect the difference in cost proportion. The main strategies of discrimination pricing are the following:

1. Customer Segmentation Pricing

Customer segmentation pricing refers to the business selling the same product or service to different customers at different prices. For example, different prices are adopted for old customers and new customers, long-term customers and short-term customers, women and men, children and the elderly, industrial users and residents. In some big cities in China, the subway tickets for primary and middle school students are sold at half price, which is lower than the price for ordinary people. Some attractions offer half-price discounts to the elderly and children.

2. Product-form Pricing

Product-form pricing means that enterprises set different prices for products of different colors, varieties and styles, but the price is not proportional to the cost of each product. For example, although the cost of fashionable clothing is similar to that of ordinary clothing, the price difference between fashionable clothing and ordinary clothing is large.

3. Location Pricing

Location pricing refers to taking different prices for the same goods in different locations, even if the cost of goods provided in different locations is the same. Typical examples are cinemas, operas and gymnasiums, where there are different seats and fares. The purpose of this is to adjust customers' needs and preferences for different locations and to balance market supply and demand.

4. Time and Season Pricing

Time and season pricing means that enterprises set different prices for products or services in different seasons, different periods or even different hours. For example, on holidays, tourist attractions charge higher fees. Another example is that a supermarket stipulates that most fresh foods are discounted by 5% after 8 p.m. and restaurants charge half price for all foods after 9 p.m. For some department stores, in the lunch break time and evening off time, the price reduction is larger, and a large number of working consumers are attracted in the absence of extended shopping mall business hours, which brings about a significant increase in sales.

Discrimination pricing can meet the different needs of customers and make more profits for enterprises, so it has been widely used in practice. However, the implementation of discrimination pricing must have certain conditions, otherwise, it will not only fail to achieve the purpose of discrimination pricing, but will even have a negative effect. These conditions include: ① The market can be segmented, and there are differences in demand between different segmented markets, so that customers will not be dissatisfied with enterprises because of different prices. ② The extra revenue of differential pricing is higher than the extra cost of implementing this strategy, so that the enterprise will be profitable. ③ Products in the low-price market cannot be transferred to the high-price market. ④ In the high-price market, competitors cannot compete with enterprises in price. ⑤ The form of differential pricing is legal.

8.3.4 Discount Pricing

The discount pricing strategy refers to the behavior of sellers in order to reward or encourage buyers, such as bulk purchase, advance payment, off-season purchase, etc., to reduce the basic price of their products and give buyers a certain price discount. Specific measures include cash discount, quantity discount, function discount, seasonal discount, etc.

1. Cash Discount

Cash discount is a kind of price discount given to purchasers in order to encourage customers to pay as soon as possible, accelerate capital turnover, reduce sales costs, and reduce enterprise risks. The commonly used financial expression is "2/10, n/30", which means: The payment period agreed by both parties is 30 days; If the buyer pays within 10 days, he will get a 2% price discount; If he pays within 30 days, there will be no discount; If he pays more than 30 days, he will pay interest. The premise of cash discount is that goods are sold on credit or by instalment. Therefore, three factors should be considered in adopting a cash discount: the discount ratio, the time limit for giving a discount, and the time limit for paying all the money.

2. Quantity Discount

Quantity discount is a discount given to the buyer because of the large quantity purchased. The purpose is to encourage customers to buy more goods. The larger the quantity of purchase, the more discounts. Its essence is to distribute part of the sales cost savings to the buyer in the form of price discounts. The purpose is to encourage and attract customers to buy goods from the enterprise in a long-term, large-scale or centralized manner.

3. Function Discount

Function discount, also known as transaction discount and trade discount, refers to the different price discounts given by enterprises according to the different functions, responsibilities and risks of middlemen in product sales, in order to compensate the related costs of middlemen. The main considerations for middlemen are: the position in distribution channels, the importance to product sales of production enterprises, purchase batches, completed promotional functions, risks undertaken, service levels, fulfillment of business responsibilities, the level of product experience in distribution and the final price on the market, etc. The purpose is to encourage middlemen to order in large quantities, expand sales, win customers, and establish long-term, stable and good cooperative relations with production enterprises. Generally speaking, the discount given to wholesalers is larger than that given to retailers.

4. Season Discount

Season discount is a kind of price discount provided by enterprises for customers who buy goods in the off-season. Because the production of some commodities is continuous, but their consumption has obvious seasonality. By offering seasonal discounts, customers can be encouraged to purchase early or off-season, which is conducive to reducing inventory, speeding up the circulation of commodities, quickly recovering funds, promoting balanced production and giving full play to production and sales potential, avoiding market risks due to seasonal changes in demand. For example, a seasonal discount is given when the merchants promote winter clothing in summer.

8.3.5　Product Portfolio Pricing Strategy

An enterprise often provides many products rather than just one product. The focus of the product portfolio pricing strategy is to formulate a set of prices to maximize the profits of the whole product portfolio. The commonly used product portfolio pricing has the following forms.

1. Product Line Pricing

Product line pricing refers to determining the price gap between different product lines according to the differences in quality, performance, grade, style, cost, customer awareness and demand intensity among the items in the product line, referring to the products and prices of competitors, so as to make different product items form different ones. Market image can attract different customer groups, expand product sales, and strive to achieve more profits. If a clothing store sets three prices for a certain type of women's wear: 150 yuan, 350 yuan and 650 yuan, it will form a low-, medium- and high-grade in the minds of consumers. When people buy clothes, they will choose different grades according to their consumption level, thus eliminating the hesitation in choosing goods. Enterprises can set the price of low-priced products at a cost-saving or even a slight loss price, which can often increase the flow of customers, make production and sales rapidly reach the desired scale and curb competition. High-priced products can establish the brand image of enterprises, quickly recover investment with excess profits, and enhance the enterprise's development stamina. Medium-priced products can play a role by giving full play to them. Scale benefit brings reasonable profits for enterprises and maintains the normal operation of enterprises. Enterprises adopting this strategy should pay attention to the appropriate division of grades. The grades of goods should neither be too fine nor too coarse, and the difference in price grades should neither be too large nor too small.

2. Selected Features Pricing

Selected features pricing refers to that, while pricing the main products, companies also set a separate price for the various choices or features that are available. Typical examples are restaurants, bars, etc. The main provision of the restaurant is meals. In addition, customers can also ask for cigarettes, alcohol, drinks and so on. Some restaurants set the price of food at a lower level, while others set the price of tobacco and alcohol at a higher level, mainly relying on the latter to make profits; others set the price of food at a higher level and set the price of alcohol at a lower level to attract a large number of alcoholics.

3. Captive-product Pricing

Captive-product pricing, also known as restricted products, refers to products that must be used with the main products. For example, camera accessories are film, razor accessories are blades, and mechanical accessories are accessories. When most enterprises adopt this strategy, the price of main products is lower, while the price of subsidiary products is higher. Companies obtain high profits from high-priced accessories and compensate for the losses caused by low prices of the major products. For example, Kodak set a low price for cameras and a high price for films, which enhanced the competitiveness of cameras in the industry and guaranteed the original profit level. However, there are risks in setting the price of accessories too high, which can easily cause competitors to produce low-cost imitations and, in turn, compete with regular commodities.

4. Two-stage Pricing

Businesses with a service nature often adopt a two-stage pricing strategy, charging a fixed fee for their services, plus a variable usage fee. For example, the telephone user's monthly telephone fee is the monthly rent plus the call fee calculated by the call time. Besides the ticket fee, tourists at scenic spots also pay extra fees for their entertainment projects. Fixed-fee pricing is generally lower in order to attract customers to use the service item, while the use-fee pricing is higher in order to ensure sufficient profits.

5. By-product Pricing

By-product pricing often produces a large number of by-products in the process of production and processing of petroleum, steel and other products. Some by-products are valuable to customers, so enterprises should not waste them in vain, but should price them reasonably and sell them to specific markets. This can not only bring a large amount of income for enterprises, but also help enterprises to set low prices for their main products and improve the competitiveness of major products. For example, the slag produced in the iron-making process is the main raw material of the cement industry.

6. Product-bundle Pricing

Companies often bundle some products together for sale at a price lower than the sum of the prices of individual products. For example, cosmetics companies bundle moisturizers, shampoos, gels, sunscreens and other products and sell them all the time. Although some consumers don't need any of them, they buy the products when they see they are much cheaper than the individual products. Bundling can, to some extent, drive consumers to buy products. However, companies should pay attention to flexibility when bundling pricing, because some rational consumers tend to buy only on demand. They only need to bundle one or more products in a portfolio, and the enterprise needs to meet their requirements.

8.3.6　International Transfer Pricing

The international transfer pricing strategy refers to the price adopted when products are transferred between the parent company of a multinational company and its subsidiaries. On the surface, the transfer price is set by a multinational company to evaluate the operating performance of its subsidiaries, but in essence, it is to avoid adverse factors to the profits of the whole company and pursue the maximization of the overall profits of the group. Therefore, the transfer price often deviates from the normal market price and maximizes the overall interests of the enterprise group through being higher or lower than the normal market price.

The main purposes of transfer pricing of transnational enterprises include: reducing risk, tax deduction, and coping with competition.

8.4　Management and Control of International Market Pricing

8.4.1　Quotation Control of Export Products

The price terms of an international sales contract may include specific factors that affect the price, such as credit, conditions of sale, and shipping. Both parties to the transaction must make it clear that the quotation shall divide the responsibilities of each party in the freightage, indicating who will pay the freight and where to start paying. The quotation must also indicate the currency, the credit terms, and the type of document required. Since different countries use different units of measurement, quantitative descriptions are necessary. For example, the reference to "tons" in the contract should be clear whether it is metric tons or U. K. tons, long tons or short tons. If the quality requirements are not specific, it will also cause misunderstanding. In addition, there should be a fully agreed opinion on the criteria for evaluating the quality of the product. For example, American customers can fully understand the meaning of "customary merchantable quality", but in other countries, there may be a completely different understanding. International trade personnel must carefully review each clause of the contract. If the review is not detailed, it may lead to changes in profits that the company is reluctant to see.

8.4.2　Price Escalation Control

Compared with domestic sales products, the products exported to the international market, due to the increase of geographical distance and economic differences, have led to the need for more transportation and insurance services for international marketing. Export products require more middlemen and longer distribution channel services, as well as various desk work and import duties required for export. All of the above costs are added to the final selling price of the product as a cost, resulting in a higher final price of the product in the international market than the domestic selling price. The phenomenon that the export price formed by the gradual addition of such export costs has gradually increased is called price increase.

There are huge differences in the prices of products sold in China and abroad. The main reason is that international sales have more marketing functions than domestic sales. It is not that companies can get more profits when they sell their products abroad. The gradual increase in the cost of each stage in the export process is the root cause of the price increase. The price upgrade does not bring any extra profits to the exporting companies. On the contrary, due to the price upgrade, consumers in the target market of the enterprise need to purchase the same goods at a higher price. The high price suppresses the demand, reduces the sales volume of the enterprise products, and has an adverse effect on the production enterprise itself. Therefore, price escalation is a necessary issue for international companies.

Companies can take several steps to reduce the negative impact of price increases. The commonly used methods are as follows:

① **Lower the net selling price**. That is, offsetting tariffs and shipping costs by lowering the net selling price. However, this kind of strategy often does not work. Firstly, because the price reduction may cause serious losses to the enterprise. Secondly, this kind of behavior of enterprises may be judged as dumping, and the anti-dumping duties imposed by the government of the importing country will make the price advantage into a bubble and will not play a role in expanding sales.

② **Change the product form**. For example, parts are shipped to the importing country and assembled locally, so that tariffs can be paid at a relatively low tax rate, which reduces the tariff burden to a certain extent, thereby lowering the price.

③ **Factory production in foreign countries**. This can greatly reduce the impact of price increases such as freight, tariffs, and brokerage margins, but it also faces the risk of changes in foreign political and economic situations.

④ **Shorten distribution channels**. This can reduce the number of transactions and thus reduce some of the intermediate costs. However, sometimes the channel is shortened, but the cost may not be reduced, because many marketing functions cannot be canceled, and there will still be costs. In countries where transaction taxes are levied according to the number of transactions, this method can be used to pay less taxes.

⑤ **Reduce product quality** means eliminating some of the costly features of the product and even reducing overall product quality. The functions that some developed countries need may be redundant in developing countries, and the elimination of these functions can achieve the goal of reducing costs and controlling prices. Reducing product quality can also reduce the cost of manufacturing a product, but there are certain risks in doing so, and companies must be cautious when making decisions.

8.4.3　Parallel Input Control

If a large company cannot effectively control prices and distribution, it is likely that the subsidiaries or branches will compete. Due to the different prices of products in different countries' markets, when products sold domestically are exported to another country, they may be sold in another country at a lower domestic sales price. For example, an American cosmetics manufacturer exported cosmetics to a developing country at a lower price, and later discovered that these cosmetics were exported to a third country, where they competed directly with the same product sold by the same company at a higher price. This is a parallel input (also known as parallel imports, or gray market) that disrupts the price market, and its roots lie in the lack of price control and effective management.

The main reasons for parallel input include: currency differences between different countries, import quotas and high tariffs, significant price differences between countries, and a high price differential between distributors and franchisees.

In order to avoid parallel markets, companies must establish a strict control system to regularly monitor the amount of the company's exports and whether it is compatible with the needs of the exporting land. In addition, companies can establish control systems that effectively control distribution channels, and can help mitigate the impact of parallel input with the help of local laws. In Taiwan, a court ruled that two companies importing Coca-Cola from the United States infringed the Coca-Cola trademark and Coca-Cola's sole authorized operator in Taiwan, prohibiting them from exporting, displaying, and selling Coca-Cola trademarks.

8.5　Issues to Be Aware of in International Market Pricing

8.5.1　Price Standardization and Price Differentiation

International companies often encounter such a problem in the process of formulating strategies: whether the price of the same product should be consistent in the world markets, or different price strategies for different countries. From the perspective of marketing practices of multinational corporations, most companies adopt price differentiation. It depends mainly on the differences in social history, cultural habits, economic development level, natural resources, government policies and other factors in different countries and regions. There are also significant discrepancies in production costs, competitive prices, distribution channels and distribution costs, product life cycles, and taxes. Companies need to comprehensively measure these differences and target different pricing strategies. However, there are also a small number of multinational companies maintaining price standardization in the international market. It is conducive to the formation of a consistent image of companies and products in the markets of various countries. Price standardization is also conducive to saving marketing costs, and at the same time facilitates the company headquarters' control over the entire marketing campaign.

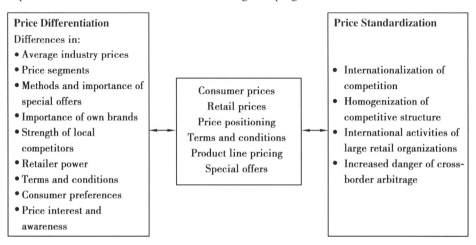

Figure 8-3　Structural Factors of Standardized versus Differentiated Pricing

8.5.2　Headquarter Pricing and Subsidiary Pricing

Many large-scale enterprises face the problem of price management in international marketing: whether the head office uniformly sets the price of goods around the world, or whether it is independently priced by subsidiaries in each country. There are usually three practices: the first is pricing by the company's headquarters; The second is separately priced by the subsidiary; The third is the common pricing by the company's headquarters and subsidiaries. Since the conditions of production, market and competition vary from country to country, it is still rare for the head office to uniformly price the subsidiaries of each country. The more common method is joint pricing by the head office and subsidiaries. The specific method is: the base company determines a base price and the floating range. The subsidiary can flexibly formulate the floating range within the scope of the head office according to the specific conditions of the host country. In this way, the head office can maintain a certain degree of control over the pricing of the subsidiaries, and the subsidiaries can have certain autonomy to adapt the prices to the specific conditions of the local market.

There are four pricing strategies for intra-company transfer products: ① sold at local manufacturing costs plus standard additions; ② the manufacturing cost of the most efficient production unit in the company plus the standard addition; ③ sold at the negotiated price; ④ sold at the market price.

Among these four methods, the transfer at the market price is most easily accepted by the tax authorities, and is most likely to be accepted by foreign branches. However, the internal transfer of the company should be based on which pricing method is appropriate, and should be determined by the nature of the subsidiary and the market situation.

Whether in the home country or in the host country, it is necessary to carefully consider the above practices, so as to avoid foreign companies evading taxes and avoiding taxes or domestic companies under-reporting overseas income.

8.5.3　Dumping and Anti-Dumping

1. Dumping

With the acceleration of economic globalization and the intensification of international market competition, dumping and anti-dumping have become a focus of international marketing. Dumping refers to the fact that an organization sells a lot of goods abroad at a price lower than the domestic market, or even lower than the cost of producing the goods, in order to defeat competitors and monopolize the whole market. In general, dumping can be divided into the following categories:

① Accidental dumping

Accidental dumping, also called "short-term dumping", often involves selling obsolete products or goods that are no longer available in the domestic market at a price below the cost of production abroad. Such dumping will have a negative impact on the similar production enterprises in the importing country in a short time, but for the consumption of the importing country, it brings cheap and high-quality goods, so the government of the importing country usually does not intervene in such dumping.

② Intermittent dumping

Intermittent dumping is selling a mass of goods abroad at a price below the domestic price or even the cost. The purpose is to crush foreign competitors, monopolize the market, and then raise the price of goods to make bigger profits. Meanwhile, companies sell at a loss in order to gain access to a foreign market, mainly to exclude foreign competitors. Once a firm's position in the market is established, it raises prices based on its monopoly. Such dumping lasts for a long time and causes great harm. It hits the national industry of the importing country, hinders the survival and development of similar enterprises in the importing country, and finally damages the interests of consumers in the importing country. Therefore, many governments resist such dumping by means of anti-dumping duties.

③ Continuous dumping

Continuous dumping, also called "long-term dumping", refers to the long-term selling of goods to foreign markets at a lower price than the domestic market, and its most striking feature is longevity. To avoid long-term losses, the export price is at least higher than the marginal cost, and at the same time, the dumping operators also expand production through economies of scale to reduce unit costs. The longest sustained type of dumping is when a firm continues to sell in one international market at a lower price than in other markets. Its applicable premise is that the marketing cost and demand characteristics of each market are different. Certainly, after crushing the competitors and completely occupying the market, the dumping people will raise their prices again to earn extra profits.

2. Anti-Dumping

The so-called anti-dumping means that the importing government aims to maintain the normal international trade order, through legislation, high anti-dumping duties levied on the dumping products and other measures to curb dumping, so as to protect the development of the domestic industry. The WTO principles provide that dumping is to be condemned if it causes material injury or obstruction to an established industry in the territory of the importing country and imposes a dumping margin not exceeding the volume of the dumped product. Anti-dumping or countervailing duties shall not be imposed if it is not concluded that the effect of dumping or subsidies will cause material injury or threat to an established industry in the country, or materially impede the construction of an established industry in the country. It can be seen that dumping must meet three conditions: Firstly, the export price of the product is lower than the normal value; Secondly, the product does cause substantial damage, threat or obstruction to the importing country; Third, there is an inseparable causal relationship between dumping and material injury, threat or obstruction. Among them, that the price is lower than the normal value is the key to the three conditions. The criterion for judging whether the export price is lower than its normal value is that, firstly, it is lower than the comparable price under normal circumstances when the same product is used for domestic consumption in the exporting country. In the absence of such a domestic price, it is below the maximum comparable price of the same product exported to a third country under normal trade conditions. Or it is below the cost of production in the country of origin plus reasonable marketing expenses and profits. Due consideration must be given to differences in conditions of specific sale, differences in taxes and other differences affecting price comparability.

Chapter Summary

- The factors influencing the pricing of international enterprises mainly include cost, competition, market demand, political factor and pricing target.
- International product pricing methods include cost-oriented pricing, demand-oriented pricing and competitive-oriented pricing.
- In addition to new product pricing, psychological pricing, differential pricing, discount pricing and product mix pricing, the international product pricing strategy also includes the international transfer pricing strategy unique to international marketing activities.
- In the process of international product price management and control, it is necessary to

properly deal with price control of export products, price rise control, parallel input, lease and relative trade price control.

Main Concepts

cost-oriented pricing, demand-oriented pricing, competition-oriented pricing, new-product pricing, psychological pricing, price discrimination, discount pricing, product portfolio pricing, quotation controls, price escalation control, parallel input control, price standardization and price differentiation, headquarter pricing and subsidiary pricing, dumping, anti-dumping

Think and Practice

1. What are the differences between the factors affecting the international market pricing and the domestic market pricing?
2. What are the main pricing strategies of international enterprises?
3. What are the main means of price control for international enterprises?
4. What's the difference between a unified price and a differential price?
5. Why has dumping become a major problem in recent years?

Case Study

IBM's pricing strategy has gradually changed from the exclusive pricing strategy to the market pricing based on market demand. Of course, IBM takes product differentiation as the basis of its pricing strategy, that is, the positioning of low prices sold through channels or personal computers should be based on the interaction with channels. The price of integrated services provided in global service units or the price of overall solutions required by large- and medium-sized customers requires complex cost calculations, but transactions with large customers need to be guided by maintaining long-term cooperative relationships. Therefore, when IBM provides solutions or participates in bidding, it will first grab business with a flexible price strategy, and then step by step achieve long-term profit recovery. This is a variant of IBM's traditional price strategy. The IBM headquarters marketing unit has left the price flexibility of products to the business sector in order to capture market share in the e-commerce era.

Discuss the following questions.

1. Why did IBM change its pricing strategy?

2. Why does an enterprise like IBM have to focus on building long-term relationships with big customers?

3. What impact does IBM's pricing have on the pricing strategies of its competitors?

Chapter 9

Distribution Strategy in the International Market

//////// **Learning Objectives** ////////////////////

- Apply the relevant theories of international marketing channels to analyze problems encountered in practice;
- Be able to make decisions on distribution channels in the international market;
- Be able to select appropriate middlemen according to conditions;
- Be able to manage distribution channels in the international market.

//////// *Key Terms* ////////////////////

distribution channel　分销渠道

vertical joint marketing system　垂直联合营销系统

horizontal joint marketing system　横向联合营销系统

product characteristic　产品特征

market characteristic　市场特征

middlemen characteristic　中间商特征

environmental characteristic　环境特征

enterprises characteristic　企业特征

intermediary　中间商

market coverage　市场覆盖

intensive distribution　密集分布

selective distribution　选择性分布

exclusive distribution　独家经销

▶ Opening Case

"Brands from China" Ride Waves of Foreign Trade

More and more Chinese vendors now sell their products globally through cross-border e-commerce platforms, and their number is on the rise, industry experts said. The increase in such transactions is also playing a substantially vital role in stabilizing China's foreign trade and economic growth amid the COVID-19 pandemic and the complex external environment, they added.

Chinese earphone maker 1MORE is reaping handsome rewards by selling in overseas markets, including the United States, Europe, Japan, the Middle East, Australia and Singapore, via Amazon, the global e-commerce giant. Lin Boqing, who created 1MORE in 2015, said Amazon offered the company helpful guidance with consumer demand analysis based on big data. It also provided professional training in operations and taught market expansion strategy. "Sales of our earphones on Amazon account for about 35 percent of the company's global sales. In 2020, sales via overseas e-commerce channels increased by 400 percent annually," Lin said.

Chinese sellers are paying more attention to building brands and expanding their presence in overseas markets, given the rapid growth in the cross-border e-commerce industry, according to Amazon Global Selling, which helps Chinese merchants sell their products abroad.

"In the past, many Chinese products had only a price advantage," said Cindy Tai, Amazon vice-president and head of Global Selling Asia. "However, we are seeing more and more differentiated and high-tech products of good design come from China, such as smart home appliances, office supplies, clothing and home furnishings."

China has a strong manufacturing base and competitive edge in supply chains, coupled with favorable policy support and the innovative spirit of Chinese entrepreneurs, Tai said. She called cross-border e-commerce an unstoppable trend that is helping drive the transformation from "Made-in-China" to "Brands-from-China". With China's advantages in those areas, "we have full confidence in the prospects of cross-border e-commerce," she said.

The number of Chinese brands that have completed their registration on Amazon has grown 40-fold in four years, and those sellers are emphasizing global expansion, with 14 percent of Chinese brands possessing trademarks in more than five countries and regions, the e-commerce giant said.

The import and export volume of China's cross-border e-commerce totaled 1.98 trillion yuan ($293.2 billion) in 2021, up 15 percent year-on-year, according to the General Administration of Customs. E-commerce exports stood at 1.44 trillion yuan, an annual increase of 24.5 percent. The country has stepped up efforts to boost the development of new forms and models of foreign trade as part of a broader push to promote high-quality development, the experts said.

(Visitors gather at the booth of Amazon Global Selling during a cross-border e-commerce expo held in Fuzhou, Fujian province, in June)

(Source: Adapted from *China Daily*)

9. 1 An Overview of International Market Distribution Strategy

9.1.1 Basic Structure of International Market Distribution Channels

Due to the existence of social division of labor, products must go through various intermediate links in the process of transferring from domestic producers to foreign final consumers or users. The differences in the characteristics of the product and the guiding ideology of the enterprise determine the different international distribution channels of the product. As can be seen from Figure 9-1, the international market distribution channel of the product can be divided into two parts, one is the distribution channel of the product in the market of the exporting country; the other is the distribution channel of the product in the market of the importing country. There are two main distribution channels for products in the exporting country market and four main distribution channels for the importing country market. In this way, there are 8 types of distribution channels for products in the international market.

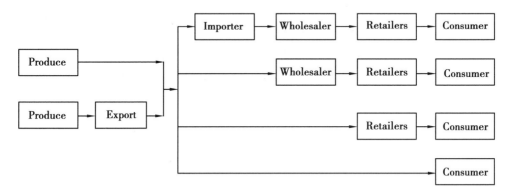

Figure 9-1   Basic Structure of Distribution Channels in the International Market

9.1.2 Development Trend of International Market Distribution Channel

Channel membership and the structure in distribution channels are not static. With the development of the economy, the change in consumption behavior, the improvement of material conditions, the change in market structure, business formats and channel organizations are constantly changing. Since the 1970s, due to global economic integration and the development of enterprise competition internationalization, large multinational corporations have increasingly become the main body of international market competition. With their abundant resources, multinational corporations often make comprehensive use of products, prices, channels and promotion strategies in the process of international market management, and require greater control over sales channels. These trends lead to the joint trend of distribution channels.

1. Development of the Vertical Joint Marketing System

The development of the vertical joint marketing system, also known as the vertical marketing system, refers to the channel system formed by the integration of different channel members such as producers, wholesalers, retailers and the like. In a vertical marketing system, one channel member has the ownership of other channel members, either granting concessions to other channel members, or having a sufficient market influence to force other channel members to take a cooperative attitude.

The vertical marketing system has the characteristics of large-scale operation, strong service function and high exchange ability, which is beneficial to avoid repeated operations, and can go to scale economy and scope economy. The emergence and development of the vertical marketing system is the product of western developed countries entering the buyer's market from the seller's market in recent decades, and the market competition intensifying, and the concentration and monopoly further developing.

2. Development of the Horizontal Joint Marketing System

The development of the horizontal joint marketing system, also known as the horizontal marketing system, refers to a number of manufacturers, wholesalers or retailers at the same level in the channel system, voluntarily forming temporary or permanent cooperative relations or forming an independent company to carry out horizontal joint operation and to jointly develop new marketing opportunities.

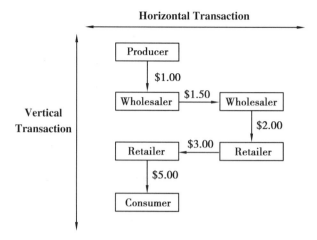

Figure 9-2   A Hypothetical Channel Sequence in the Consumer Market

9.1.3   Basic Elements Affecting the Design and Selection of International Distribution Channels

The design of international market distribution channels makes it an important activity in enterprises' international marketing. It is to plan the marketing network of an enterprise across the border from the perspective of the producer. Its central problem is to determine the best network way to reach the international target market. The selection of an international market distribution channel requires the enterprise to make a comprehensive analysis of various environmental factors, including customer factors, the product nature, middleman factors, competition factors, enterprise factors, environmental factors and the rights and obligations of the channel members.

1. Product Characteristics

Different products have special requirements for channels because of their different characteristics. For products, such as live perishable products, products with a short life cycle and fashionable products, it is obvious that the most direct channels should be taken. Special products with large volume, heavy weight and technical strength are suitable for the shortest possible channels. Products with high unit prices and requiring more additional services are mostly sold directly by manufacturing companies or go through only one intermediate link; On the contrary, the more standardized the product, and the more familiar with the customer is, the longer and wider the channel, as shown in Table 9-1. When the new product has not yet been accepted by the market and the demand is unstable, it is usually necessary for the production enterprises to send people directly to engage in marketing and market development. With the improvement of market acceptance, the channels can also be changed. For example, a sports juice drink that initially serves only sports teams, gymnasiums and fitness clubs. Then, with the popularity of recipients, it begins to enter supermarkets, convenience stores and fast food restaurants.

Table 9-1   A Comparison between Product Characteristics and Distribution Channel

Factors	Product Characteristics: High or Low (Large or Small)	Channel Characteristics: Long or Short
Price	high	short
	low	long
Perishability	high	short
	low	long
Weight	large	short
	small	long
Technical complexity	high	short
	low	long
Fashion	high	short
	low	long

2. Market Characteristics

If the market potential is large, companies need to use middlemen. If the market potential is small, the enterprise can consider the promotion of the direct use of the salesman. If the frequency of the customer's purchase of goods is high, companies should select more middlemen. If customers are concentrated, a large number of purchases can be sold directly without intermediaries. For example, if industrial users are concentrated because of large purchase quantities, they would prefer to trade directly with suppliers to save circulation costs. For the same purpose, large retailers are also trying to bypass the wholesalers and find the shortest buying channel. For new and high-tech products and special products, it is not suitable for users to use middlemen extensively because users need complicated and serialized services.

3. Middlemen Characteristics

In general, different intermediaries have different abilities in promotion, negotiation, storage, communication and credit. If the importers are professional and experienced, who are familiar with the channels of the domestic market and know all kinds of import regulations, they are especially suitable for foreign enterprises who are not familiar with the host country. Direct import retailers have their own import department to control market conditions, while wholesalers can purchase in large quantities. Therefore, enterprises must consider the advantages and disadvantages of different types of intermediaries in carrying out various tasks when establishing channels.

4. Environmental Characteristics

In the international market, most enterprises try to avoid using the same marketing channels as their competitors. Some companies often use the same channels as competing products. For example, companies that produce food and other products with less involvement of buyers but a large brand difference, want to sell their products alongside those of competitors for consumers to choose from. Enterprises' use of marketing channels is not only constrained by the channels used by competitors, but also needs to understand the scale of various intermediaries in the market, and the strengths and weaknesses of various functional tasks. For example, in a certain market, there are many large retailers with large purchase quantities, which is enough to match the output of production enterprises. In this case, the enterprise can sell products directly to retailers, and do not need wholesalers to change hands, so the channel is shorter. In contrast, with a large number of small and medium retailers and fierce competition, better marketing benefits can be achieved through the long channels of wholesalers.

5. Enterprises Characteristics

For companies that are not only large-scale and well-known, but also have strong capital, excellent products, and outstanding advantages, they have greater initiative in choosing sales channels and middlemen, and can even establish their own sales companies. This sales channel can be short. In addition, the "product portfolio" of an enterprise also affects its choice of marketing channels. If the product portfolio is deep, it is suitable for narrow channels. At the same time, the enterprise's marketing strategy will also affect its channel design. If an automobile manufacturer wants to provide timely service to customers, it will have to establish numerous service outlets, widely distributed spare parts storage sites, or faster transportation vehicles. In addition, enterprises themselves have different desires to control channels. In order to control the sales channels of products, some manufacturers are willing to adopt short channels even though the cost is high, because it can increase the sales force, keep the product inventory fresh, and control the retail price. If manufacturers want to completely control the market positioning, price and image of their products, they may have to set up special shops or special counters. On the contrary, companies can sell through more middlemen.

6. Channel Members' Mutual Rights and Obligations

After choosing the model of international sales channels and specific middlemen, the rights and obligations of each member in the channel must be clarified. Only in this way can companies better deal with the interests and strengthen the cooperation of channel members. The rights and obligations of channel members are determined around the core of interests, including price policies, trading conditions, regional rights of middlemen, and specific services provided by various parties.

In terms of price policy, the manufacturer should establish a price catalogue, which clearly specifies different discounts or price concessions for different types of intermediaries or for different quantities of goods.

In terms of sale and purchase, for the middlemen who pay in advance or on time, the enterprise should give different discounts according to the time of payment, which can stimulate the enthusiasm of the middlemen, and at the same time help the manufacturer's loan recovery, and speed up the turnover of funds.

In terms of the regional rights of intermediaries, manufacturers should make clear provisions on the regional division, coverage, rights and responsibilities of intermediaries.

For example, the scope, jurisdiction, responsibilities, and remuneration of franchising should be clearly defined in the franchising agreement. On one hand, it can reduce unnecessary disputes and conflicts. On the other hand, it can maximize the enthusiasm of intermediate traders.

In terms of the specific services to be provided by both parties, there may be conflicts in interests between manufacturers and intermediaries in terms of advertising, capital input, personnel training, etc., so the best form is to specify it by agreement or contract. For example, an agreement under which the manufacturer gives 5% to the middlemen who advertise a product, gives preference to the middlemen who serve the advertisement in times of scarcity, and encourages the middlemen to assume their functions.

9.2 International Marketing Channel Members

International marketing channel members refer to all kinds of intermediaries who join in the circulating process of commodities in the international market. International middlemen can be divided into domestic middlemen and foreign middlemen. Because international middlemen play a key role in bridging and connecting enterprises in the international market, enterprises should regard middlemen not only as customers, but also as strategic partners. Enterprises should reach a consensus, that is, the middleman who serves the ultimate customer of the enterprise can help the enterprise to establish customers' trust and loyalty to the enterprise.

9.2.1 Basic Types of Members (Intermediaries) in International Marketing Channels

In the process of international marketing, international intermediaries play an important role as intermediaries and bridges. Therefore, in order to grasp the features of different types of intermediaries and give full play to the role of various types of intermediaries in international marketing channels, it is necessary to classify intermediaries.

1. Export Middlemen

Export middlemen refer to middlemen located in the country of production. When a manufacturing enterprise cannot deal with foreign customers directly, export middlemen can take advantage of the domestic importer's international marketing knowledge and experience to service the manufacturing enterprises. According to whether export middlemen own the commodities, export middlemen can be divided into export distributors and export agents. Export distributors have the ownership of goods, while the export agent just accepts the commission, buys and sells the goods in the name of the commissioner, receives a commission, and does not have the ownership of the goods.

① **Export dealers**. Export dealers include five types: export companies, export direct wholesalers, export resellers, foreign importers and international trading companies.

② **Export agents**. The difference between export agents and exporters is that the export agents generally do not buy goods from domestic vendors in their own names, but only accept the entrustment of the vendors, and carry out export business on behalf of the principals under specified conditions. Export agents do not need to have the ownership of commodities, but after successful transactions, the principal should pay a certain commission. In the international market, export agents mainly include sales agents, manufacturers' export agents, exporting countries, brokers and export commissioners. These agents can be either an organization or a natural person.

2. Import Middlemen

Import middlemen means middlemen who engage in the import business and who sell imported goods, mainly including import dealers and foreign import agents.

① **Import dealers**. Any trading enterprise that purchases goods from abroad directly and sells them to the domestic market can be called an import dealer. The import dealer owns the ownership of the goods and earns profits through the import business. In fact, it should undertake all the risks from import to sale. The functions of import dealers are similar to the domestic wholesalers, but the difference is that import dealers' target is foreign enterprises. There are two main modes of management of import dealers: one is to import goods according to the requirements of the domestic market firstly, and then resell them to domestic wholesalers, retailers or industrial users; The other is to first deal with domestic buyers according to the sample, and then purchase the goods abroad, responsible for all transportation, insurance and customs clearance. Import dealers operate a wide variety of goods, but they tend to operate high-profit, and fast turnover goods. Many importers, in addition to operating their own import business, are also entrusted by foreign exporters as their agents in the local market.

② **Import agent**. Import agents generally accept imports entrusted by domestic vendors and are responsible for arranging sales, providing services and collecting commissions in the domestic market under specified conditions, but they do not undertake credit, exchange and market risks and do not have the ownership of the goods. Its functions mainly include three aspects: one is to buy and import goods on behalf of domestic buyers; the other is to sell consignment goods on behalf of foreign exporters; and the third is to act as a representative for foreign manufacturers or exporters to sell goods. The main types of import agents are foreign import agents, import commissioners, import international brokers, finance brokers, etc.

From the perspective of international marketing, the intermediaries in international marketing channels include not only the export intermediaries and import intermediaries mentioned above, but also some other types of intermediaries. In addition, manufacturers in exporting countries should set up their own export agencies and sales agencies abroad, which should also be part of international sales channels.

9.2.2 The Selection of Members (Intermediaries) in International Marketing Channels

When enterprises decide to choose international marketing channels, the choice of international middlemen is directly related to the operational efficiency of marketing channels and the realization of the whole marketing plan. Choosing international middlemen should focus on a long-term plan and should be based on a detailed investigation and a full understanding of foreign markets. The selective norms of international middlemen generally include the following aspects.

1. The Condition of the Target Market

The purpose of selecting middlemen for enterprises is to bring their products into foreign target markets, so that foreign end-users or consumers who need their products can purchase them conveniently. Therefore, when choosing sales channels, enterprises should pay attention to whether the selected middlemen have the sales channels they need in the target market, such as branches, subsidiaries, sales places, etc.

2. Geographical Location

International middlemen should have geographical location superiority. Geographical location should be consistent with the products, services and coverage areas of manufacturers. Specifically, if it is a wholesaler, its geographical location should be convenient for transportation and storage of products. If it is a retailer, it should have a larger passenger flow, more concentrated consumers, complete road traffic networks, fast means of transportation and so on.

3. Business Conditions

An international middleman should have good business conditions, including business premises, business equipment, etc. For example, in order to support the retailer's business operation effectively, the lighting facilities, counters and other equipment in the retailer's business place should be complete.

4. Business Ability and Business Nature

Middlemen's business ability refers to their management ability, marketing ability and customer service ability. The business ability of international middlemen is the key factor to determine the success of sales. The business characters of middlemen refer to the business scope of middlemen and their coverage and penetration into the target market. It is necessary to make a comprehensive study of the business characters of middlemen. Generally speaking, professional chain sales companies have a strong marketing ability for those goods with high value, strong technology, strong brand attraction and more after-sales service. Various small and medium department stores and grocery stores are strong in operating convenience products and low-to-medium grade shopping items. When examining the business ability of middlemen, there are several specific indicators as follows:

① **Business history**. International middlemen should have a long business history and establish a good image among customers.

② **Staff quality**. Employees of international middlemen should be highly qualified, with a remarkable ability to use various promotion methods and means, and be willing to promote the sales of products directly. They have rich product knowledge, abundant experience and skills in the sales of related products. They have higher service skills, and answer the customer's questions at any time, and provide customers with services such as installation, maintenance and so on.

③ **Business performance**. International middlemen should have good performance, and they should have perfect regulations and good results in operating income, repayment speed and profit level.

5. Credit Conditions of Middlemen

Credit conditions of middlemen refer to the financial status, business style and business reputation of middlemen. New customers who do not know much about their credit status should be treated with caution and avoid being deceived. International middlemen should have high prestige and a good reputation among customers, win the trust of customers, and establish long-term and stable business relationships with customers. Middlemen with a high reputation are often those who are willing to visit or even buy goods at a higher price from target consumers or secondary marketers. Such middlemen not only have a better image in the heart of consumers, but also can help manufacturers establish a brand image.

6. Attitude of Cooperation

When choosing middlemen, enterprises should pay attention to analyzing the willingness of marketing cooperation with other channel members so as to select good partners. For marketing channels as a whole, the benefit of each member comes from the cooperation and mutual benefit creation activities between members. From this point of view, they share the task of marketing commodities and "bundle" each other's interests through marketing. Only when all members have common aspirations, common aspirations and a spirit of cooperation, can it be possible to establish an effective sales channel. Therefore, the middleman chosen by the manufacturer should meet the requirements of the established marketing channel function in terms of business direction and professional ability, and be willing to cooperate with the manufacturer to undertake some marketing functions, such as joint promotion. A good cooperative relationship between producers and intermediaries is beneficial not only to manufacturers and consumers, but also to intermediaries.

9.3　International Marketing Channel Strategy

The decision of international marketing channels refers to the activities where enterprises analyze and evaluate different schemes according to their objectives, abilities, conditions, production characteristics, and the structural characteristics of the target marketing channel. They then choose their own marketing channel mode in the target market.

9.3.1　Market Coverage

The amount of market coverage that a channel member provides is important. Coverage is a flexible term. It can refer to geographical areas of a country (such as cities and major towns) or the number of retail outlets (as a percentage of all retail outlets). Regardless of the market coverage measures used, the company has to create a distribution network (dealers, distributors and retailers) to meet its coverage goals.

As shown in Figure 9-3, three different approaches are available:

- Intensive distribution. This calls for distributing the product through the largest number of different types of intermediary and the largest number of individual intermediaries of each type.

- Selective distribution. This entails choosing a number of intermediaries for each area to be penetrated.

- Exclusive distribution. This involves choosing only one intermediary in a market.

Channel coverage (width) can be identified along a continuum ranging from wide channels (intensive distribution) to narrow channels (exclusive distribution).

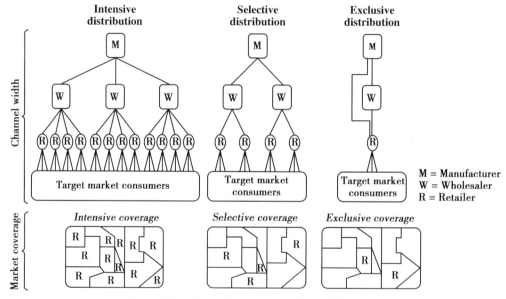

Figure 9-3 Three Strategies for Market Coverage

9.3.2 Standardization and Differentiation of Marketing Channels

If the length and width of the marketing channels build the marketing model of the company in a specific market, then the standardization and differentiation of marketing channels is to solve the problem of enterprises using a unified marketing model in multiple countries as well as the problem of designing different marketing models for different countries. Whether the enterprises adopt the standardized marketing model or the differentiated marketing model in foreign markets should be decided according to the marketing characteristics, consumption characteristics, market competition characteristics of each country and the characteristics of the enterprise and its products.

1. The Standardization of Marketing Channels

The standardization of marketing channels means that enterprises directly adopt a unified marketing model in foreign markets. The main reason for companies to adopt this standardized marketing model is that the tendency for this demand to converge is increasingly evident with the integration of the global economy. Despite the limitations of many conditions, the marketing model of many industrial products or certain consumer products has shown a trend of unification and standardization in many countries or regions.

The adoption of a standardized marketing model can bring benefits to enterprises, helping enterprises achieve scale economies effect and improving the experience curve effect accumulated in marketing experience by using marketers and marketing actions. Using a standardized marketing model, the biggest attraction for multinational consumers is that they can use fixed purchase patterns and marketing channels to buy products or services that they are familiar with in different countries or regions. However, a standardized marketing model may not allow effective product marketing activities in the host market, given the different market environments of each country. Therefore, some companies tend to differentiate marketing channels.

2. The Differentiation of Marketing Channels

The differentiation of marketing channels, also known as diversification, refers to the use of different marketing modes by enterprises according to the specific conditions of different countries. In international marketing practice, the reasons for most companies using differentiated marketing design are mainly the following ones:

① Differences in the marketing environment in different countries or regions.

In different countries or regions, the number and size of wholesalers, retailers and the services they may provide, and the conditions of the storage and transportation of goods vary greatly, leading to differences in the marketing patterns of enterprises. For example, the marketing model of PepsiCo is to set up bottling plants in target market countries and then truck them to retail outlets. However, in remote areas with small populations and difficult transportation, the cost of using trucks to transport goods is too high, they have to switch to other marketing methods.

② Differences in consumption characteristics between countries and consumer purchase patterns.

For similar products, consumers in different countries often have their own consumption habits and purchasing patterns, and they always use specific channels that they are familiar with. The selection of marketing models for different countries or regions has to take the differences in consumer buying patterns into account.

③ Differences in the way companies enter different countries or regions.

The way companies enter a market limits the choice of their international marketing channels for the target market. For example, the way of exporting products, whether indirect or direct, enterprises have basically no control over the domestic marketing channels of importing countries, and have to accept marketing channels arranged by intermediaries. For another example, as for the form of licensing trade or joint venture, the choice of marketing channels by enterprises is affected and restricted by the licensee or the joint venture party. Taking a step back, even if the company enters different target markets in the same way, due to the different sales potential and competitive conditions in the local market, the marketing strategies adopted by the companies are often different, and the selected marketing model is difficult to be consistent.

9.3.3　Decision-making on Creating New Channels or Using Existing Channels

1. Advantages and Disadvantages of New Channels

The so-called new channels are the establishment of specialized channels or networks for product marketing after an enterprise enters a country's market. New channels have the following advantages than using existing ones abroad:

① **Helping to establish market awareness and expand product sales.** Through the company's self-established marketing agency abroad, it is conducive to focusing on the marketing of the company's products, which is very beneficial for the product to open the market and increase its popularity. General foreign marketers, who sell many products at the same time, do not pay special attention to a certain product. This is not good for products, especially those that have newly entered a country's market.

② **It is conducive to strengthening control**. First of all, enterprises can set up their own marketing channels to establish a relatively complete and reasonable product line, strengthen the product sales plan to implement control, and enrich the product color and price levels. Foreign marketers tend to promote high-margin products for their own purposes, which is detrimental to the sales of products across the board. If the company establishes its own marketing channels, it can sell all the products of the company, and the market coverage is wide. Secondly, through new marketing channels, enterprises can also effectively get feedback on product quality, control product quality, and ensure that product quality is not affected during the marketing process. Moreover, enterprises through their own new marketing channels are also conducive to strengthening product price control. By setting up its own marketing agency, it will reduce the intermediate links and overcome the problem that it is difficult for exporters to control the final price of products due to the increase in intermediate links, which is conducive to price control.

③ **It is helpful to provide perfect services**. The marketing organization set up by enterprises abroad can not only strengthen the marketing of specific products, but also help to provide perfect after-sales service. If foreign intermediaries sell too many products, they are unable to concentrate on expanding the market of a particular product and provide perfect after-sales service for the products they sell.

④ **It is conducive for enterprises to accumulate international marketing experience**. For enterprises that have just entered the foreign market, it is also beneficial to get closer to the target market by setting up their own marketing agencies, understand the situation of the target market, and carry out targeted marketing activities. And it is helpful for enterprises to get familiar with the whole process of foreign market development, accumulate rich international marketing experience, and lay a good foundation for further expanding the international market.

However, when companies set up their own marketing agencies in foreign markets, the investment in rebuilding marketing networks is large, the cost is high, and the risk is also high. This strategy is often appropriate for large and powerful companies.

2. Advantages and Disadvantages of Using Existing Channels

The use of existing marketing channels refers to companies entrusting existing middlemen in the target country's market to market products. In international markets, most products are marketed by local middlemen because of financial constraints or other reasons. It has the following advantages:

① **Low cost**. Marketing products through the original intermediary abroad, companies have no necessity to invest in the establishment of corresponding marketing subsidiaries. Although companies need to increase agency fees and other expenses, the cost of product marketing is much lower than the cost of rebuilding marketing agencies.

② **Entering the market quickly**. Since the original foreign middlemen understand the local market and already have a certain marketing network, corporate products can quickly enter the market through them. If enterprises set up their own marketing agencies, not only do they need to invest a lot of manpower and material resources, but also they need a considerable amount of time to run, so it takes a longer time.

③ **Be less risky**. Firstly, enterprises setting up their own marketing agencies abroad may not understand the characteristics of the local market, so it is difficult for them to open the market. Secondly, every company has its own marketing agency and needs a lot of investment. Once the market changes, it is hard to launch out and the risk is high.

Of course, the use of existing foreign middlemen will also face weak corporate control of the market, and services may not keep up with the problems.

3. The Choice of New or Old Channels

The choice of new or old channels should be based on the following factors:

① **Marketing conditions**. If the original market system of the target country is perfect, the distribution network is sound, and the conditions of the distributors are better, there is no need for the company to re-establish the corresponding distribution system. Conversely, if the market system in the target country is not perfect and it is impossible to find a suitable distributor, the company must establish its own distribution network or it cannot open the market.

② **The characteristics of the policy or sociocultural environment**. In some countries, it is not possible for enterprises to establish their own distribution channels and networks when entering countries because of government regulations or cultural conventions.

③ **The characteristics of market competition**. In the target country market, due to the large number of competitors and the fact that most of them occupy favorable distributors, enterprises consider establishing their own distribution channels in order to compete with competitors. If the market is not competitive, it may be better to choose suitable local distributors for the enterprises.

④ **The conditions of the enterprise**. Because the reconstruction channel needs a lot of investment, it is possible for enterprises with sufficient capital to consider setting up their own distribution agencies. Instead, existing local distribution networks could be used.

⑤ **Product characteristics**. The new channel is beneficial to those enterprises with more product lines and more technical products. On the contrary, if the product variety is small or the technology is not strong, there is no need to set up a distribution agency.

⑥ **Cost-benefit comparison**. Using existing channels and rebuilding new channels have their own advantages and disadvantages. When making a choice, an enterprise must carefully weigh the advantages and disadvantages of the two and make a prudent decision by comparing the costs and benefits.

9.4　International Marketing Channel Management

International marketing channels in international marketing are complex and changeable, so the management of international marketing channels becomes a significant subject. International marketing channels are mainly composed of middlemen. Thus, supporting the work of middlemen, effectively evaluating their performance, reducing conflicts among channel members, promoting cooperation among channel members, and improving the effectiveness of channel management, has become the main content of channel management.

1. Support for International Middlemen

Enterprises often have different opinions and disagreements with international middlemen in terms of marketing objectives, product portfolio, promotion activities, sales remuneration and customer service in the international market. They complain that middlemen cannot be aligned with production enterprises or actively cooperate with the unified development strategy of the production enterprise. In order to establish an unobstructed international sales channel, the production enterprise must carefully analyze the causes of disagreements and take effective measures to stimulate the motivation of international middlemen.

Giving support to the middle, and stimulating the motivation of international middlemen is an important aspect of international marketing channel management. The main support measures for international middlemen are:

① **Support for promotion services**. Enterprises can assist middlemen to carry out promotion activities, stimulate the motivation of middlemen, and promote the smooth operation of international sales channels through cooperative advertising, merchandise display, product exhibitions and operational performances, and new product information release conferences, etc. Apple Computer has been very successful in promoting sales support.

② **Financial support**. Enterprises can give international middlemen preferential treatment on payment to make up for the lack of funds for middlemen, such as allowing international middlemen to pay in installments and deferred payments. However, the international market is changing. The measures of installment payment and deferred payment can not only improve the initiative of the middlemen and achieve the purpose of motivation, but also increase the risks of the producers. Therefore, producers should have a detailed understanding of the credit status of international middlemen, and only when they are sure that they can recover the payment can they use the form of financial support.

Enterprises also increase commissions, raise discounts or use special subsidies and other measures to solve the problem of high operating costs of middlemen, or increase their profits of distribution so as to improve the initiative of their distribution.

③ **Management support**. Enterprises can assist international middlemen in business management, training marketing personnel, to improve marketing effectiveness. Management support is especially important for some mechanical equipment products, high-tech products that require technical support, and some service industries that require specification and standardization. Enterprises can also support middlemen through spiritual encouragement and material rewards. For example, regular dealer meetings are held to recognize middlemen with outstanding distribution performance and to give certain rewards or opportunities for free travel.

2. Evaluate International Middlemen

Enterprises regularly assess and evaluate international middlemen to understand whether their activities meet the company's distribution goals, and whether they meet the company's profit plan, which is the prerequisite for ensuring a smooth and efficient distribution system.

Figure 9-4 shows the most important criteria (qualifications) for selecting foreign middlemen, grouped into five categories.

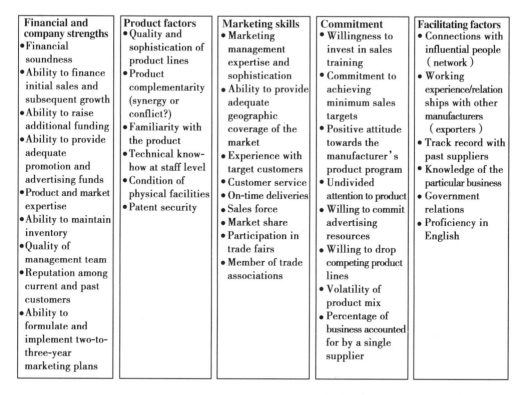

Financial and company strengths	Product factors	Marketing skills	Commitment	Facilitating factors
• Financial soundness • Ability to finance initial sales and subsequent growth • Ability to raise additional funding • Ability to provide adequate promotion and advertising funds • Product and market expertise • Ability to maintain inventory • Quality of management team • Reputation among current and past customers • Ability to formulate and implement two-to-three-year marketing plans	• Quality and sophistication of product lines • Product complementarity (synergy or conflict?) • Familiarity with the product • Technical know-how at staff level • Condition of physical facilities • Patent security	• Marketing management expertise and sophistication • Ability to provide adequate geographic coverage of the market • Experience with target customers • Customer service • On-time deliveries • Sales force • Market share • Participation in trade fairs • Member of trade associations	• Willingness to invest in sales training • Commitment to achieving minimum sales targets • Positive attitude towards the manufacturer's product program • Undivided attention to product • Willing to commit advertising resources • Willing to drop competing product lines • Volatility of product mix • Percentage of business accounted for by a single supplier	• Connections with influential people (network) • Working experience/relationships with other manufacturers (exporters) • Track record with past suppliers • Knowledge of the particular business • Government relations • Proficiency in English

Figure 9-4 Criteria for Evaluating Foreign Middlemen

▶ Case 9-1

Wuliangye: a Model for Chinese Enterprises to "Go Global"

On October 17, 2018, the Czech "2018 China Investment Forum" closed in Prague. As the main global partner, Wuliangye, a Chinese national brand, epitomizes the deepening of opening-up and practical cooperation under the "16 + 1 cooperation" initiative under the Belt and Road Initiative and serves as a model for Chinese enterprises to "go global", Chinese brands to "go global" and Chinese culture to "go global".

Wuliangye has been actively participating in major public events and holding high-end special events in countries and regions along the Belt and Road. It appeared on important international stages such as G20 Hangzhou Summit, Summer Davos Forum, Xiamen BRICS Summit, Astana Expo, etc., and held high-end tasting events in Russia, Austria, Switzerland, Czech Republic, Greece, Israel, etc. The company also participated in international exhibitions in Singapore, Russia, Japan, Panama, France and other places, reached strategic cooperation with internationally renowned brands, jointly established the Belt and Road International Wine Alliance, and promoted national brands to "go global". The company has also reached strategic cooperation with internationally renowned brands, established the Belt and Road International Wine Alliance, promoted the "going out" of national brands, built international brands, and contributed to the transformation of Chinese manufacturing to Chinese creation, Chinese speed to Chinese quality, and Chinese products to Chinese brands.

Chapter Summary

- The international market distribution channel refers to the path that products flow from a country's producers to foreign end consumers and users, and is an important part of the overall strategy of the company's international marketing. The basic structure of the international market sales channel can be divided into two parts, one is the distribution channel of the product in the export market; the other one is the distribution channel of the product in the import market.

- Selecting international market distribution channels requires enterprises to conduct comprehensive analysis of various environmental factors, including customer factors, product nature, middleman factors, competition factors, enterprise factors, environmental factors and rights and obligations of channel members.

- The international marketing channel member refers to various types of middlemen involved in the process of international marketing and the circulation of goods. International middlemen can be divided into two categories: export middlemen and import middlemen. The former can be divided into export dealers and export agents, and the latter mainly include import dealers and foreign import agents.

- The selection criteria of international middlemen generally include the following aspects: the status of the target market, the geographical location, operating conditions, operational capabilities and business nature, credit conditions of middlemen, and attitude of cooperation.

- International marketing channel decision-making refers to the activities of an enterprise to select its marketing channel mode in the target market by analyzing and evaluating different programs based on its own objectives, capabilities, product characteristics and structural characteristics of the target marketing channel. The decision of international marketing channels mainly involves the decision of the length and width of the marketing channels, the decision of the standardization and differentiation of marketing channels, and the decision of building new channels and using the existing channels.

- The main content of international marketing channel management includes effectively evaluating their performance, reducing conflicts among channel members, promoting cooperation among channel members, and improving the effectiveness of channel management.

❯ Main Concepts

international marketing channel, vertical marketing system, horizontal marketing system, export middlemen, import middlemen, wide distribution, exclusive distribution, selective distribution, standardization of marketing channel, differentiation of marketing channel, new channel

❯ Think and Practice

1. Briefly describe the basic concepts of international sales channels.
2. What is the basic structure of the international marketing channel?
3. Briefly describe the classification, basic characteristics and functions of international middlemen.
4. How to motivate international middlemen?
5. How to solve the conflict in distribution channels?

❯ Case Study

The New Railway Line between China and Europe Will
Change the Pattern of Trade between China and Europe

The railway freight volume between China and Europe is rising rapidly. From 2013 to 2016, the freight weight increased fourfold. Ronald Kleijwegt, an expert in the railway freight industry, said that western enterprises welcome the development of railway freight in China and Europe because it helps them reduce costs. Take the high-tech electronics industry as an example. Consumers of high-tech electronic products want to receive goods quickly, but it is very expensive to make these products in China's coastal areas and then ship them to Europe.

Discuss the following questions.

1. What role does channel development and management play in the Belt and Road?

2. What is the relationship between the choice of distribution channels and goods?

Chapter 10

Promotion Strategy in the International Market

///////// *Learning Objectives* /////////////////////

- Master the content of international advertising decision and international sales promotion decision;

- Learn to select and formulate targeted marketing promotion strategies according to the characteristics of the international market, and use non-price factors to win advantages in the market competition;

- Learn to use decision-making methods of international public relations and promotion mix.

///////// *Key Terms* ///////////////////////////

salesperson　销售员

bi-directional　双向的

rapidity　快速

selectivity　选择性

flexibility　灵活性

region-oriented mode　区域导向模式

product-oriented mode　产品导向模式

customer-oriented mode　客户导向模式

mixed mode　混合模式

publicity　宣传

permeability　渗透性

expressiveness　表现力

objective setting　目标设定

budget decision　预算决策

message decision　信息决策

unique selling proposition (USP)　独特的销售主张

media decision　媒体决策

agency selection　机构选择

Fairs and Exhibitions (EXPO)　展览会

lottery ticket　彩票

coupon　优惠券

public relation　公共关系

▶ **Opening Case**

Users of Live Streaming E-commerce Increase

Users of live streaming e-commerce platforms reached 469 million in China by June 2022, up 204 million from March 2020, and accounted for 44.6 percent of the total internet users in the country, said the Academy of China Council for the Promotion of International Trade in a report on Nov 15.

As per the report that focuses on the development trend of China's e-commerce, between May 2021 and April 2022, China's major short-video platform Douyin launched over 9 million livestreams every month, selling at least 10 billion pieces of goods, the total sales of which grew 2.2 times year-on-year. By March 2022, number of views of livestreams on Taobao reached over 50 billion.

The report noted that digital techs have become the new driver in consumption upgrade. On the one hand, digital techs have expedited the forming of new business patterns, such as cloud shopping and cloud concert. On the other hand, digital techs have pushed ahead refining the consumption structure.

The report deemed e-commerce is playing a key role in China's economic recovery and development against the background of a complicated international and domestic environment.

First, e-commerce has become a major force to boost consumption and supply. In the first nine months of this year, the online retail sales of physical commodity recorded at 8.24 trillion yuan ($1.15 trillion), up 6.1 percent on a yearly basis, far higher than the total retail sales of consumer goods over the same period. Online sales of food, clothing and other daily necessities grew 5. 6 percent, 4. 7 percent and 5. 2 percent respectively, guaranteeing the supplies for daily life.

Second, the emerging of new consumption scenarios has boosted the service sectors. By June this year, remote-work users in China reached 461 million, 43.8 percent of the total internet users of the country. So far, online medical service users stand at 300 million, 28.5 percent of the total internet users.

Third, cross-border e-commerce has become an important tool to stabilize foreign trade and promote consumption. Data from the Ministry of Commerce shows that foreign trade via cross-border e-commerce in the first half this year increased 28.6 percent from a year earlier.

(Source: Adapted from *China Daily*)

10.1 International Market Promotion and the Promotion Mix Strategy

10.1.1 International Market Promotion

The most fundamental purpose for enterprises adopting appropriate product strategies, pricing strategies, and distribution strategies is selling products, which involves promotion. Promotion is the communication between the enterprise and the consumer. It is an activity that the enterprise carries out on the current consumer and potential consumer, and aims to influence the consumer's purchase behavior. Enterprises disseminate information on products or services to help consumers understand the benefits of goods or services, inspire their desires, promote them to take action and ultimately achieve the purpose of sale.

As we all know, the competition in the international market is very fierce. This kind of competition is not only manifested in product quality, price, service, etc., but also prominently displayed in the competition of information dissemination. When products are similar in performance, price and service, the success or failure of the promotion determines the success or failure of the company's operation in the international market. It can be said that whoever has achieved success in information communication has achieved a decisive advantage in sales.

In international marketing, promotion is the closest link to culture. It is difficult to develop a promotion program that is truly international, because the market environment of each country is very different, especially the cultural background and values are very different. Therefore, adapting the corporate promotion strategy to the cultural differences in the world's markets is a very complex issue for international marketers.

10.1.2　Elements of International Promotion

1. Language Differences

A slogan or advertising copy that is effective in one language may mean something different in another language. Thus the trade names, sales presentation materials and advertisements used by firms in their domestic markets may have to be adapted and translated when used in other markets.

There are many examples of unfortunate translations of brand names and slogans. General Motors has a brand name for one of its models called the Vauxhall Nova—this does not work well in Spanish-speaking markets because there it means "no go". In Latin America, "Avoid Embarrassment—Use Parker Pens" was translated as "Avoid Pregnancy—Use Parker Pens". Scandinavian vacuum manufacturer Electrolux used the following in a U.S. ad campaign: "Nothing sucks like an Electrolux."

A Danish company made up the following slogan for its cat litter in the U.K. market:

"Sand for Cat Piss". Unsurprisingly, sales of the firm's cat litter did not increase! Another Danish company translated "Teats for baby's bottles" as "Loose tits". In Copenhagen Airport the following poster could be seen until recently: "We take your baggage and send it in all directions." Thus, a slogan used to express the desire to give good service might instead cause concern about where the baggage might end up.

2. Economic Differences

In contrast to industrialized countries, people in developing countries may be more likely to have radios than television sets. In countries with low levels of literacy, written communication may not be as effective as visual or oral communication.

3. Sociocultural Differences

Dimensions of culture (religion, attitudes, social conditions and education) affect how individuals perceive their environment and interpret signals and symbols. For example, the use of color in advertising must be sensitive to cultural norms. In many Asian countries, white is associated with grief; hence an advertisement for a detergent where whiteness is emphasized would have to be altered for promotional activities in, say, India.

4. Legal and Regulatory Conditions

Local advertising regulations and industry codes directly influence the selection of media and the content of promotion materials. Many governments maintain tight regulations on content, language and sexism in advertising. The type of product that can be advertised is also regulated. Tobacco products and alcoholic beverages are the most heavily regulated in terms of promotion. However, the manufacturers of these products have not abandoned their promotional efforts. Camel engages in corporate-image advertising using its Joe Camel. Regulations are found more in industrialized economies than in developing economies, where the advertising industry is not yet highly developed.

5. Competitive Differences

As competitors vary from country to country in terms of number, size, type and promotional strategies used, a firm may have to adapt its promotional strategy and the timing of its efforts to the local environment.

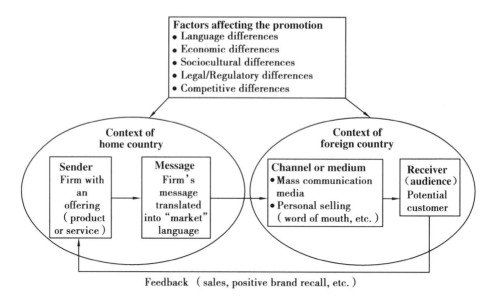

Figure 10-1　Elements of International Promotion

10.2　Personal Selling Strategies in International Marketing

10. 2. 1　Characteristics and Types of Personal Selling in International Marketing

Personal marketing in international marketing refers to the process of activities in which the company sends full-time or part-time sales personnel to directly contact foreign consumers and users, negotiate, publicize, and introduce goods and services to achieve sales purposes. Although this kind of promotion method is relatively old, it is still an effective promotion method in current international marketing, especially in the export of industrial supplies, because in modern marketing, most of the final transactions are achieved by the face to face contact between leading salesmen and users.

Salesperson is a unique bridge between enterprises and consumers or users. It is the key to achieving the promotion objectives, and the main role of sales activities. The quality of salesperson plays an important role in realizing the promotion target, expanding sales, and developing the international market. In international marketing, salesperson should not only have the decisive decision-making ability, research ability and cultural adaptability, but also must have sales skills and good moral cultivation.

The fundamental task of human selling in international marketing can be summarized into three aspects: The first is to facilitate the occurrence and realization of actual trading behaviors, to achieve the basic objectives of marketing, and to achieve marketing achievements. The second is to establish a good relationship with customers. Long-term customer contact is the source of enterprise profits. In the era of prominent relationship marketing, enterprise international marketing in this relationship is particularly important. Third, international marketing work itself also contains the collection of international market information, providing a scientific basis for the further marketing planning of enterprises.

1. Characteristics of Personal Selling in International Market

Compared with other ways of promotion, personal selling has the following advantages.

① Personal selling is direct and effective

Personnel marketing can be on the spot to demonstrate the use of products, increase the buyers' understanding of product specifications, performance, use, language and other aspects, eliminate the differences and all kinds of doubts due to social culture, ideology, aesthetic, customs and habits. Personal selling has a direct and obvious effect on understanding customers' purchase motivation, inducing buyers' curiosity, and eliminating strangeness and fear.

② The bi-directional and rapidity of information communication

On the one hand, salesperson can directly and accurately convey the information of enterprises, products or services to buyers or potential buyers, for the benefit of buyers' understanding. On the other hand, salesperson can hear the opinions and requirements of buyers and potential buyers face to face, and other relevant information, and timely feedback these valuable opinions to the decision-makers of the enterprise. According to the feedback of information, decision makers make necessary supplements and modifications to the enterprise's business plan.

③ High selectivity and flexibility

Salesperson can judge the choice of objects with large purchase possibilities based on their own knowledge, experience, and market research, so that they promote purchases and improve efficiency in a short period of time. Salesperson can also make targeted explanations according to the characteristics of different customers, timely adjust marketing methods, and facilitate transactions.

④ A long-term business relationship

Through the long-term door-to-door service of sales personnel and various flexible sales techniques, the salesman can establish a good relationship and deep friendship with the purchaser and potential buyers, thus consolidating and winning more buyers and establishing long-term, and stable business relationships. In addition, the characteristics of personal sales have determined that this promotion method also has its shortcomings. First, it is impossible for salespeople to spread across the entire target market, and instead they make selective pilot sales. Secondly, the high cost of personnel promotion increases the cost of sales and increases the price of commodities, which is not conducive for enterprises to compete in the market. Finally, in international marketing, salesmen must work in different cultural backgrounds in different countries. The overall quality and personal ability of sales personnel are very high, and it is difficult for companies to find suitable international salesperson.

2. The Composition of Sales Force in International Marketing

To establish a perfect personal marketing network, international marketing enterprises need to carry out scientific planning on the composition of international marketing personnel. The composition of salesperson in international marketing can be divided into three categories, namely the home country salesperson, the target market country local salesperson, and third country salesperson. For a certain enterprise, the main basis for the enterprise to make decisions on the composition of export personnel is the requirements of the enterprise, the availability of salesperson and qualification and other conditions. With the acceleration of the pace of international economic globalization and the deepening of the degree of enterprise internationalization, the composition of salesperson is also changing. The proportion of salesperson in the home country is decreasing, while the proportion of local salesperson in the target market is rising.

① Salesperson of the home country

When marketing products are high-tech products, or the sale of products requires a wealth of relevant information, it is still the best decision to choose the home country's sales force as the international sales force. The main advantages of selecting natives as international salesperson are: better technical training, a better understanding of the company and the product line, a stronger independent working ability and higher working efficiency, and sometimes more authoritative in the eyes of foreign consumers. Of course, there are some disadvantages for people from their home countries to be international marketing personnel, mainly due to cultural and legal barriers. Few people are willing to live overseas for a long time.

② Salesperson of the target country

There are many advantages in employing local people as export sales personnel. Local people can overcome cultural and legal barriers and have a better understanding of local customers or consumers, which is more conducive for enterprises to establish a good relationship with local consumers. In addition, savings in travel, subsidies and other related costs have been made from a cost perspective. The trend toward hiring locals is clear: one study found that the percentage of Americans in managerial and technical positions in foreign subsidiaries has fallen from more than 85 percent to about 45 percent, and more companies are relying on local talents.

③ Salesperson of a third country

More and more international enterprises make a third country person act as the salesperson. Often the nationality of a third country person has little to do with which country he or she works for or goes to. A German, for example, works for an American company in Argentina. It used to be rare for nationals and third country staff to work abroad permanently, but now there is a new breed of "global managers". This phenomenon not only reflects the trend of enterprise internationalization, but also indicates that talents do not belong to a certain country. The advantage of hiring people from third countries is that they are multilingual and familiar with a particular industry or country.

10.2.2　The Organization Mode of Personal Selling in International Marketing

[**Box 10-1**]

Haier's Internationalization Strategy

Haier's strategic development can be broadly viewed as a sequence of phases, each lasting approximately seven years. Through analysis of each phase, this paper seeks to determine the main features of Haier's internationalization strategy, how it differs from traditional western models, the principle features of Haier's management system and how successful Haier's strategy has been.

"Human Value Maximization" Runs Through Haier's Six Strategic Development Stages

01	02	03	04	05	06
Brand Strategy 1984–1991	Diversification Strategy 1991–1998	Globalization Strategy 1998–2005	Global Branding Strategy 2005–2012	Networked Strategy 2012–2019	Ecosystem Brand Strategy 2019–
Quality products created by quality talent	Liquid assets driven by motivated talent	An international brand built by intertional talent	A globalized brand developed by localized Haier talent	User experience scenarios created with EMC	

Personnel selling in the international market generally adopts the following four organizational modes:

1. Region-oriented Mode

The region-oriented mode means that a company selects the salesperson according to the regions. This model makes the sales staff's responsibilities clear, facilitates to understand the customers and market conditions in the region in detail, and plans the sales work in this area. It is also easy to grasp the focus of sales and establish long-term relationships with customers, and travel costs can be cut back. This model is suitable for enterprises with a large number of products in the same region. If there are many kinds of products in the same region and the technology is complicated, it is not conducive to the salesman's familiarity with the performance, structure and characteristics of various products, which hinders the development of effective consultation and maintenance services, etc. In the international market, the general practice is that an agent is responsible for the product's sales in this country. Therefore, the company's international marketing professionals responsible for a category of products can be responsible for sales activities in several countries.

2. Product-oriented Mode

With a product-oriented mode, enterprises select the sales person according to the exported products. The sales personnel are responsible for one or a few categories. This organizational form is suitable for product sales when there are many types of products, and they are highly technical and have no correlation between products. The disadvantage of this method is that, due to the large geographical span, the travel cost is relatively high. In addition, because there are different salesmen of different products in the same market, it is not conducive to formulating a unified promotion strategy in the same market.

3. Customer-oriented Mode

The customer-oriented sales organization mode classifies the customers of the company, and each salesperson conducts its sales promotion activities for a certain type of customer. The criteria for dividing customers can be occupation, industry characteristics, size, and functional status. The advantage of this organizational model is that the salesperson can have a very deep understanding of the consumer psychology and consumption habits of the customer group they are responsible for, and it is convenient to observe the customer's needs and to conduct sales activities. However, this organizational model may result in overlapping or ambiguous sales targets due to the insufficiency of the standards used in classifying customers. It also causes problems like the product-based organizational model. Also, when objects are dispersed, sales expenses increase.

4. Mixed Mode

The mixed mode is the combination of the three structural models to organize the salesperson in the international market. When the company is large in scale, with many products, a wide market and scattered customers, it is impossible to effectively improve the sales efficiency by any of the above three methods. In this case, the enterprise can adopt the above three organizational forms. Two or even three hybrid models sell a variety of products to many different types of customers in different regions.

10.2.3   Management of Personal Selling in International Marketing

1. Recruitment of Salesperson in International Marketing

The internationalization of business makes the demand for overseas salesmen increase constantly. At the same time, because the quality and enthusiasm of overseas salesperson directly affect the effect of promotion and the reputation of the enterprise, the selection and recruitment of international salesperson is a very critical task.

A qualified international salesperson must have some basic quality conditions, such as:

- Be smart and fast to respond.
- Have a friendly attitude and a good appearance.
- Have strong language skills.
- Be aggressive and persevering.
- Be loyal to the company and the job.

- Be good at collecting and analyzing information.
- Have relatively extensive external relations.
- Obey the law.
- Have certain business knowledge and sales skills.
- Be knowledgeable.

2. Training of Salesperson in International Marketing

The training content of international sales staff varies according to the training objects. For salesperson from the company's home country, due to their lack of understanding of the cultural background and language habits of the target market, it is necessary to focus on the language, the cultural background of the target market country and possible problems in working overseas. For local sales personnel from target market countries, training should focus on the understanding of the enterprise, products, as well as the teaching of marketing skills and corporate culture identification. In specific, training methods can be flexible and effective cooperation. The content of the training can include aspects as below.

- **Language ability**. It is mainly aimed at salesmen from abroad. To meet the requirements of direct contact with customers, international sales staff should not only be able to speak the local language fluently, but also improve their language skills and enhance communication skills, to lay a solid foundation for sales work.
- **Differences in cultural customs**. In international marketing, the culture and customs of different target market countries have great differences. Only by understanding and mastering these differences can one improve the probability of success of marketing. For example, if a salesman of an American company sells products in Japan, he will find that there is a big difference between selling products to the Japanese and selling products in the United States. Japanese seldom directly express their views in the communication process, and more of them are silent. This is quite different from the way Americans express their opinions, and they like to express their opinions through arguments.
- **Knowledge of the enterprise**. Make sales personnel understand the history of the enterprise, the company's mission or strategic outlook, corporate culture, production process, technical capacity, organizational structure, product direction, rules and regulations, to master the overall situation of the enterprise.
- **Knowledge of products and technology**. This is the most important requirement for a skilled salesperson. They should master the variety of products, use, price, packaging,

use methods, operation and maintenance, manufacturing process and other knowledge.

- **Knowledge of markets**. Salesperson should have a deeper understanding of market conditions, competition, demand distribution, national policies, regional characteristics, and can foresee the future trend of change.

- **Knowledge of customers**. Understand customers' purchasing motivation, purchasing habit, demand situation, purchasing system, department, management organization and so on, so that they can grasp the key of marketing.

- **Marketing skills**. The proficiency of a salesman depends on the skill of selling, including how to find customers and take the initiative to approach them, how to deal with people and customers, how to overcome the psychological and technical barriers to successfully reach a deal, and how to maintain contact with customers, and consolidate the relationship between production and marketing.

- **Procedures and responsibilities**. Enable sales staff to master all aspects of making plans, arranging time, negotiating, entering into contracts, settlement methods, spending ranges, travel, etc., in order to save costs, avoid losses, and increase sales.

10.3 Advertising Strategy in the International Market

10.3.1 Meaning and Characteristics of International Advertising

International advertisement is a kind of mass communication activity in which advertisers transmit relevant information on commodities and services to international audiences through mass media in a paid way, to influence the attitudes of audiences, and then induce or persuade them to take purchasing actions. International advertising can be used not only to create a long-term image of the product, but also to stimulate sales quickly. International advertisements can usually reach buyers spreading over a wide area economically and effectively. Simply put, advertising has the following characteristics:

1. Publicity

The so-called publicity of advertising, as its name implies, is a public statement, which shows that the products provided by enterprises are standard and legal. Because advertisements are published publicly, most people receive the same information, which makes the buyer know that the purchase of the product can be understood and recognized by the public, and it is possible to collect and compare the information of various similar products.

2. Permeability

Because modern people make more purchasing decisions through advertisements, enterprises can make their products popular through multi-channel and large-scale advertising, and show their scale, fame and achievements.

3. Expressiveness

Advertising carries a variety of carriers, and expressive techniques are rich and colorful. Through smart use of printing, audio and color, advertising can show the characteristics of products and services by dramatic means.

10.3.2　Constraints on International Advertising

1. Characteristics of the Product

The characteristics of products require the same products from different countries, such as technological products, especially high-tech products, such as computers, photocopiers, etc. The characteristics of consumer demand and the way of use are comparatively consistent, so standardization strategies can be used. However, for products with low technological content, such as crafts, food and daily necessities, there is a big difference in the demand of consumers in different countries, and differentiation strategies are often needed.

2. Characteristics of Consumers

If the characteristics of consumers are like those of target consumers in other countries, standardized advertising strategies can be adopted. In different countries, people are likely to buy similar products for very different reasons. Advertising activities must consider the following reasons.

① **Companies should consider the purchase motivation and use habits**. If different markets have a very similar purchase motivation for the same product, the standardization strategy can be adopted. If the purchase motivation is not the same, the differentiation strategy should be adopted. For example, when Americans purchase food or commodities, they are accustomed to buying a lot of the same goods at a time, while consumers in Western European countries prefer to buy them several times, which requires relevant enterprises to focus on advertising. Advertising in the United States should emphasize that the product has a long fresh-keeping performance to meet the needs of consumers to buy in large quantities, while advertising in Western Europe should promote the convenience of the product and guide consumers to increase the frequency of purchase.

② **It is necessary to analyze the attitudes and purchasing points of consumers in different countries to enterprises' products or services**. For example, when buying food, consumers in some countries consider the nutritional content of food, while consumers in other countries may pay more attention to the taste of food. Watermelons sold in the U.S. market are marked with sugar content to meet people's need to limit sugar intake, while Chinese consumers prefer watermelons with a high sugar content. Therefore, such products in advertising call for the use of the differentiation strategy.

③ **We should also analyze the differences of cultural backgrounds among different consumers**. For countries with similar cultural backgrounds, standardized advertising strategies can be adopted, such as in East Asia or even across Asia. However, if the cultural background significantly differs, a differentiation strategy should be employed.

3. The Adaptability of Advertising Laws and Regulations

The adaptability of advertising laws and regulations formulated by different countries in the world has some regulations on advertising management. There are different restrictions on the types, prices, brochures, advertising methods and advertising media of products. If the advertisements produced do not violate the advertisement laws and regulations of various countries, standardization strategies can be adopted to promote the advertisements to all countries in the world. If the advertisements produced violate the advertisement laws and regulations of some countries, differentiation strategies can only be adopted. In order to save advertising costs, companies can make advertisements that do not violate national advertising laws and regulations on the basis of full study of national advertising laws and regulations and adopt standardized strategies to promote them all over the world.

Many countries have corresponding regulations and legal restrictions on advertising. Enterprises must attach great importance to transnational advertising activities and study adaptive countermeasures. Generally speaking, the policy and legal restrictions on advertising activities include advertising costs, advertising media, advertising products, advertising prices, payment methods, reproductions, illustrations and other aspects of advertising programs. For example, in Germany, comparative advertising is illegal. Advertisers cannot say that their products are better than other new products, let alone that their products are the best. In Kuwait, only 32 minutes of television commercials are allowed every day and must be broadcast at night. In China, the law restricts the publication and broadcasting of tobacco advertisements in the main media. Similar regulations exist for alcohol advertising.

The main differences of advertising laws in different countries lie in:

① **There are different restrictions on commodities**. For example, some countries prohibit the advertising of cigarettes, alcoholic drinks, medicines, etc.

② **There are different restrictions on advertising content**. For example, some countries do not allow the broadcasting of horrible, disrespectful and vulgar pictures.

③ **There are different restrictions on advertising methods**. For example, since Canada requires comparative advertising, advertisers must be able to prove the superiority of their products. Otherwise, they will be regarded as cheating and liable.

④ **Time limit for advertising broadcasting is different**. In some countries, advertisements are not allowed on Saturdays, Sundays and holidays, while in others, advertisements are only allowed from 6 p.m. to 8 p.m. every night.

⑤ **Different taxes are levied on advertisements**. For example, in Italy, all kinds of advertising media are taxed, ranging from 4% to 15%, while in Austria, the highest advertising tax is 30%.

In fact, companies in many countries mix standardized advertising strategies with differentiated advertising strategies. The company uses successful advertising ideas or programs in some countries and regions to compare with other advertisements in the countries and regions where the advertisements will be launched to determine whether successful advertisements are appropriate and successful in the new countries and regions. If appropriate, standardize advertising strategies; if not very appropriate, make appropriate modifications in order to be more effective and achieve better results.

10.3.3 Advertising Decisions in the International Market

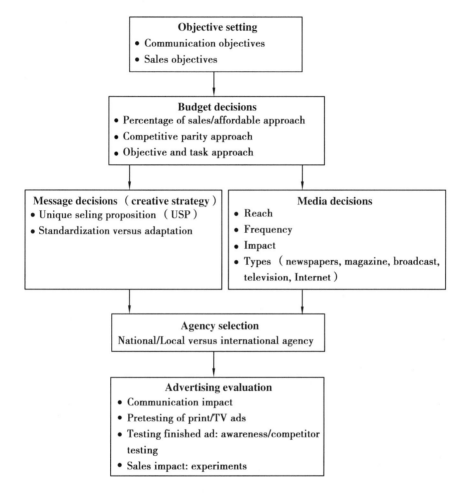

Figure 10-2 The Major International Advertising Decisions

1. Objective Setting

Although advertising methods may vary from country to country, the major advertising objectives remain the same. Major advertising objectives (and means) might include:

- Increasing sales from existing customers by encouraging them to increase the frequency of their purchases; maintaining brand loyalty via a strategy that reminds customers of the key advantages of the product; stimulating impulse purchases;

- obtaining new customers by increasing consumer awareness of the firm's products and improving the firm's corporate image among a new target customer group.

2. Budget Decisions

Controversial aspects of advertising include determining a proper method for deciding the size of the promotional budget, and its allocation across markets and over time.

In theory, the firm (in each of its markets) should continue to put more money into advertising, as money spent on advertising returns more money than money spent on anything else. In practice, it is not possible to set an optimum advertising budget. Therefore, firms have developed more practical guidelines. The manager must also remember that the advertising budget cannot be regarded in isolation, but has to be seen as one element of the overall marketing mix.

3. Message Decisions (Creative Strategy)

This concerns decisions about what unique selling proposition (USP) needs to be communicated, and what the communication is intended to achieve in terms of consumer behavior in the country concerned. These decisions have important implications for the choice of advertising medium, since certain media can better accommodate specific creative requirements (the use of color, written description, high definition, demonstration of the product, etc.) than others.

An important decision for international marketers is whether an advertising campaign developed in the domestic market can be transferred to foreign markets with only minor modifications, such as translation into appropriate languages. Complete standardization of all aspects of a campaign over several foreign markets is rarely attainable. Standardization implies a common message, a creative idea, media and strategy, but it also requires that the firm's product has a USP that is clearly understood by customers in a cross-cultural environment.

Standardizing international advertising can lead to a number of advantages for the firm. For example, advertising costs will be reduced by centralizing the advertising campaign in the head office and transferring the same campaign from market to market, as opposed to running campaigns from different local offices.

However, running an advertising campaign in multiple markets requires the balance between conveying the message and allowing for local nuances. The adaptation of global ideas can be achieved by various tactics, such as adopting a modular approach, adapting international symbols and using international advertising agencies.

▶ **Case 10-1**

Regionalization of International Advertising

Kraft has designed different advertisements for its cheese products in different countries, based entirely on its findings: nearly 95% of housewives in Puerto Rico use cheese in various foods; 65% in Canada use cheese in breakfast toast; and 35% in the United States use snacks.

Renault also designs different advertisements in different countries. In France, Renault is portrayed in its advertisement as a kind of "supercar", which is interesting to drive in high-speed companies and cities. In Germany, Renault advertising focuses on promoting safety, solid engineering technology and internal comfort. In Italy, Renault advertising emphasizes good driving performance and easy acceleration. In Finland, the advertising highlights a solid and complete structure and reliability.

Implications: Whether it is an international food production company or an international automobile production company, it is necessary to design and produce advertisements based on the living needs and values of people in the region.

4. Media Decisions

Based on the various media used in advertising, advertising then can be broadly classified into several categories: Auditory, such as radio advertising; Visual, such as newspapers and magazines; Audio-visual, such as television advertisements. An advertisement consists of various forms, with rich content, and it's still developing unceasingly. In recent years, the online advertisement has gained a huge development.

Furthermore, media selection can be based on the following criteria:

- Reach: the total number of people in a target market exposed to at least one advertisement in a given time period ("opportunity to see", or OTS);
- Frequency: the average number of times within a given time period that each potential customer is exposed to the same advertisement;
- Impact: depends on compatibility between the medium used and the message.

① Types and characteristics of media

Advertising media mainly include newspapers, magazines, radio, television, online, outdoor (placards, banners, screens, etc.), the use of transportation facility, shops and mailings. Among which, newspapers, magazines, radio and television are the four major media, in addition to the newly emerged internet medium of advertising.

- **Internet advertisement**. With the development of information technology, new advertisements based on the Internet have appeared, and some people say that the Internet is the fifth largest medium for advertising. E-commerce refers to all kinds of commercial activities conducted by buyers and sellers in accordance with certain standards by using the modern open Internet, including electronic business advertising, electronic purchase and transaction, exchange of electronic transaction certificates, electronic payment and settlement, online after-sales service, etc. Internet advertising has become an important part of modern electronic commerce. The general procedure for advertising through the Internet is for companies to set up their own websites on the Internet and then to present their products and services, and publish various business information through the websites. In this medium, customers can quickly find the information they need by means of an online search tool. It can also deliver advertising messages such as global advertisements. The Internet can be regarded as being cheap and informative compared with those of other media. Enterprises in the international marketing is faced with global consumers and users, therefore online advertising can bring a lot of opportunities to these enterprises.

- **Magazine advertisement**. Magazine ads are exquisitely printed, have clear promotional objects, and are good at expressing the texture of the product. But the advertisement general cycle of this medium is usually long, with poor timeliness, and a high production cost. The percentage of international advertisers using foreign consumer magazines is relatively low, mainly because they have a large circulation or few magazines that can provide a reliable circulation. In the present, more and more U.S. publishing houses are now publishing overseas editions, such as *Reader's Digest International*, *Playboy* and *Science America*.

- **Broadcast advertisement**. The information dissemination of the broadcast advertisement is timely and quick, and the effect of the advertisement can be expressed through language and sound effects, which is capable of giving the customer a clear impression of the advertisement. The limitation of broadcast advertising is that the information it conveys depends entirely on sound transmission, which disappears quickly and is difficult to preserve. Moreover, the mere use of sound to describe and present products is often not intuitive, and can easily lead to misinterpretation.

- **Television advertisement**. This combines sound, image and music. It is one of the most important kind of advertisement medium in the present day. It has wide coverage, deep influence, strong appeal and promptness. Its shortcoming is that it has a fleeting dissemination of information, information is not easy to retain, and advertising pertinence is poor, with a high cost of investment. Because of its great entertainment value, television advertising has become the main medium of communication in most countries. Most densely populated areas have television broadcasting facilities, such as China, where television advertising has a large audience. However, in some countries with a relatively small number of television sets and poor TV transmitting technology, the spread of television advertising will be greatly reduced.

Table 10-1   Use of Different Advertising Media in the Countries Concerned

Types of Advertising Media	Countries
Mixed advertising	The United States, Japan, United Kingdom, Canada, Netherlands, Finland, Spain, Brazil, Venezuela, Argentina, Liberia, India, Pakistan, Kuwait, Thailand
Newspaper advertisements	Sweden, Norway, Australia, New Zealand, South Africa, Malaysia, Singapore, Egypt, Sri Lanka, Jamaica, Ghana
Magazine advertisement	Germany and Italy
Television and Radio Announcements	Ireland, Greece, Colombia, Mexico, Panama, Costa Rica, Portugal, Philippines
Other types of advertising	France, Switzerland, Austria, Denmark, Peru, Lebanon, Syria, Indonesia, Nigeria

Note: There are other types of advertising media such as movies, outdoor, transportation, direct mails, etc.

② Combination of medium

The systematic and effective combination of all kinds of advertisement media can improve the efficiency of advertising. For example, the newspaper medium is less infectious than the television medium, but the combination of newspaper and television according to the specific content of the advertisement can achieve good results. When the product was just introduced into the market, the newspaper media can be used to introduce the advantages and uses of the product in detail. After the introductory advertisement lasts for a certain period of time, a brief television advertisement is introduced to impress the customer and to establish the image of the product.

- **Mix of different media**. Different advertising media have different functions, and this is to give full play to the role of different advertising media, and save the advertising expenses of enterprises. It's important we should make a scientific collocation between different advertising media.

- **Timing of different media**. According to the content of the advertisements, the advertisements of different media can be reasonably matched in time. If the audience is expected to recognize and accept the advertisement in a very short frame of time, then different advertising media are needed to arrange and publicize the product at the same time. If the audience is expected to keep receiving the advert for a longer period of time, and this is needed to be done at a lower cost, different advertising media need to be arranged in different time periods. As mentioned above, the cooperation of newspapers and television media needs to be arranged at different times, which can make the advertisement work continuously and save the cost of advertisement.

- **Geographical mix of advertising media**. The role of advertising media varies from region to region, and from country to country. Geographical factors need to be taken into account in the allocation of advertisements. For example, in the economically developed countries where the number of people accessing the Internet is high, advertising through the Internet can work well in such countries, while in less developed countries where the Internet coverage is low, it is difficult to achieve the desired objectives if the Internet advertising is used.

5. Agency Selection

① Types of international advertising agency

There are two main types of international advertising agencies: local advertising agencies and foreign advertising agencies, and they all exist in various forms.

- **Local advertising agencies**. This includes advertising agencies without foreign affiliates and advertising agencies with foreign affiliates.

- **Foreign Advertising Agencies**. This includes local advertising agencies and cooperative advertising agencies.

② Considerable factors in the selection of an international advertising agency

● Whether the operating capability of the advertising company is available, including: operational equipment, manpower, creativity, production, implementation and survey testing, the easiest way to understand the ability of an advertising agency is through their current customer.

● How rich the advertising company's experience and performance is. A word-of-mouth advertising company always has its successful track record. However, it is not enough to know the advertising company only from the "fame". It is also necessary to know the past customers of the advertisers in the past, which industry it is familiar with, what products they deal with and whether its advertising experience and actual achievements are beneficial to the advertising agency activities.

● The size of the advertising item. If there are many advertising projects with high requirements, a large-scale advertising agency is required to be competent. But if there are few advertising items with a small scale, then it is not necessary to find a large agency. An important customer for a small agency may be better than an additional small customer for a large agency. Small goods need not be heavily advertised.

● Whether the advertising agency has considerable financial strength. If the agency is small, it will be difficult to provide satisfactory service to advertisers. Therefore, the company should look for those who have the financial strength, and is good at operations to do the advertisement.

Besides these, companies should also know the standard for charging fees and methods. For example, when entrusting an agent to do an investigation, research or perform a service, the charging standard of each enterprise is usually different. Hence a prior investigation and comparison need to be carried out to make a better choice.

10.4 Sales Promotion Strategy in the International Market

10.4.1 The Meaning of International Sales Promotion

Among the various elements of marketing mix, sales promotion is most frequently used, but its meaning is ambiguous. Sales promotion consists of a series of promotional tools, which is the result of long-term efforts of enterprises all over the world to compete for products. At the same time, many tools are being created in the promotion practice of enterprises.

1. Sales Promotion Concept

In the international market, if companies combine the means of sales promotion and advertising, they are more likely to succeed while entering into the market. In recent years, there is a development trend that the scope and extent of sales promotion have been accelerating. The factors that lead to the rapid growth of sales promotion are those such as, a large number of brands, more marketing-minded competitors, inflation and recession making consumers more easily accept the impact of promotions, the effectiveness of advertising due to increased costs, and messy media and legal restrictions decreasing. Sales promotion is characterized by irregularity, non-periodicity, flexibility, diversity, and obvious short-term benefits.

2. Purpose of Sales Promotion

The purpose of business promotion is usually to induce consumers to try or buy new products directly, to guide consumers to increase the use of existing products, to directly attract consumers to buy at the retail level. Since the 1990s, many international enterprises attach great importance to the use of sales promotion means. They have set up sales promotion departments under the direct leadership of marketing managers and formulated sales promotion cost budgets. This is because sales promotion plus advertising has a quick effect. When Coca-Cola promoted Fanta drinks in developing countries, it used sales promotion methods such as giving ballpoint pens and pencils, coupled with advertising, which attracted a large number of consumers and prompted middlemen to purchase in large quantities, and thus it entered and occupied the market in these countries.

10.4.2 Sales Promotion in the International Market

Sales promotion in international marketing is of great significance for enterprises to enter the international market quickly and promote the sales of products. Sales promotion methods in international marketing mainly include foreign product catalogues, sample exhibitions, publications of institutions or companies, trade fairs and expositions, point-of-sale publications and consumer promotional materials.

1. Catalogue of Foreign Products

The foreign product catalogue is an international promotion way that can be preserved for a long time and can accurately introduce and publicize enterprises and products. This method is suitable for the situation where foreign consumers live very scattered or do not visit frequently. It provides consumers with an opportunity to study and choose goods carefully. When making catalogues of foreign products, enterprises should highlight the following characteristics. Firstly, it can arouse the interest of customers and stimulate their enthusiasm for reading. To use the appeal of color and exquisite printing to make consumers have strong desire. Secondly, reflect the characteristics of manufacturers. It is necessary to introduce the history, honor and the related product series of the manufacturer so as to give customers a sense of dependence. Of course, this kind of introduction should also highlight the attraction, meticulous design and excellent arrangement. Thirdly, it is necessary to provide purchase information so as to facilitate purchase. Specific items such as product specifications and contact methods should be clearly defined in the catalogue. Fourthly, let customers have the desire to own. Highlight the value of the product and arrange the application occasions and procedures, so that customers have the desire to own. Fifthly, companies should clarify the ways of communication and provide customers with convenient channels for suggestions and opinions.

In addition, the catalogue of foreign products should consider the culture and customs suitable for the foreign market. When using some proper nouns and new vocabulary, it is necessary to consider the acceptance ability of local customers and understand their thinking mode.

2. Samples

Sample publicity gives people a real sense of the product, which cannot be achieved in any other way. Giving samples has become an important way for some well-known international companies to open up overseas markets.

3. Publications of Institutions or Companies

These publications can be distributed in a wide range of areas, such as consumers, distributors or other agencies. Corporate publications can publicize products, and publish the latest information about enterprises. Corporate publications can be published in the country where the company is located. For large multinational corporations, when their business and market coverage cover many countries, publications can also be published and distributed in the target market country.

4. Fairs and Exhibitions（EXPO）

International trade fairs and exhibitions, also known as expositions, are a good way to promote international businesses. They gather a large number of exporters and provide opportunities to promote products. There are many ways of exposition, including comprehensive and professional expositions according to products, national and international expositions according to the country of exhibitors, temporary and permanent expositions according to time, and trade fairs open to the business community and to the public according to visitors. For example, the Hanover Trade Fair in Germany is one of the largest trade fairs in the world. It brings together products from more than 20 industries and is a well-known comprehensive exposition. The International Air Exposition in Paris is one of the largest professional expositions in the aviation industry in the world. About 100 major international expositions are held in Germany every year, with about 87,000 enterprises participating, 40% of which come from more than 150 countries and regions outside Germany. In China, the famous Canton Fair provides an opportunity for Chinese enterprises to show and promote their products to foreign customers and enjoys a high reputation at home and abroad.

The Expo provides an opportunity for enterprises from all over the world to exchange information and conclude transactions. In trade fairs, enterprises can buy and sell goods and negotiate contracts. Therefore, in the international marketing of enterprises, it is regarded as a basic marketing strategy. Through the way of exposition, enterprises can get to know more ideal agents and distributors, and enter the market of their country through them. If enterprises have good products, winning prizes at exhibitions can greatly improve the reputation of enterprises and products, expand their international influence and promote the export of products. In addition, the way of exposition can also help enterprises to understand the international market situation of their products, such as product quality, price, packaging and sales situation, competitors' product situation, and collect information on international market technology and economy, so as to facilitate the timely adjustment or correct selection of enterprises' international marketing strategies.

5. Various Lottery Tickets and Coupons

Lottery tickets and coupons are a kind of certificate of reduction issued by enterprises to customers. With this certificate, consumers can get preferential treatment when buying goods. There are many ways to issue lottery tickets and coupons. They can be distributed along with the last purchase to encourage continuous purchase, or can be presented with advertisements or other ways. In international marketing, the use of lottery tickets and coupons depends on the degree of acceptance of consumers in different countries. For example, in the United States, lottery tickets can be distributed independently, while in Canada, they are distributed in advertisements to retailers.

Sales promotion has attracted more and more attention from some large international companies. They invest huge amounts of money in the hope that products will be accepted by customers as soon as possible. Some famous brands, such as Procter & Gamble and Nestle, have actively implemented their sales promotion plans. The usual way is to give the right to invest and use funds to the local branches and make sales promotion plans according to the local objective environment. In this way, companies can fully consider and better adapt to the local consumers' brand preferences, purchase frequency, use quantity, target price, as well as the maturity and promotion of the market. The laws of some countries have various restrictions on business promotion methods, such as the prohibition of lottery sales and gift giving, and the restriction on retail rebates. In some countries, the sales promotion must be approved. Individual countries have stipulated that competitors cannot conduct sales promotion at a higher cost than other companies selling the same type of product. Therefore, when using sales promotion methods in international marketing, companies should pay attention to the legal restrictions of various countries, understand the effective ways of various countries, and strengthen cooperation with retailers in various countries, so that international sales promotion can play a good role.

10.4.3   The development of International Sales Promotion Strategies

Sales promotion activities have the characteristics of strong promotion pertinence, being flexible and diverse, and remarkable short-term promotional effects. However, sales promotion activities are not as routine as advertising, personnel marketing and public relations. They are usually carried out to solve specific promotional problems or achieve temporary promotional purposes. Such as introducing new products, promoting overstocked goods, enhancing the effect of advertising or personnel marketing, and often combined with other promotion methods such as advertising or personnel marketing. When adopting sales promotion in the international market, companies should pay special attention to the restrictions on sales promotion activities in different countries or regions, the cooperative attitude of dealers and the degree of competition in the local market.

Sales promotion strategies for international enterprises should focus on choosing appropriate promotion methods and means, as well as creating efficient promotion tools.

1. Understand and Analyze the Restrictions and Regulations on Sales Promotion in Different Countries

Many countries restrict the application of sales promotion methods in local markets. For example, some countries stipulate that enterprises must obtain the consent of the relevant government departments in advance to carry out sales promotion activities in the local market. Some countries restrict the scale of sales promotion activities of enterprises and others restrict the form of sales promotion, stipulating that gifts must be related to the goods promoted. Other national laws limit cash discounts and quantity discounts. Under New Zealand law, coupons can only be converted into cash. The legitimacy, impartiality and honesty of sales promotion activities in Britain have special explanations. Enterprises engaged in international marketing must be familiar with these regulations in order to avoid falling into misunderstanding and suffering undue losses.

2. Determine a Reasonable Sales Promotion Budget

The budget of sales promotion is directly related to the scale of sales promotion. Within a certain scale, there is a positive correlation between the cost and the effect of sales promotion, but when the cost of sales promotion reaches a certain level, the effect will decrease, and finally there will be a negative correlation with the cost of sales promotion. Enterprises must correctly determine the scale of sales promotion. Generally speaking, when the unit product promotion cost is the lowest, the scale of sales promotion is the best. Neither below nor above this scale can give full play to the effect of sales promotion expenses.

3. Make a Reasonable Choice of Time for Sales Promotion

Choosing the time of sales promotion has two meanings: one is to determine the starting time of sales promotion activities, such as whether to launch promotional activities as soon as new products are introduced into the market, etc. The second is to determine the duration of sales promotion activities. The time for enterprises to carry out sales promotion activities should depend on the situation of products, regions and population. Too short timing of the sales promotion activities can make many potential consumers have no chance to buy products and fail to achieve the expected promotion purpose. Too long a time may create a bad impression on consumers, who tend to believe that enterprises are eager to deliver goods and promote unsalable products.

4. Investigate the Target Market Situation Deeply

① **The cooperative attitude of distributors**. The success or failure of sales promotion activities in the international market of enterprises is closely related to the support of local distributors or intermediaries. Before deciding to carry out sales promotion activities, it is necessary to carefully understand the cooperative attitude of distributors.

② **The level of competition in the target market and the strategies employed by competitors**. The situation of competitors in the target market will directly affect the decision-making of sales promotion activities of enterprises. For example, when introducing products in a less competitive market, it is necessary to study how to formulate a sales promotion plan suitable for the enterprise. But if there is a fierce competition in the market and competitors introduce new promotional measures to attract customers to compete for the market, the enterprise must take actions against the competitors. When enterprises carry out sales promotion activities in overseas target markets, they may face opposition or obstruction from local competitors, or even be prohibited by local chambers of commerce or government departments through laws or regulations. Therefore, when enterprises decide to carry out some sales promotion activities in a market, they must take into account the degree of competition and the trend of competitors.

In conclusion, the promotion strategy of the international market is more complicated than that of the domestic market. Enterprises engaged in international businesses need to adopt corresponding ways to overcome the obstacles caused by geographical and cultural factors according to the actual situation of target market countries. Only in this way can they successfully carry out international marketing and make their products across national boundaries and move towards the international market.

10.5 International Public Relation Strategy

Public relations are of great significance for enterprises to carry out international operations. As enterprises try to cross national boundaries for marketing activities, the degree of acceptance of the enterprise by local governments and the public determines the popularity of enterprises' products to a certain extent, so public relations in the international market is often more important than in the domestic market. To enter the international market smoothly, high-quality products are important, but what's more important is to make the international community understand, recognize and accept the enterprise itself and its products. Corporate public relations activities are an effective means for enterprises to establish a good image and win the understanding, trust and support of intermediaries and the public in the target market. Effective public relations, together with other ways of promotion, can timely overcome the cultural and other obstacles in international businesses, to eventually achieve the goal of occupying the international market. Public relations are an indispensable means of promotion in international marketing activities, and one of the important strategies for enterprises to win in the international market.

The international public relation is an international communication way based on the relationship between international marketing enterprises and the public of the host country.

The main purpose of public relations activities in international marketing is to establish a good social image and reputation of enterprises. To achieve this goal, the public relations department should accomplish the following tasks:

1. Strengthen the Relationship with the Media

Mass media bears the social functions of disseminating information and guiding public opinions. The media's reports on enterprises have a strong guiding role for the public, and thus affect the public image of enterprises to a large extent. Enterprises must make full use of the media to serve them, establish a good cooperative relationship with them, actively provide information to enable the media to understand the enterprise, and actively create events with news value to strive for active media coverage.

▶ **Case 10-2**

The Marketing Communication Strategies behind
the New Traffic "IP" Bing Dwen Dwen

On February 4, 2022, the Beijing Winter Olympics officially kicked off. Along with the opening ceremony, Bing Dwen Dwen, the mascot of the Winter Olympics, was on the hot search list. This lovely IP image has become a new Internet celebrity in just a few days, attracting huge traffic on social media. In the official flagship store of tmall Olympics, Bing Dwen Dwen related products, such as thermos cups, key chains, satchels, badges, etc., were snapped up as soon as they went online. Bing Dwen Dwen's emoticons have become an important medium for group communication of generation Z. From home to abroad, the discussion on Bing Dwen Dwen has become increasingly fierce.

2. Improve Relationships with Consumers

Improving the relationship with consumers is a top priority for almost any reputable company in the world. It is of great significance for enterprises to use public relations to communicate with society, to enhance understanding, and to make consumers have good feelings for the image of enterprises and their products.

3. Adjust the Relationship between Adjustment and Government

Unlike domestic enterprises, international enterprises are facing various demands or pressures from various countries and governments. On the one hand, enterprises must adjust their behaviors to adapt to the changes in government policies at any time. On the other hand, they should make every effort to coordinate possible conflicts. This is an important task of corporate public relations. Public relations departments must strengthen their contacts with government officials of the host country, understand their intentions, understand the laws of the host country, and strive for a mutual understanding to achieve the survival and development of enterprises. To achieve this goal, enterprises can engage in some public welfare activities, such as donating to public utilities, supporting disabled persons, sponsorship, culture, education, health, environmental protection, etc., and establish an image of actively contributing to the social and economic development of target market countries.

4. Make Different Public Relations Activities in Different Periods and Stages

In the initial stage of entering the host country, there are many problems and public relations tasks. The focus of the work is to win acceptance by the host country's government and nationals. In the mid-term stage, companies should pay attention to the political situation and policy trends of the host country, as well as the risk of transferring corporate profits to the home country. The focus of the work is to expand the influence of enterprises in the host society and establish a good reputation. Finally, even in the withdrawal phase, attention should be paid to maintaining good relations with the host country in order to safeguard the interests of other parties.

Chapter Summary

- Promotion strategies in the international market include personal selling, advertising, sales promotion, and public relations.

- The personal selling of international marketing activities is a process in which the company sends full-time or part-time sales personnel to directly contact foreign consumers and users, negotiate, publicize, and introduce products and services to achieve sales purposes.

- International advertising activities are influenced by product characteristics, consumer hotspots and advertising laws and regulations in various regions. Therefore, the biggest problem in the formulation of advertising is the standardization and regionalization of advertising decisions.

- There are many ways to promote international businesses, including foreign product catalogs, trade fairs and exhibitions, etc. In formulating international promotional activities, it is necessary to fully study the actual situation of the target country, overcome regional and cultural barriers, and adopt targeted promotional activities to improve the awareness of the enterprise.

- In addition to fulfilling the functions of domestic public relations activities, international public relations activities also need to adjust relations with the host government and engage in different public relations activities in different periods, different stages, and different regions.

Main Concepts

international personal selling, international advertising, international sales promotion, international public relations

Think and Practice

1. Outline the elements of international promotion.
2. List the four organizational modes of personal selling in the international market.
3. Describe the three types of international advertising.
4. Explain the main sales promotion methods in international marketing.
5. Why and how should international marketers develop international public relation strategies?

Case Study

Chinese Companies Score Big at World Cup

Although failing to qualify for the FIFA World Cup finals soccer tournament now underway in Qatar, China is making a huge contribution to the largest global sporting event.

Chinese products, infrastructure projects and sponsors have won praise from appreciative fans and potential customers.

A range of Chinese items are available at the tournament, including key rings, horns, flags, clothing and shoes from Yiwu, Zhejiang, and Jinjiang, Fujian province, as well as fireworks from Liuyang, Hunan province.

Market observers said the abundance of such products is due to China's industrial upgrading boom, well-developed supply chains, and green transformation.

Even without the presence of the Chinese team at the tournament, Chinese sponsors are enthusiastic about the Qatar World Cup, and they have been warmly welcomed by the host country.

According to Global Data, a data analytics and consulting company based in London, 20 Chinese companies have provided more sponsorships for the 2022 World Cup than rivals from other countries. These companies rank top globally with spending of nearly $1.4 billion, exceeding the $1.1 billion outlay from U.S. companies.

Discuss the following questions.

1. Why are Chinese companies willing to connect with the World Cup even though it costs quite a lot to be a sponsor?

2. Comment on international advertising strategies.

References

［1］菲利普・凯特奥拉,布鲁斯・莫尼,玛丽・吉利,等.国际营销(英文版)［M］.18版.北京:中国人民大学出版社,2020.

［2］菲利普・科特勒,加里・阿姆斯特朗.市场营销原理［M］.17 版. 北京:清华大学出版社,2021.

［3］田盈,徐亮,等.国际市场营销(双语版)［M］. 北京:人民邮电出版社,2013.

［4］斯文德・霍伦森. 国际市场营销学(英文版)［M］. 8 版.北京:清华大学出版社,2021.

［5］HOFSTEDE G. Culture's Consequences: Comparing Values, Behaviors, Institutions and Organizations across Nations［M］. Thousand Oaks, CA: Sage Publications Inc., 2001.

［6］季羡林. 季羡林谈东西方文化［M］. 北京:当代中国出版社,2016.

［7］小威廉・D. 佩罗,约瑟夫・P. 坎农,E. 杰,等.国际市场营销(英文版)[M].16版.北京:中国人民大学出版社,2020.

［8］陈文汉,孙畅,等.国际市场营销[M]. 2 版.北京:清华大学出版社,2020.

［9］BAACK D W, CZARNECKA B, BAACK D. International Marketing[M]. London: Sage Publications Ltd., 2018.

［10］达娜-尼科莱塔・拉斯库.国际市场营销学[M] . 3 版.北京:机械工业出版社,2010.

［11］徐小贞. 国际市场营销(英文版)[M]. 2 版.北京:高等教育出版社,2017.

[12] 迈克尔·钦科陶,伊卡·龙凯宁.国际市场营销学[M]. 10 版.北京:中国人民大学出版社,2015.

[13] 沃伦·基根,马克·格林.全球营销(英文版)[M]. 8 版.北京:中国人民大学出版社,2019.

[14] 斯文德·霍伦森.国际市场营销学[M]. 7 版.张昊,等译.北京:机械工业出版社,2019.